A VISUAL EXPLORATION OF SCIENCE

A VISUAL GUIDE TO THE UNIVERSE

Rosen YA

ALBERTO HERNÁNDEZ PAMPLONA

This edition published in 2018 by
The Rosen Publishing Group, Inc.
29 East 21st Street
New York, NY 10010

Library of Congress Cataloging-in-Publication Data

Names: Pamplona, Alberto Hernández.
Title: A visual guide to the universe / Alberto Hernández Pamplona.
Description: New York : Rosen Publishing, 2018. | Series: A visual exploration of science | Audience: Grades 7–12. | Includes bibliographical references and index.
Identifiers: LCCN 2017002116 | ISBN 9781508175858 (library-bound)
Subjects: LCSH: Cosmology—Juvenile literature. | Universe—Juvenile literature. | Solar system—Juvenile literature. | Astronomy—Juvenile literature.
Classification: LCC QB983 .H47 2018 | DDC 523.1—dc23
LC record available at https://lccn.loc.gov/2017002116

Manufactured in the United States of America

Metric Conversion Chart

1 inch = 2.54 centimeters; 25.4 millimeters
1 foot = 30.48 centimeters
1 yard = .914 meters
1 square foot = .093 square meters
1 square mile = 2.59 square kilometers
1 ton = .907 metric tons
1 pound = 454 grams
1 mile = 1.609 kilometers
1 cup = 250 milliliters
1 ounce = 28 grams
1 fluid ounce = 30 milliliters
1 teaspoon = 5 milliliters
1 tablespoon = 15 milliliters
1 quart = .946 liters
355 degrees F = 180 degrees Celsius

Original Idea Sol90 Publishing
Project Manegement Nuria Cicero
Editorial Coordination Diana Malizia
Editorial Team Alberto Hernández, Virginia Iris Fernández, Mar Valls, Marta de la Serna, Sebastián Romeu. Maximiliano Ludueña, Carlos Bodyadjan, Doris Elsa Bustamante, Tania Domenicucci, Andrea Giacobone, Constanza Guariglia, Joaquín Hidalgo, Hernán López Winne.
Proofreaders Marta Kordon, Edgardo D'Elio
Design Fabián Cassan
Layout Laura Ocampo, Carolina Berdiñas, Clara Miralles, Paola Fornasaro, Mariana Marx, Pablo Alarcón

Photography Age Fotostock, Getty Images, Science Photo Library, Graphic News, ESA, NASA, National Geographic, Latinstock, Album, ACI, Cordon Press

Infographic Coordination Paula López

Infographies Sol90 Images www.sol90images.com , Paula López, Guillermina Eichel, Pablo Gentile, Maru Hiriart, Maureen Holboll, Clarisa Mateo, Sol Molina, Vanina Ogueta, Gastón Pérsico, Cecilia Szalkowicz, Paula Simonetti

Illustrations Sol90 Images www.sol90images.com , Guido Arroyo, Pablo Aschei, Gustavo J. Caironi, Hernán Cañellas, Leonardo César, José Luis Corsetti, Vanina Farías, Joana Garrido, Celina Hilbert, Isidro López, Diego Martín, Jorge Martínez, Marco Menco, Ala de Mo
Diego Mourelos, Eduardo Pérez, Javier Pérez, Ariel Piroyansky, Ariel Roldán, Marcel Socías, Néstor Taylor, Trebol Animation, Juan Venegas, Coralia Vignau, 3DN, 3DOM studio, Constanza Vicco, Diego Mourelos.

Contents

EAGLE NEBULA
Stars are forming within this pillar of interstellar dust.

The Secrets of the Universe

There was a time when people believed that the stars were bonfires lit by other tribes in the sky, that the universe was a flat plate resting on the shell of a giant turtle, and that the Earth, according to the Greek astronomer Ptolemy, was at the center of the universe. From the most remote of times, people have been curious about what lies hidden beyond the celestial sphere. This curiosity has led them to build telescopes that show with clarity otherwise blurry and distant objects. In this book you will find the history of the cosmos illustrated with spectacular images that show in detail how the cosmos was formed, the nature of the many points of light that adorn the night sky, and what lies ahead. You will also discover how the suns that inhabit space live and die, what dark matter and black holes are, and what our place is in this vastness. Certainly, the opportunity to

compare the destiny of other worlds similar to ours will help us understand that for the time being there is no better place than the Earth to live. At least for now.

In the Milky Way—according to mathematical and physical calculations—there are more than 100 billion stars, and such a multitude leads to the question: Is it possible that our Sun is the only star that possesses an inhabited planet? Astronomers are more convinced than ever of the possibility of life in other worlds. We just need to find them. Reading this book will let you become better acquainted with our neighbors in the solar system—the other planets—and the most important characteristics that distinguish them. All this information that explores the mysteries of space is accompanied by recent images captured by the newest telescopes. They reveal many details about the planets and their satellites, such as the volcanoes and craters found on the surface of some of them. You will also learn more about the asteroids and comets that orbit the Sun and about Pluto, a dwarf planet, which was recently visited by a space probe for the first time. About twenty-five years ago, astronomers began observing frozen worlds, much smaller than a planet, in a region of the solar system called the Kuiper belt. We invite you to explore all of this. The images and illustrations that accompany the text will prove very helpful in studying and understanding the structure of all the visible and invisible objects (such as dark matter) that form part of the universe. There are stellar maps showing the constellations, the groups of stars that since ancient times have served as a guide for navigation and for the development of calendars. There is also a review through history: from Ptolemy, who thought the planets orbited around the Earth, and Copernicus, who put the Sun in the center, and Galileo, the first to aim a telescope skyward, up to the most recent astronomical theories, such as those of Stephen Hawking, the genius of space and time who continues to amaze with his discoveries about the greatest mysteries of the cosmos. You will find these and many more topics no matter where you look in this fantastic book that puts the universe and its secrets in your hands.

What Is the Universe?

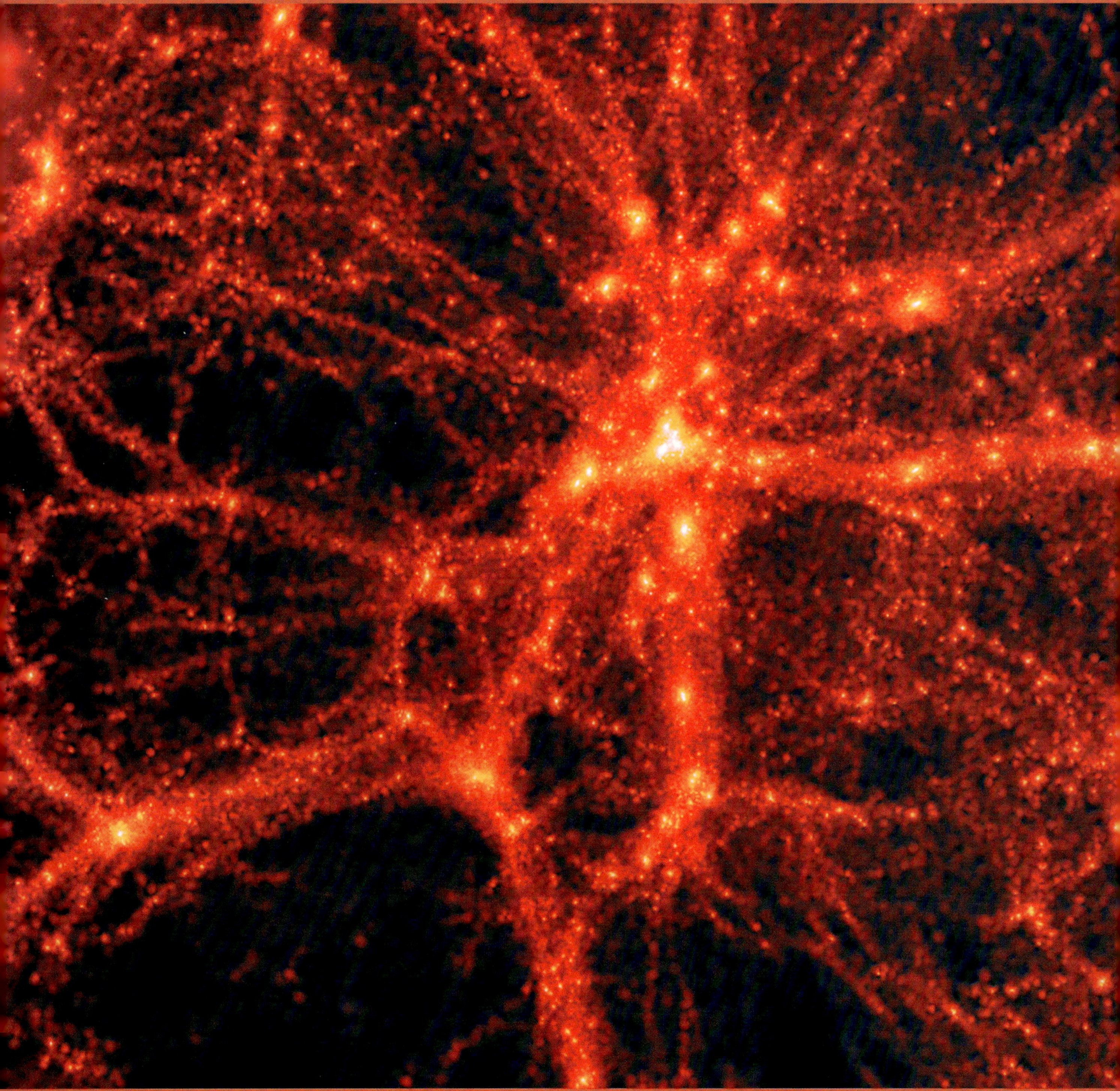

The universe is everything that exists, from the smallest particles to the largest ones, together with all matter and energy. The universe includes visible and invisible things, such as dark matter, the great, secret component of the cosmos. The search for dark matter is currently one of the most important tasks of cosmology. Dark matter may

ARK MATTER
vidence exists that dark matter, though
visible to telescopes, betrays itself by the
avitational pull it exerts over other heavenly
dies.

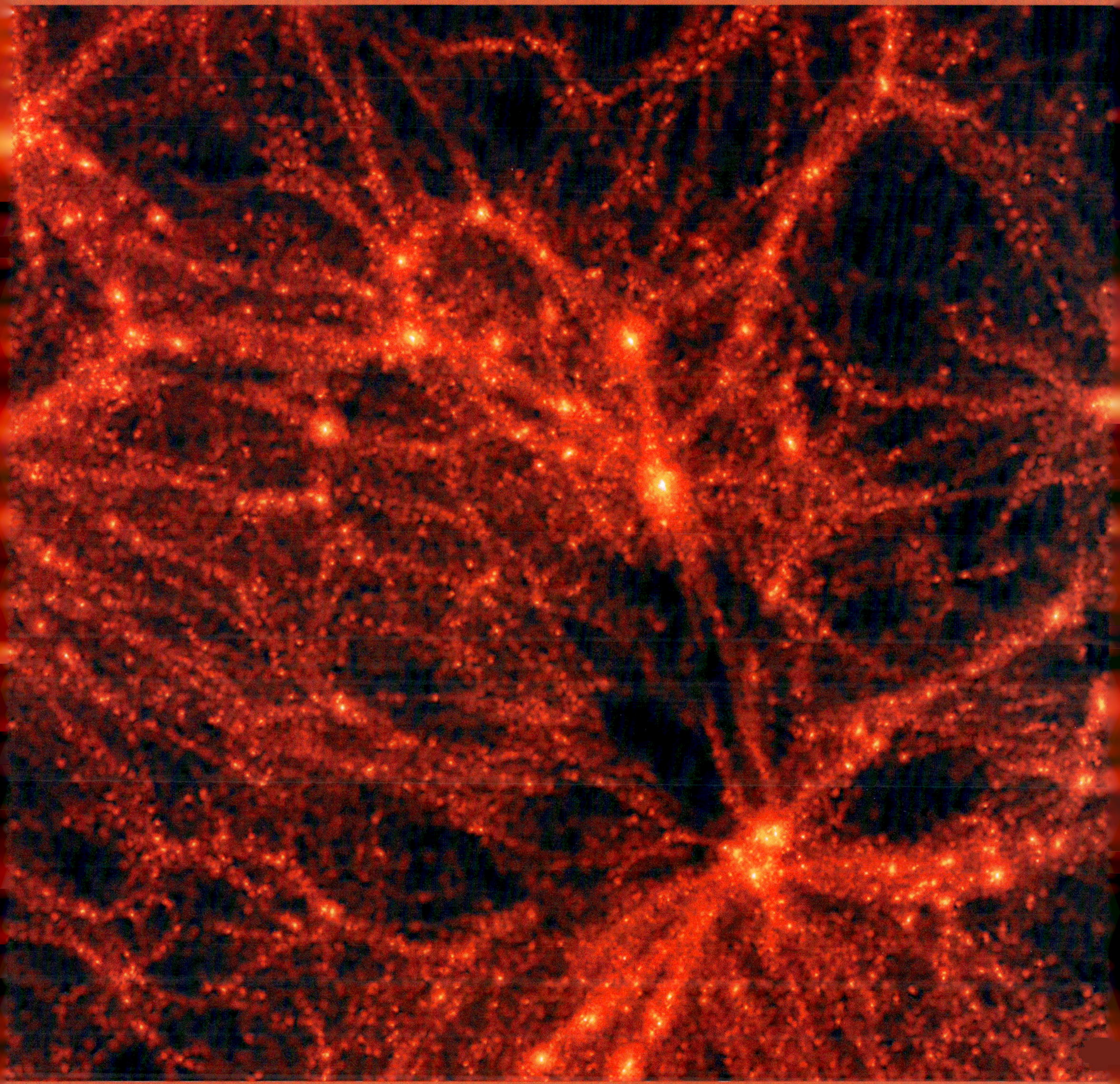

iterally determine the density of all of space, as well as decide the destiny of he universe. Did you know that, second by second, the universe grows and grows? The question that astronomers are asking—the question that concerns them the most—is how much longer the universe can continue to expand like a balloon before turning into something cold and dark. ●

X-Ray of the Cosmos

The universe, marvelous in its majesty, is an ensemble of a hundred billion galaxies. Each of these galaxies (which tend to be found in large groups) has billions of stars. These galactic concentrations surround empty spaces, called cosmic voids. The immensity of the cosmos can be better grasped by realizing that the size of our fragile planet Earth, or even that of the Milky Way, is insignificant compared to the size of the remainder of the cosmos.

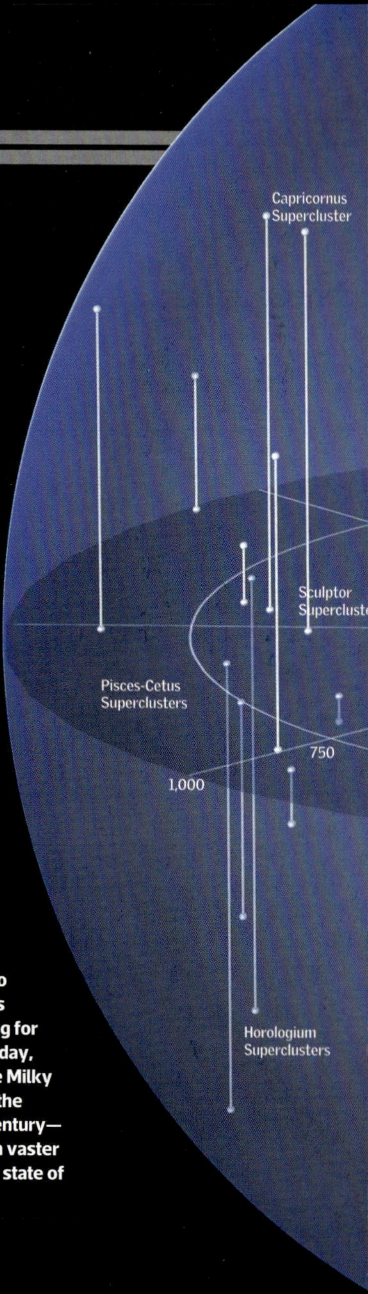

The Universe

Originating nearly 14 billion years ago in an immense explosion, the universe today is too large to be able to conceive. The innumerable stars and galaxies that populate it promise to continue expanding for a long time. Though it might sound strange today, for many years, astronomers thought that the Milky Way, where the Earth is located, constituted the entire universe. Only recently—in the 20th century—was outer space recognized as not only much vaster than previously thought but also as being in a state of ongoing expansion.

1.

EARTH **Originated, together with the solar system, when the universe was already 9.1 billion years old. It is the only known planet that is home to life.**

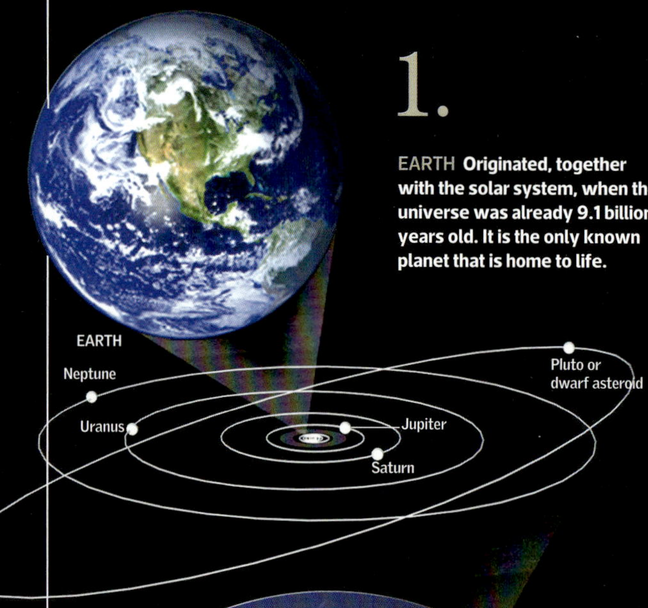

2.

NEAR STARS **Found closer than 20 light-years from the Sun, they make up our solar neighborhood.**

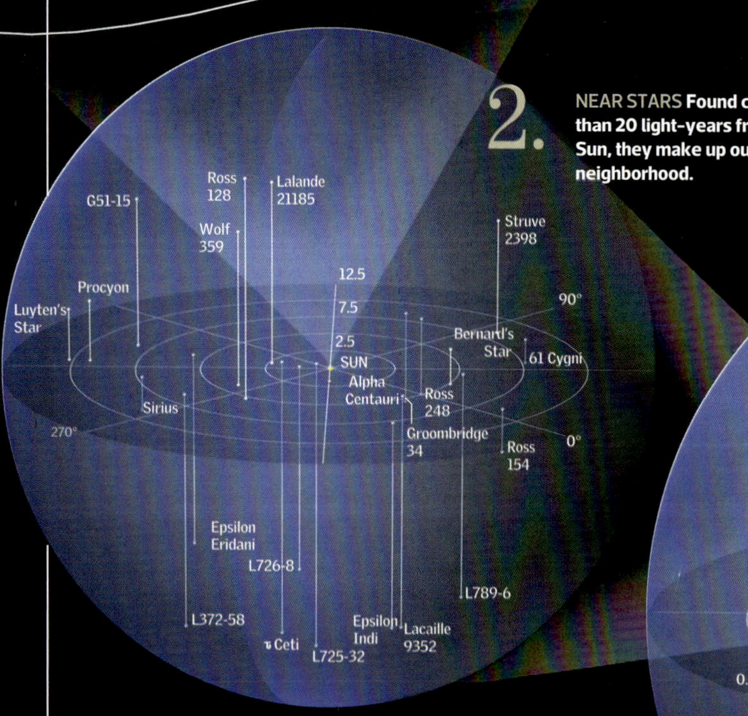

3.

NEIGHBORS **Within a space of one million light-years, we find the Milky Way and its closest galaxies.**

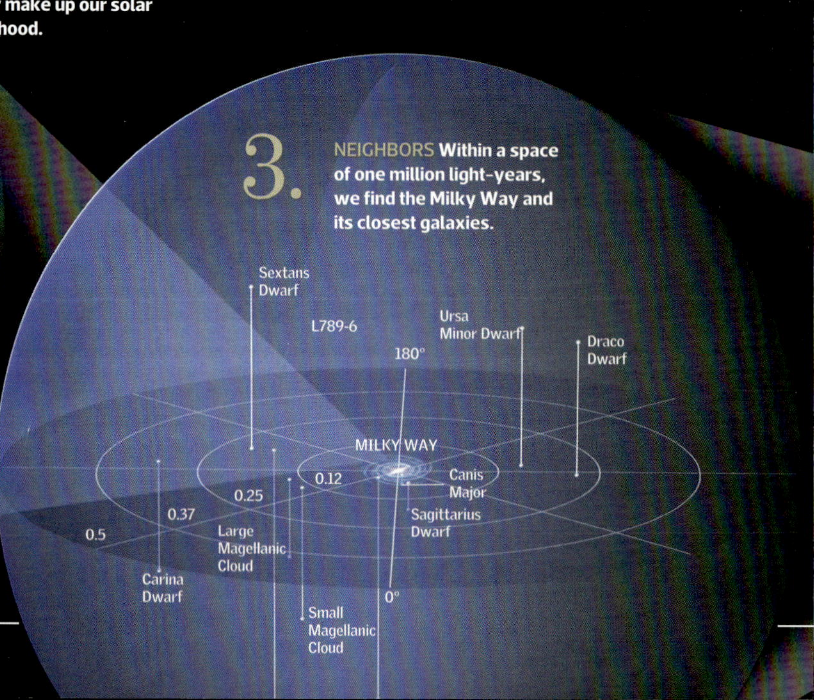

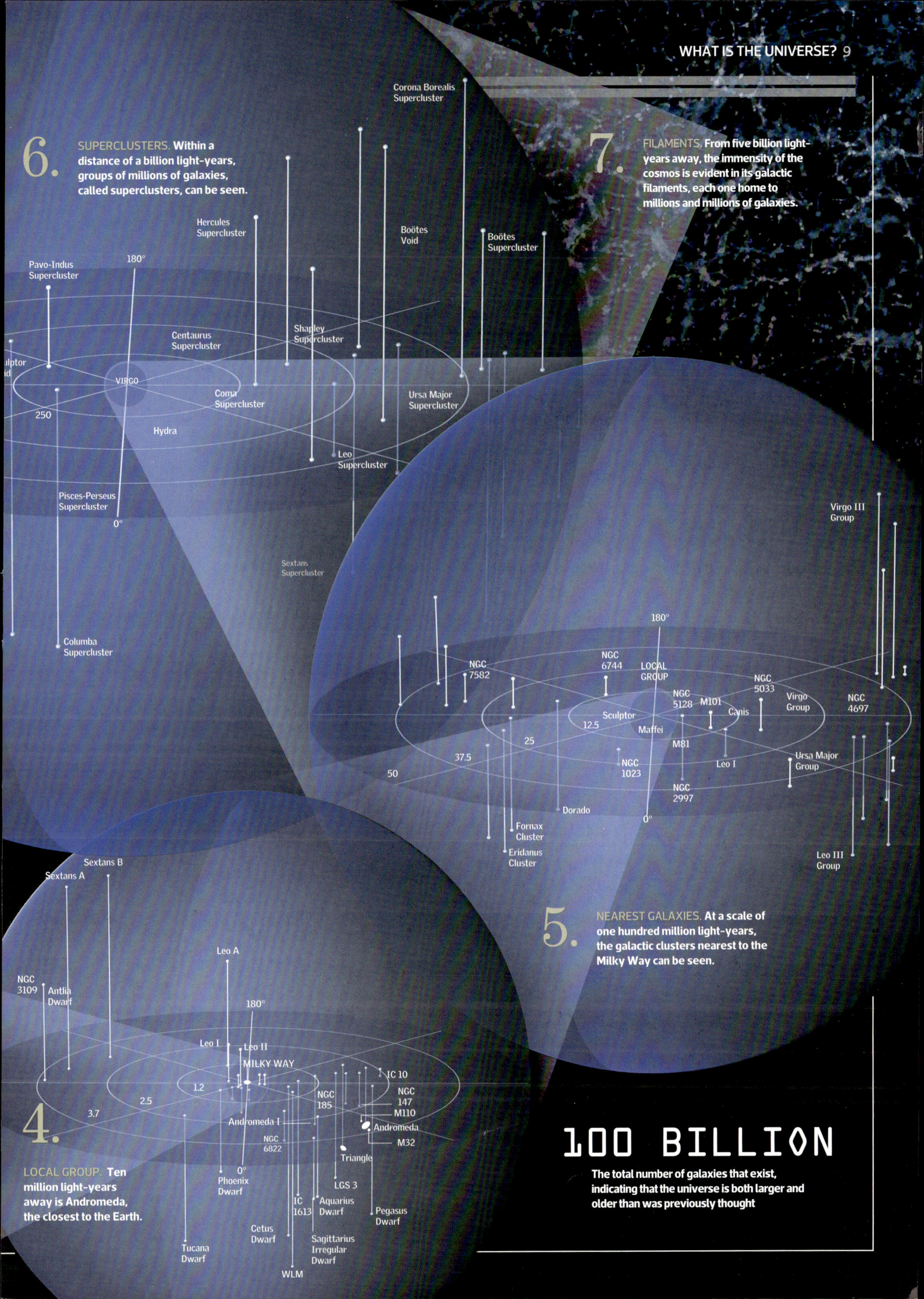

6. SUPERCLUSTERS. **Within a distance of a billion light-years, groups of millions of galaxies, called superclusters, can be seen.**

7. FILAMENTS. **From five billion light-years away, the immensity of the cosmos is evident in its galactic filaments, each one home to millions and millions of galaxies.**

5. NEAREST GALAXIES. **At a scale of one hundred million light-years, the galactic clusters nearest to the Milky Way can be seen.**

4. LOCAL GROUP. **Ten million light-years away is Andromeda, the closest to the Earth.**

100 BILLION

The total number of galaxies that exist, indicating that the universe is both larger and older than was previously thought

The Instant of Creation

It is impossible to know precisely how, out of nothing, the universe began to exist. According to the big bang theory—the theory most widely accepted in the scientific community—in the beginning, there appeared an infinitely small and dense burning ball that gave rise to space, matter, and energy. This happened 13.7 billion years ago. The great, unanswered question is what caused a small dot of light—filled with concentrated energy from which matter and antimatter were created—to arise from nothingness. In very little time, the young universe began to expand and cool. Several billion years later, acquired the form we know today.

Energetic Radiation

The burning ball that gave rise to the universe remained a source of permanent radiation. Subatomic particles and antiparticles annihilated each other. The ball's high density spontaneously produced matter and destroyed it. Had this state of affairs continued, the universe would never have undergone the growth that scientists believe followed cosmic inflation.

HOW IT GREW

Cosmic inflation was an expansion of the entire universe. The Earth's galactic neighborhood appears fairly uniform. Everywhere you look, the types of galaxies and the background temperature are essentially the same.

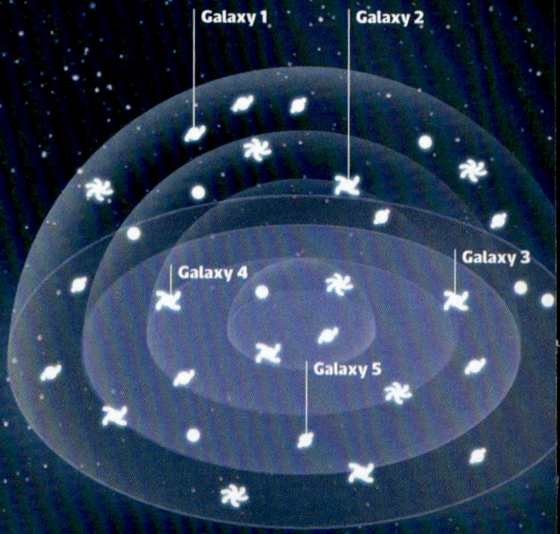

TIME	0	10^{-43} sec	10^{-38} sec
TEMPERATURE	–	10^{32}° F (and C)	10^{29}° F (and C)

1 Scientists theorize that, from nothing, something infinitely small, dense, and hot appeared. All that exists today was compressed into a ball smaller than the nucleus of an atom.

2 At the closest moment to zero time, which physics has been able to reach, the temperature is extremely high. Before the universe's inflation, a superforce governed everything.

3 The universe is unstable. Only 10^{-38} seconds after the big bang, the universe increases in size more than a trillion trillion trillion times. The expansion of universe and the division of its forces be

ELEMENTARY PARTICLES

In its beginnings, the universe was a soup of particles that interacted with each other because of high levels of radiation. Later, as the universe expanded, quarks formed the nuclei of the elements and then joined with electrons to form atoms.

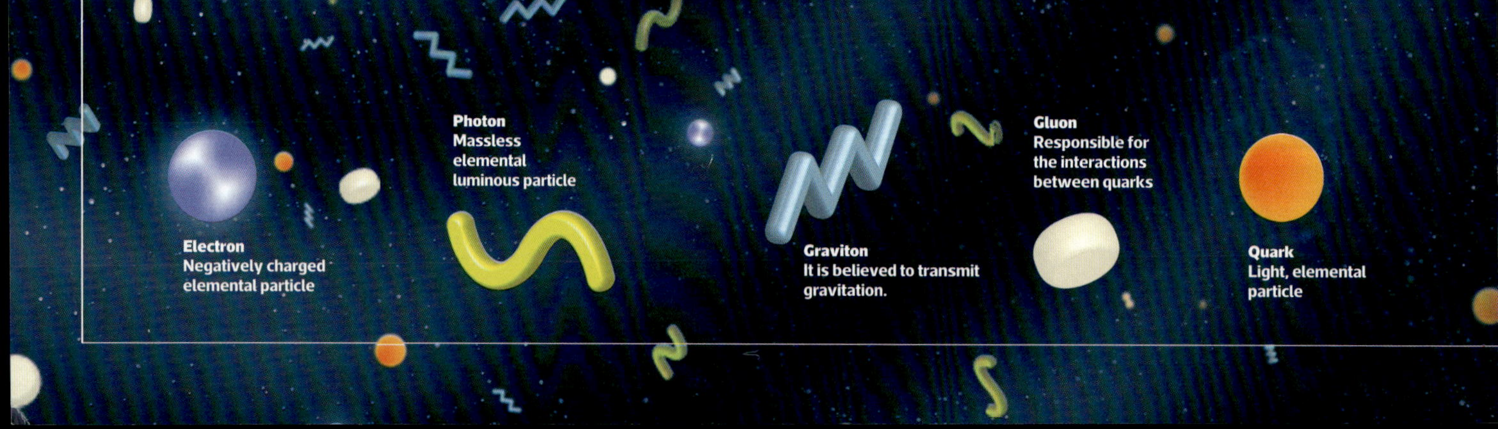

:osmic Inflation Theory

Although big bang theorists understood the universe as originating in an extremely small, hot, and condensed ball, they could not understand the reason for its staggering growth. In 1981, physicist :an Guth proposed a solution to the problem with his inflationary theory. an extremely short period of time (less than a thousandth of a second), e universe grew more than a trillion trillion trillion times. Near the end of is period of expansion, the temperature approached absolute zero.

WMAP (WILKINSON MICROWAVE ANISOTROPY PROBE)

NASA's WMAP project maps the background radiation of the universe. In the image, hotter (red-yellow) regions and colder (blue-green) regions can be observed. WMAP makes it possible to determine the amount of dark matter.

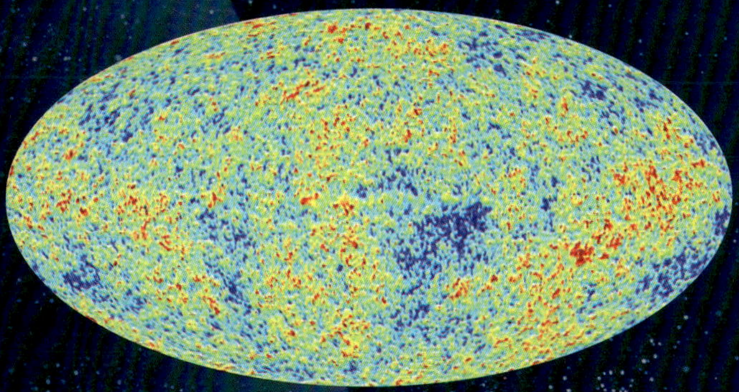

OW IT DID NOT ROW

ad the universe ot undergone flation, it would be a ollection of different egions, each with s own particular ypes of galaxies nd each clearly istinguishable from he others.

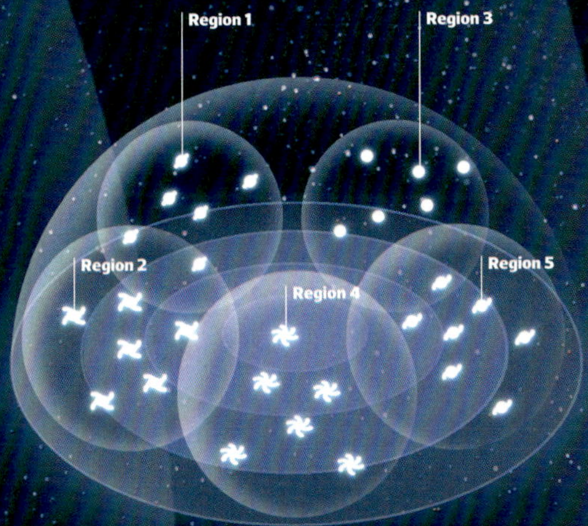

THE SEPARATION OF FORCES

Before the universe expanded, during a period of radiation, only one unified force governed all physical interactions. The first distinguishable force was gravity, followed by electromagnetism and nuclear interactions. Upon the division of the universe's forces, matter was created.

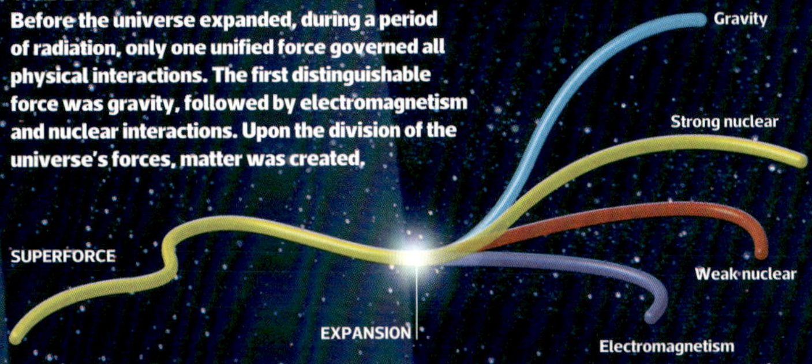

10^{-12} sec — 10^{15}° F (and C)

4 The universe experiences a gigantic cooldown. Gravity has already become distinguishable, and the electromagnetic force and the strong and weak nuclear interactions appear.

10^{-4} sec — 10^{12}° F (and C)

5 Protons and neutrons appear, formed by three quarks apiece. Because all light is trapped within the web of particles, the universe is still dark.

1 sec — The neutrinos separate from the initial particle soup through the disintegration of neutrons. Though having extremely little mass, the neutrinos might nevertheless form the greatest part of the universe's dark matter.

5 sec — 9×10^{9}° F (5×10^{9}° C)

6 The electrons and their antiparticles, positrons, annihilate each other until the positrons disappear. The remaining electrons form atoms.

3 min — 2×10^{9}° F (1×10^{9}° C)

7 The nuclei of the lightest elements, hydrogen and helium, form. Protons and neutrons unite to form the nuclei of atoms.

FROM PARTICLES TO MATTER

The quarks, among the oldest particles, interact with each other by forces transmitted through gluons. Later protons and neutrons will join to form nuclei.

1 A gluon interacts with a quark.

2 Quarks join by means of gluons to form protons and neutrons.

3 Protons and neutrons unite to create nuclei.

The Transparent Universe

With the creation of atoms and overall cooling, the once opaque and dense universe became transparent. Electrons were attracted by the protons of hydrogen and helium nuclei, and together they formed atoms. Photons (massless particles of light) could now pass freely through the universe. With the cooling, radiation remained abundant but was no longer the sole governing factor of the universe. Matter, through gravitational force, could now direct its own destiny. The gaseous lumps that were present in this process grew larger and larger. After 100 million years, they formed even larger objects. Their shapes not yet defined, they constituted protogalaxies. Gravitation gave shape to the first galaxies some 500 million years after the big bang, and the first stars began to shine in the densest regions of these galaxies. One mystery that could not be solved was why galaxies were distributed and shaped the way they were. The solution that astronomers have been able to find through indirect evidence is that there exists material called dark matter whose presence would have played a role in galaxy formation.

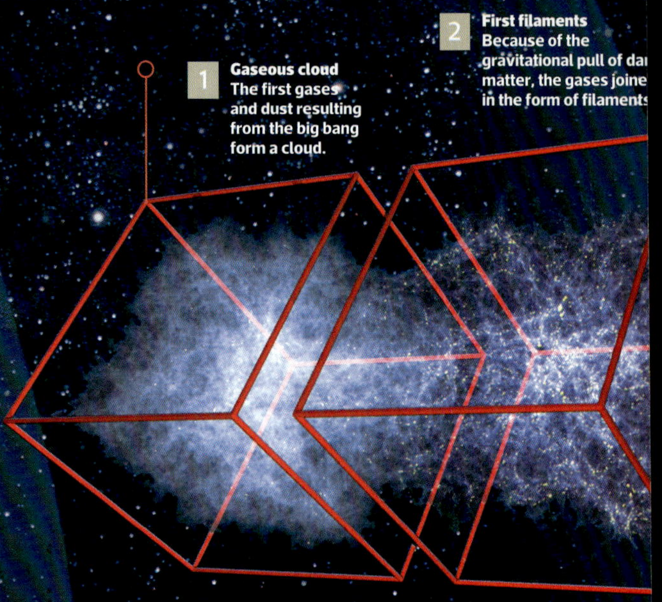

DARK MATTER

The visible objects in the cosmos represent only a small fraction of the total matter within the universe. Most of it is invisible even to the most powerful telescopes. Galaxies and their stars move as they do because of the gravitational forces exerted by this material, which astronomers call dark matter.

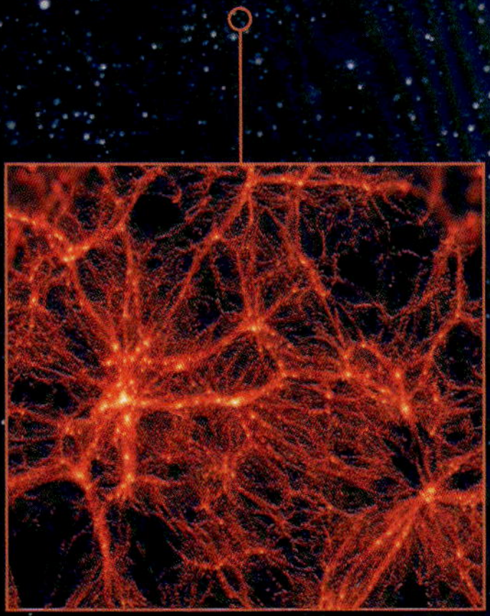

EVOLUTION OF MATTER

What can be observed in the universe today is a great quantity of matter grouped into galaxies. But that was not the original form of the universe. What the big bang initially produced was a cloud of uniformly dispersed gas. Just three million years later, the gas began to organize itself into filaments. Today the universe can be seen as a network of galactic filaments with enormous voids between them.

TIME (in years)	380,000	500 million
TEMPERATURE	4,900° F (2,700° C)	-405° F (-243° C)

8 380,000 years after the big bang, atoms form. Electrons orbit the nuclei, attracted by the protons. The universe becomes transparent. Photons travel through space.

9 Galaxies acquire their definitive shape: islands of millions and millions of stars and masses of gases and dust. The stars explode as supernovas and disperse heavier elements, such as carbon.

FIRST ATOMS

Hydrogen and helium were the first elements to be formed at the atomic level. They are the main components of stars and planets. They are by far the most abundant elements in the universe.

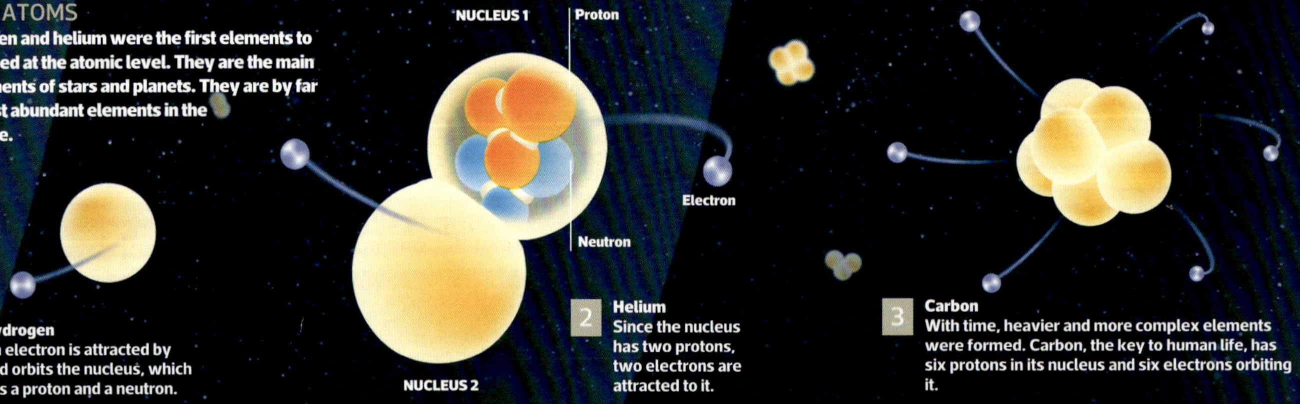

Filament networks
The universe has large-scale filaments that contain millions and millions of galaxies.

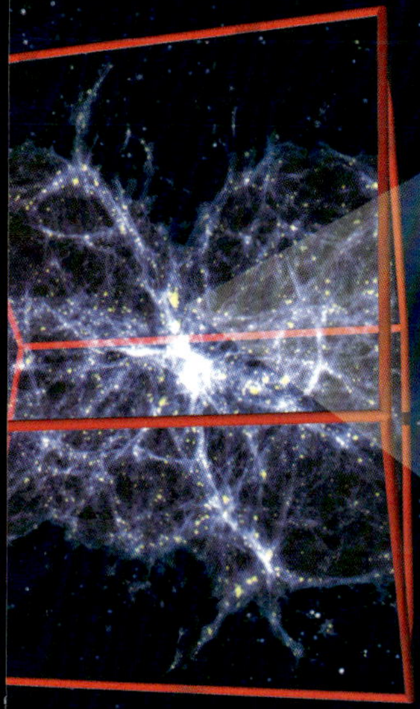

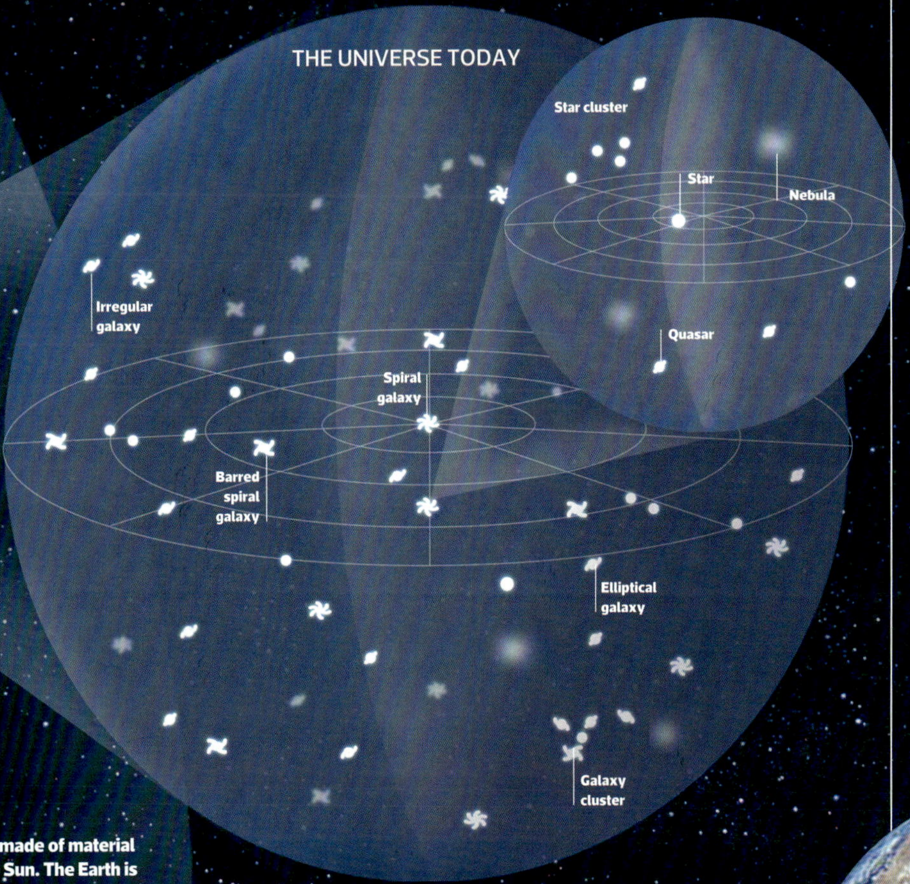

9.1 billion

THE EARTH IS CREATED

Like the rest of the planets, the Earth is made of material that remained after the formation of the Sun. The Earth is the only planet known to have life.

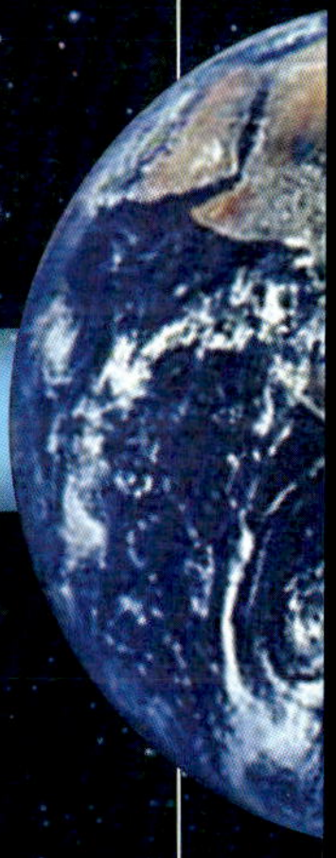

9 billion

-432° F (-258° C)

10 **Nine billion years after the big bang, the solar system emerged. A mass of gas and dust collapsed until it gave rise to the Sun. Later the planetary system was formed from the leftover material.**

13.7 billion

-454° F (-270° C)

11 **The universe continues to expand. Countless galaxies are surrounded by dark matter, which represents 27 percent of the mass and energy in the universe. The ordinary matter, of which stars and planets are made, represents just 5 percent of the total. The predominant form of energy is also of an unknown type. Called dark energy, it constitutes 68 percent of the total mass and energy.**

TIMESCALE

The vast span of time related to the history of the universe can be readily understood if it is scaled to correspond to a single year—a year that spans the beginning of the universe, the appearance of humans on the Earth, and the voyage of Columbus to America. On January 1 of this imaginary year—at midnight—the big bang takes place. *Homo sapiens* appears at 11:56 P.M. on December 31, and Columbus sets sail on the last second of the last day of the year. One second on this timescale is equivalent to 500 true years.

BIG BANG occurs on the first second of the first day of the year.

THE SOLAR SYSTEM is created on August 24 of this timescale.

COLUMBUS'S ARRIVAL takes place on the last second of December 31.

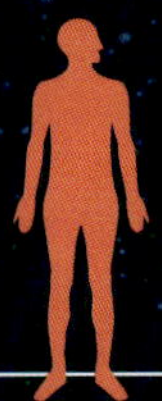

JANUARY

DECEMBER

Everything Comes to an End

The big bang theory helped solve the enigma of the early moments of the universe. What has yet to be resolved is the mystery surrounding the future that awaits. To unravel this mystery, the tota mass of the universe must be known, but that figure has not yet been reliably determined. The most recent observations have removed some of this uncertainty. It seems that the mass of the univers is far too little to stop its expansion. If this is this case, the universe's present growth is merely the last step before its total death in complete darkness.

Flat Universe

1 There is a critical amount of mass for which the universe would expand at a declining rate without ever totally stopping. The result of this eternal expansion would be the existence of an ever-increasing number of galaxies and stars. If the universe were flat, we could talk about a cosmos born from an explosion, but it would be a universe continuing outward forever. It is difficult to think about a universe with these characteristics.

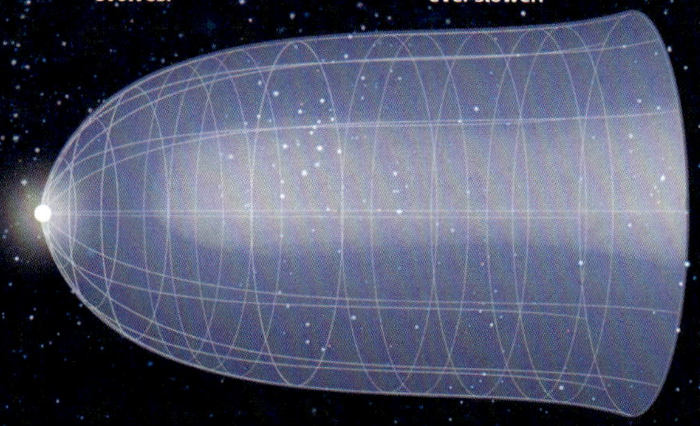

THE HAWKING UNIVERSE

The universe was composed originally of four spatial dimensions without the dimension of time. According to Stephen Hawking, since there is no change without time, one of these dimensions transformed spontaneously on a small scale into a temporal dimension, and the universe began to expand.

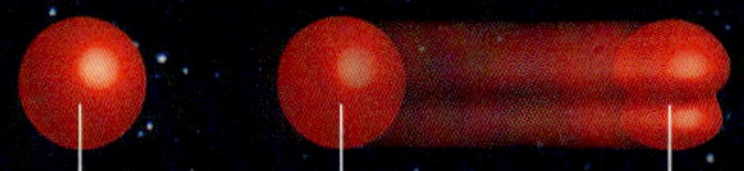

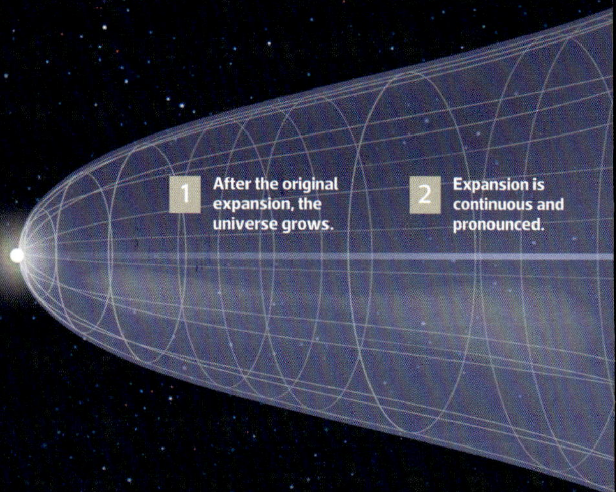

Closed Universe

2 If the universe had more than critical mass, it would expand until reaching a point where gravity stopped the expansion. Then, the universe would contract in the Big Crunch, a total collapse culminating in an infinitely small, dense, and hot spot similar to the one from which the universe was formed. Gravity's pull on the universe's excess matter would stop the expansion and reverse the process.

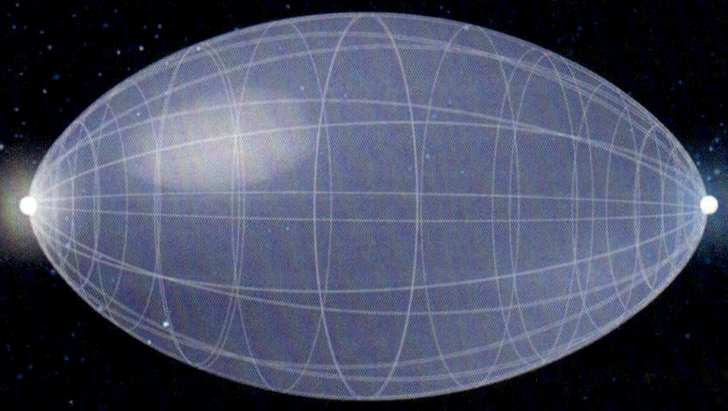

HOW IT IS MADE UP

Dark energy is hypothesized to be the predominant energy in the universe. It is believed to speed up the expansion of the universe.

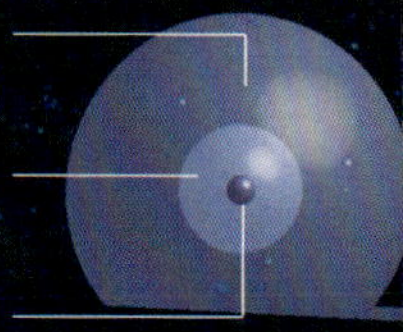

DISCOVERIES

The key discovery that led to the big bang theory was made in the early 1920s by Edwin Hubble, who discovered that galaxies were moving away from each other. In the 1940s, George Gamow developed the idea that the universe began with a primordial explosion. A consequence of such an event would be the existence of background radiation, which Arno Penzias and Robert Wilson accidentally detected in the mid-1960s.

1920s

GALACTIC EXPANSION

By noting a redshift toward the red end of the spectrum, Hubble was able to demonstrate that galaxies were moving away from each other.

1940s

GAMOW'S SUSPICION

Gamow first hypothesized the big bang, holding that the early universe was a "cauldron" of particles.

1965

BACKGROUND RADIATION

Penzias and Wilson detected radio signals that came from across the entire sky—the uniform signal of background radiation.

Self-generated Universes

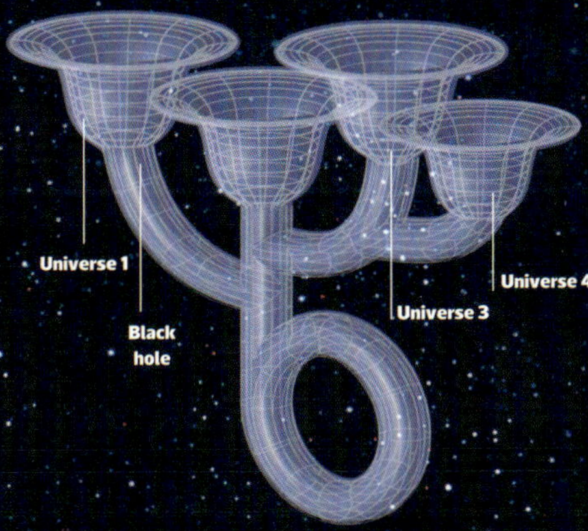

3 **A less widely accepted theory about the nature of the universe suggests that universes generate themselves. If this is the case, universes would be created continuously like the branches of a tree, and they might be linked by supermassive black holes.**

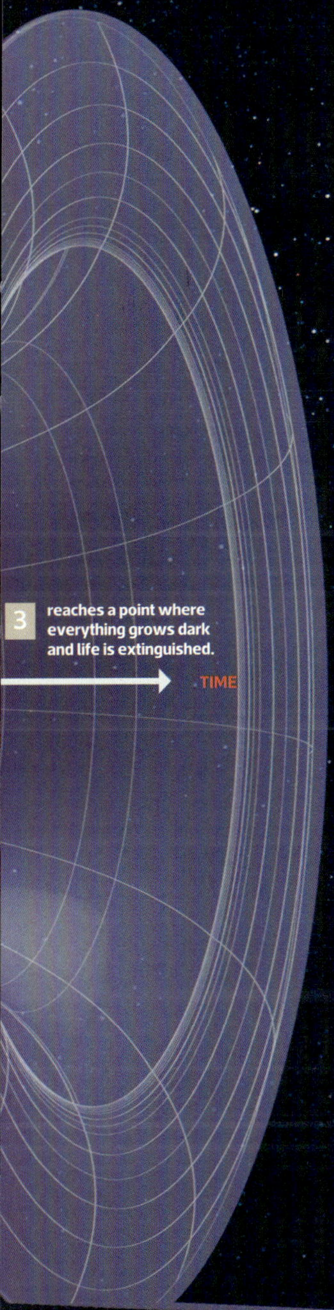

Open Universe

4 **The most accepted theory about the future of the cosmos says that the universe possesses a mass smaller than the critical value. The latest measurements seem to indicate that the present time is just a phase before the death of the universe, in which it goes completely dark.**

BLACK HOLES

Some theorists believe that, by entering a black hole, travel through space to other universes might be possible because of antigravitational effects.

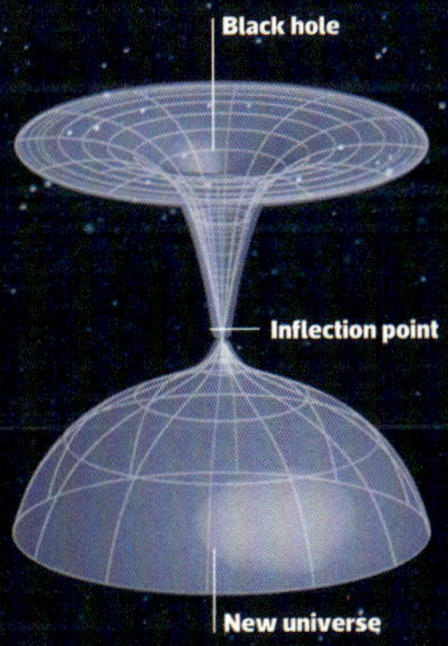

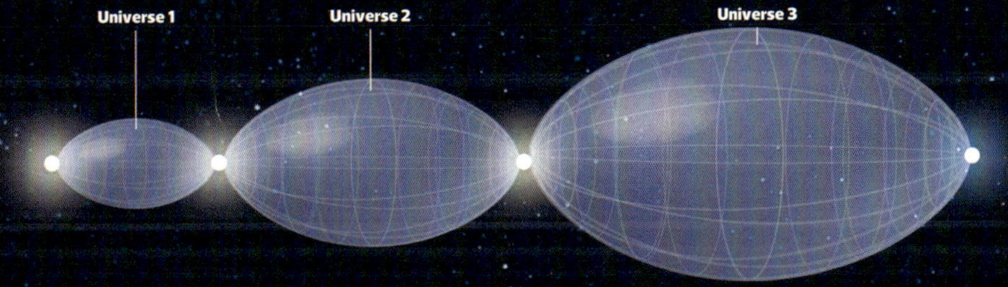

Baby Universes

5 **According to this theory, universes continuously sprout other universes. But in this case, one universe would be created from the death or disappearance of another. Each dead universe in a final collapse, or Big Crunch, would give rise to a supermassive black hole, from which another universe would be born. This process could repeat itself indefinitely, making the number of universes impossible to determine.**

The Forces of the Universe

The four fundamental forces of nature are those that are not derived from basic forces. Physicists believe that, at one time, all physical forces functioned as a single force and that during the expansion of the universe, they became distinct from each other. Each force now governs different processes, and each interaction affects different types of particles. Gravity, electromagnetism, strong nuclear interactions, and weak nuclear interactions are essential to our understanding of the behavior of the many objects that exist in the universe. In recent years, many scientists have tried with little success to show how all forces are manifestations of a single type of exchange.

General Theory of Relativity

The biggest contribution to our comprehension of the universe's internal workings was made by Albert Einstein in 1915. Building on Newton's theory of universal gravitation, Einstein thought of space as linked to time. To Newton, gravity was merely the force that attracted two objects, but Einstein hypothesized that it was a consequence of what he called the curvature of space-time. According to his general theory of relativity, the universe curves in the presence of objects with mass. Gravity, according to this theory, is a distortion of space that determines whether one object rolls toward another. Einstein's general theory of relativity required scientists to consider the universe in terms of a non-Euclidian geometry, since it is not compatible with the idea of a flat universe. In Einsteinian space, two parallel lines can meet.

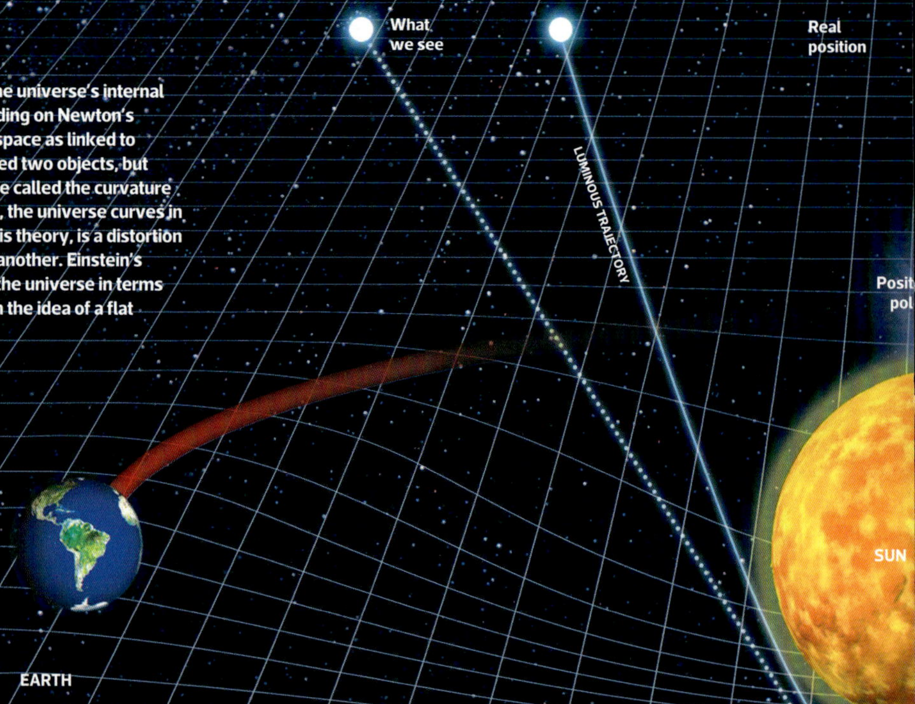

$$E=mc^2$$

In Einstein's equation, energy and mass are interchangeable. If an object increases its mass, its energy increases, and vice versa.

Gravity

1 Gravity was the first force to become distinguishable from the original superforce. Today scientists understand gravity in Einstein's terms as an effect of the curvature of space-time. If the universe were thought of as a cube, the presence of any object with mass in space would deform the cube. Gravity can act at great distances (just as electromagnetism can) and always exerts a force of attraction. Despite the many attempts to find antigravity (which could counteract the effects of black holes), it has yet to be found.

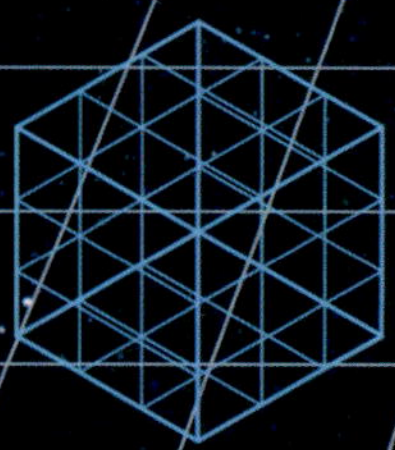

The universe, if it were empty, could be pictured in this way.

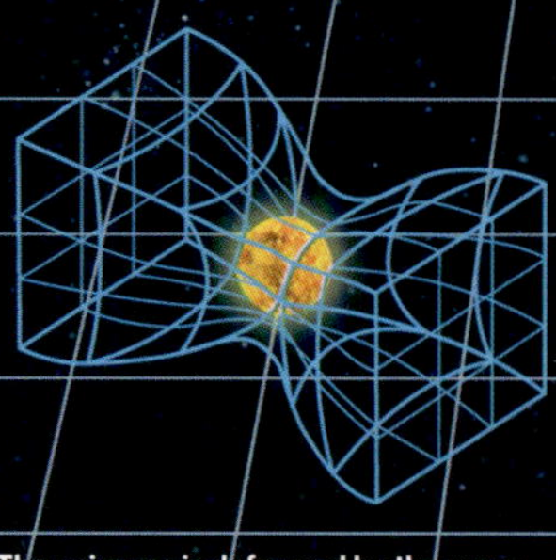

The universe is deformed by the mass of the objects it contains.

UNIVERSAL GRAVITATION

The gravitation proposed by Newton is the mutual attraction between bodies having mass. The equation developed by Newton to calculate this force states that the attraction experienced by two bodies is directly proportional to the product of their masses and inversely proportional to the square of the distance between them. Newton represented the constant of proportionality resulting from this interaction as G. The shortcoming of Newton's law, an accepted paradigm until Einstein's theory of general relativity, lies in its failure to make time an essential component in the interaction between objects. According to Newton, the gravitational attraction between two objects with mass did not depend on the properties of space but was an intrinsic property of the objects themselves. Nevertheless, Newton's law of universal gravitation was a foundation for Einstein's theory.

NEWTON'S EQUATION

Two bodies with mass attract each other. Whichever body has the greatest mass will exert a greater force on the other. The greater the distance between the objects, the smaller the force they exert on each other.

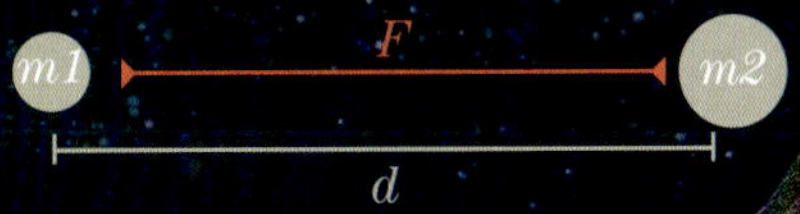

$$F = \frac{G \times m1 \times m2}{d^2}$$

Strong Nuclear Force

3 **The strong nuclear force holds the protons and neutrons of atomic nuclei together. Both protons and neutrons are subject to this force. Gluons are particles that carry the strong nuclear force, and they bind quarks together to form protons and neutrons. Atomic nuclei are held together by residual forces in the interaction between quarks and gluons.**

1 Quarks and gluons
The strong nuclear interaction takes place when the gluon interacts with quarks.

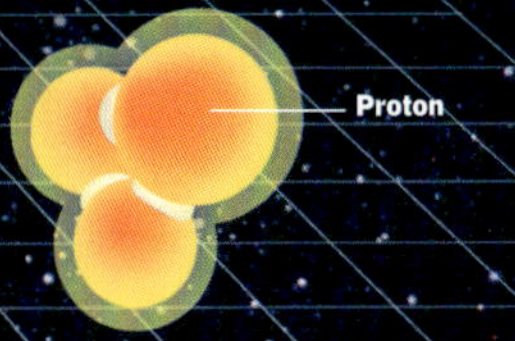

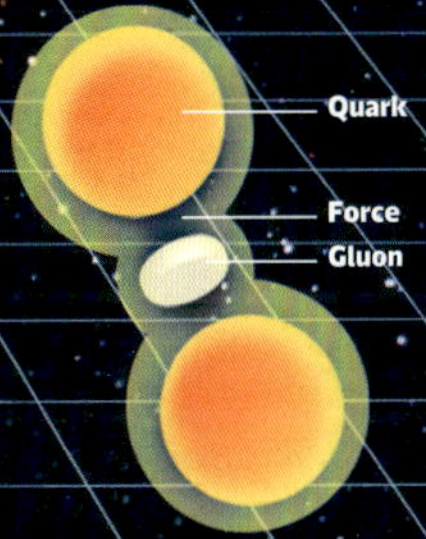

2 Union
Quarks join and form nuclear protons and neutrons.

Electromagnetism

2 **Electromagnetism is the force that affects electrically charged bodies. It is involved in the chemical and physical transformations of the atoms and molecules of the various elements. The electromagnetic force can be one of attraction or repulsion, with two types of charges or poles.**

Attraction
Two atoms are drawn together, and the electrons rotate around the new molecule.

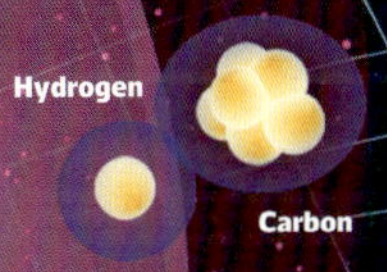

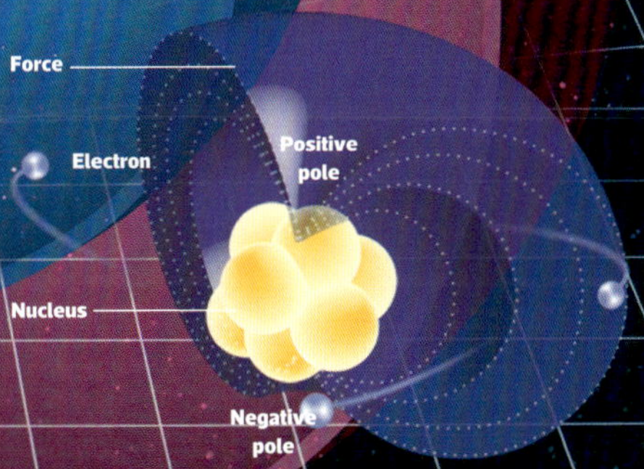

MOLECULAR MAGNETISM

In atoms and molecules, the electromagnetic force is dominant. It is the force that causes the attraction between protons and electrons in an atom and the attraction or repulsion between ionized atoms.

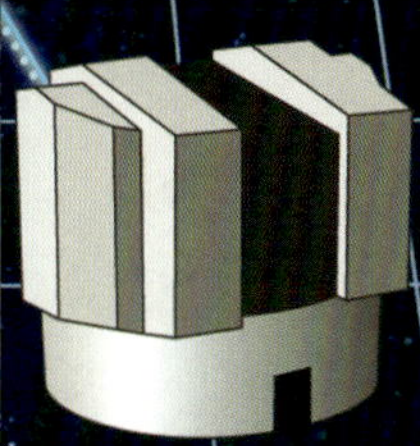

BENDING LIGHT

Light also bends because of the curvature of space-time. When seen from a telescope, the real position of an object is distorted. What is perceived through the telescope is a false location, generated by the curvature of the light. It is not possible to see the actual position of the object.

Weak Nuclear Force

4 **The weak nuclear force is not as strong as the other forces. The weak nuclear interaction influences the beta decay of a neutron, which results in a proton and the emission of an electron and a neutrino. This force takes part in the natural radioactive phenomena associated with certain types of atoms.**

1 Hydrogen
A neutron's *down* quark transforms to an *up* quark.

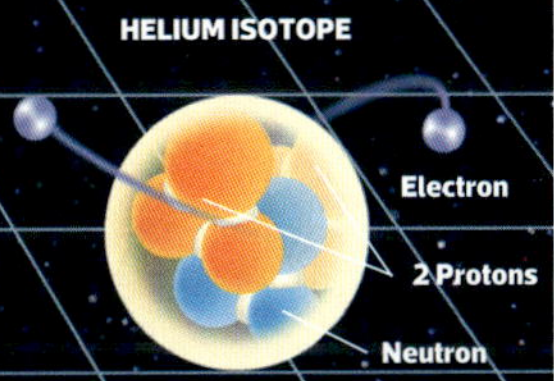

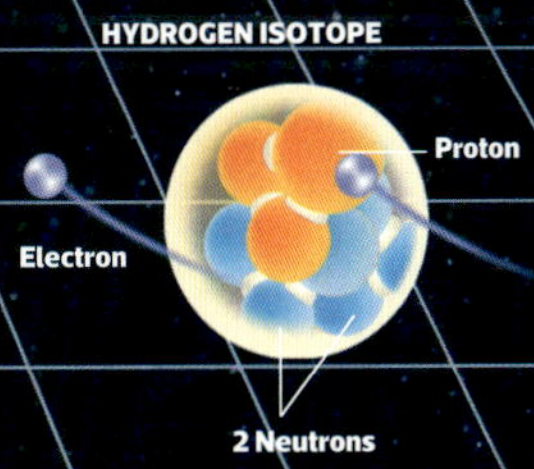

2 Helium
The neutron becomes a proton, and the hydrogen atom becomes a helium atom.

What Is in the Universe?

The universe is populated on a grand scale by strands of superclusters surrounding vacant areas. Sometimes the galaxies collide with each other, triggering the formation of stars. In the vast cosmos, there are also quasars, pulsars, and black holes. Thank to current technology, we can enjoy the displays of light and shadow that make

ETA CARINAE NEBULA
With a diameter of more than 200 light-years, it is one of biggest and brightest nebulae of our galaxy. This young, supermassive star is expected to become a supernova in the near future.

p, for example, the Eta Carinae Nebula shown), which is composed of jets of ot, fluorescent gases. Although not all he objects in the universe are known, it an be said without a doubt that most of the atoms that make up our bodies have been born in the interior of stars. ●

Luminous

For a long time stars were a mystery to humans, and it was only as recently as the 19th century that astronomers began to understand the true nature of stars. Today we know that they are gigantic spheres of incandescent gas—mostly hydrogen, with a smaller proportion of helium. As a star radiates light, astronomers can precisely measure its brightness, color, and temperature. Because of their enormous distance from the Earth, stars beyond the Sun only appear as points of light, and even the most powerful telescopes do not reveal any surface features.

Hertzsprung-Russell (H-R) Diagram

The H-R diagram plots the intrinsic luminosity of stars against their spectral class, which corresponds to their temperature or the wavelengths of light they emit. The most massive stars are those with greatest intrinsic luminosity. They include blue stars, red giants, and red supergiants. Stars spend 90 percent of their lives in what is known as the main sequence.

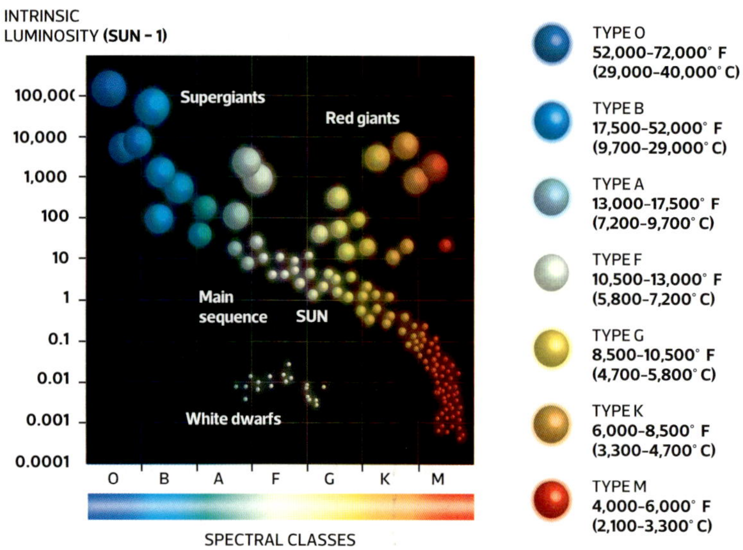

Light-years and Parsecs

In measuring the great distances between stars, both light-years (ly) and parsecs (pc) are used. A light-year is the distance that light travels in a year—5.9 trillion miles (10 trillion km). A light-year is a unit of distance, not time. A parsec is equivalent to the distance between the star and the Earth if the parallax angle is of one second arc. A pc is equal to 3.26 light-years, or 19 trillion miles (31 trillion km).

COLORS The hottest stars are bluish-white (spectral classes O, B, and A). The coolest stars are orange, yellow, and red (spectral classes G, K, and M).

PRINCIPAL STARS WITHIN 100 LY FROM THE SUN

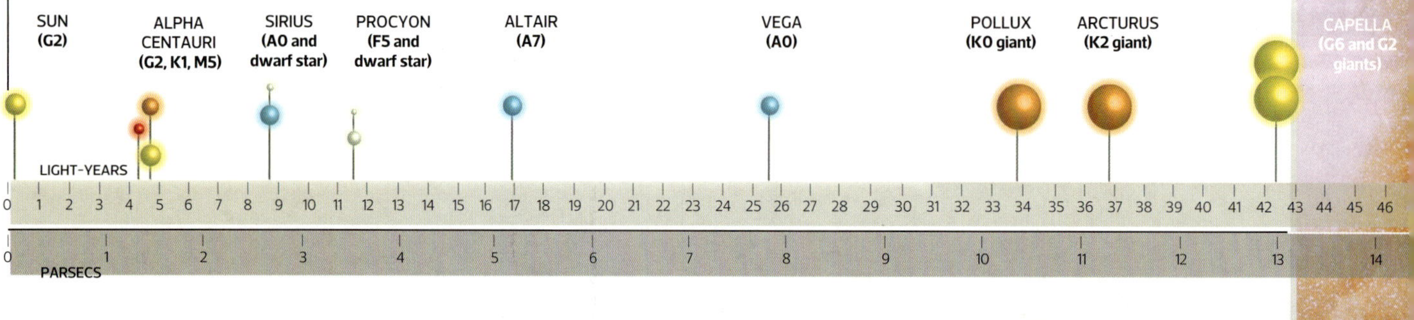

GLOBULAR CLUSTER
More than a million stars are grouped together into a spherical cluster called Omega Centauri.

OPEN CLUSTER
The Pleiades are a formation of some 400 stars that will eventually move apart.

Measuring Distance

When the Earth orbits the Sun, the closest stars appear to move in front of a background of more distant stars. The angle described by the movement of a star in a six-month period of the Earth's rotation is called its parallax. The parallax of the most distant stars are too small to measure. The closer a star is to the Earth, the greater its parallax.

PARALLAX

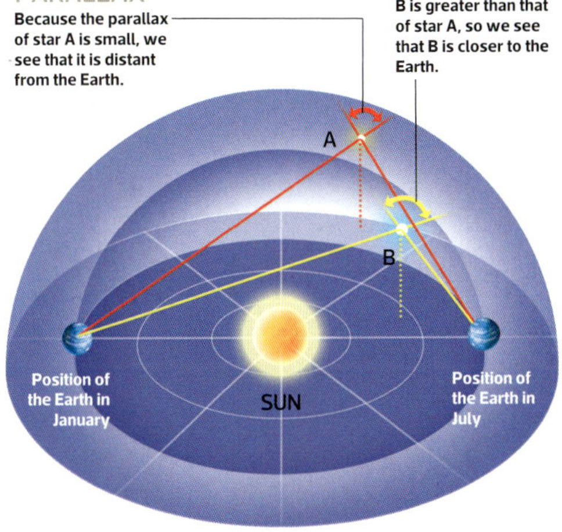

Spectral Analysis

The electromagnetic waves that make up light have different wavelengths. When light from a hot object, such as a star, is split into its different wavelengths, a band of colors, or spectrum, is obtained. Patterns of dark lines typically appear in the spectrum of a star. These patterns can be studied to determine the elements that make up the star.

DOPPLER EFFECT

When a star moves toward or away from an observer, its wavelengths of light shift, a phenomenon called the Doppler effect. If the star is approaching the Earth, the dark lines in its spectrum experience a blueshift. If it moves away from the Earth, the lines experience a redshift.

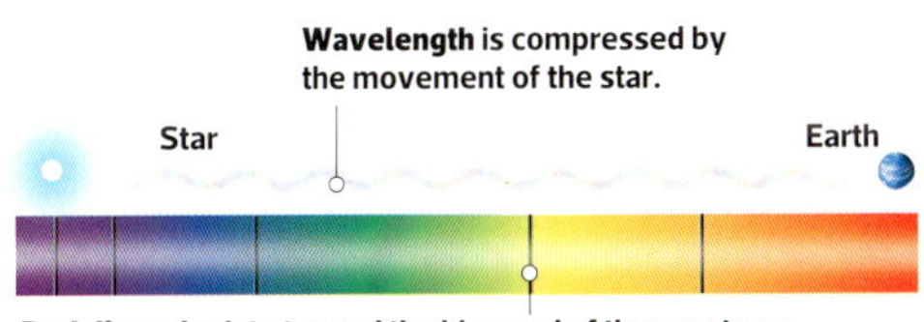

BLUESHIFT of a star moving toward the Earth.

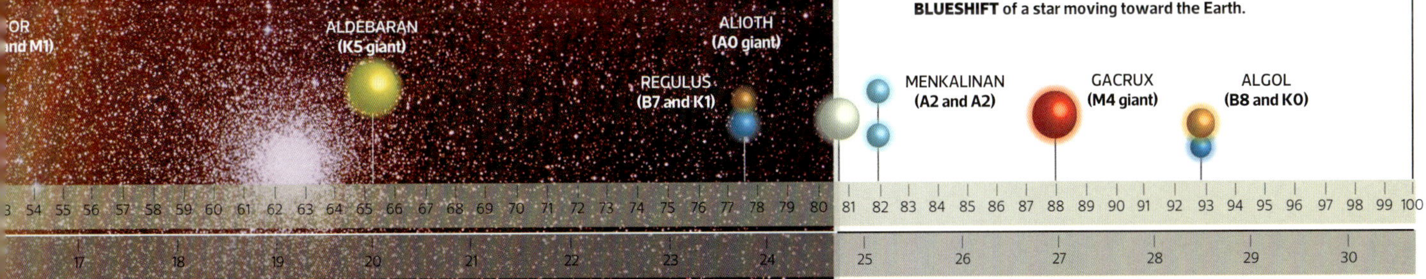

Stellar Evolution

Stars are born in nebulae, which are giant clouds of gas (mainly hydrogen) and dust that float in space. Stars can have a life span of millions, or even billions, of years. The biggest stars have the shortest lives, because they consume their nuclear fuel (hydrogen) at a very accelerated rate. Other stars, like the Sun, burn fuel at a slower rate and may live some 10 billion years. Many times, a star's size indicates its age. Smaller stars are the youngest, and bigger stars are approaching their end, either through cooling or by exploding as a supernova.

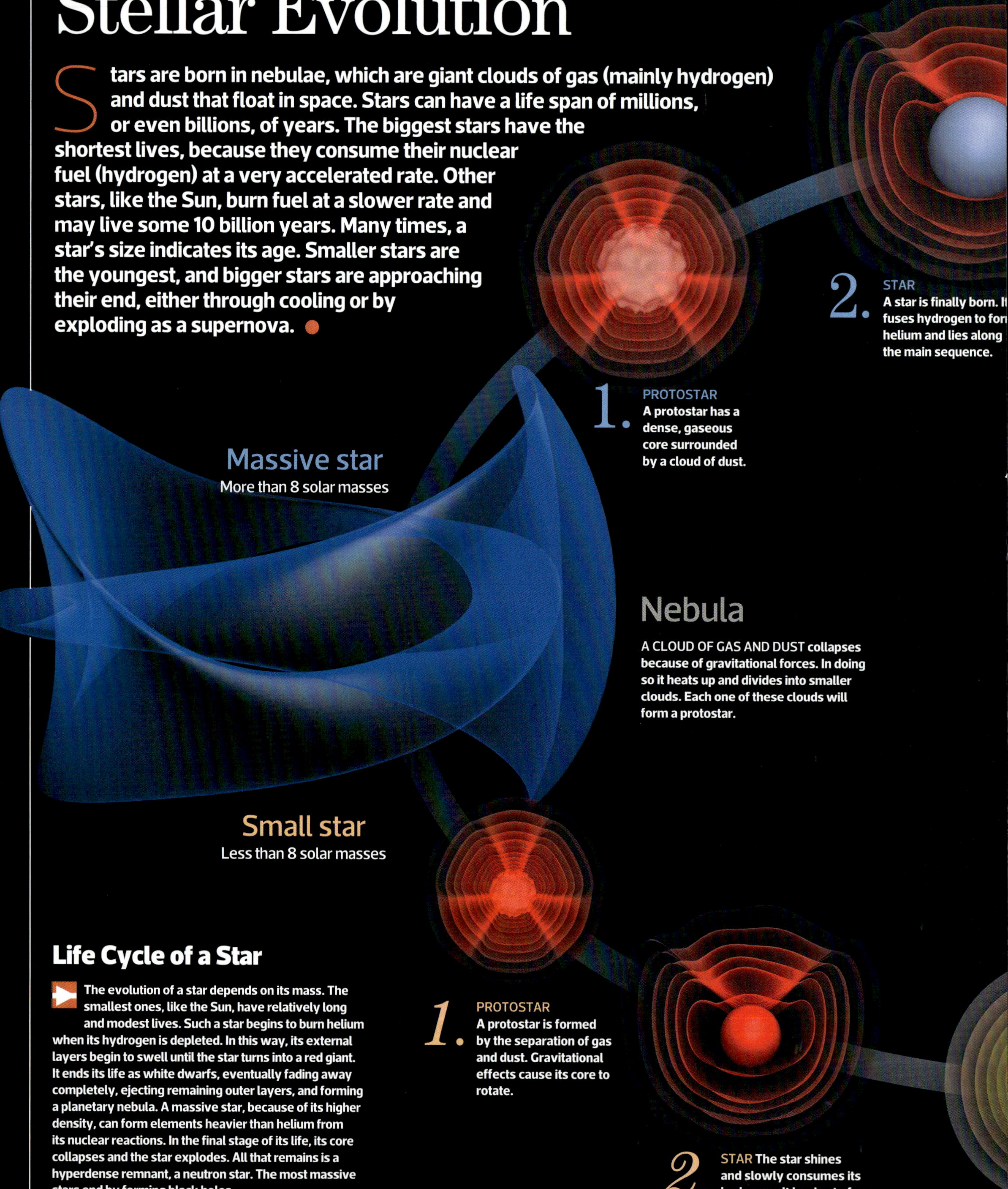

1. PROTOSTAR
A protostar has a dense, gaseous core surrounded by a cloud of dust.

2. STAR
A star is finally born. It fuses hydrogen to form helium and lies along the main sequence.

Massive star

More than 8 solar masses

Nebula

A CLOUD OF GAS AND DUST collapses because of gravitational forces. In doing so it heats up and divides into smaller clouds. Each one of these clouds will form a protostar.

Small star

Less than 8 solar masses

1. PROTOSTAR
A protostar is formed by the separation of gas and dust. Gravitational effects cause its core to rotate.

2. STAR The star shines and slowly consumes its hydrogen. It begins to fuse helium as its size increases.

Life Cycle of a Star

The evolution of a star depends on its mass. The smallest ones, like the Sun, have relatively long and modest lives. Such a star begins to burn helium when its hydrogen is depleted. In this way, its external layers begin to swell until the star turns into a red giant. It ends its life as white dwarfs, eventually fading away completely, ejecting remaining outer layers, and forming a planetary nebula. A massive star, because of its higher density, can form elements heavier than helium from its nuclear reactions. In the final stage of its life, its core collapses and the star explodes. All that remains is a hyperdense remnant, a neutron star. The most massive stars end by forming black holes.

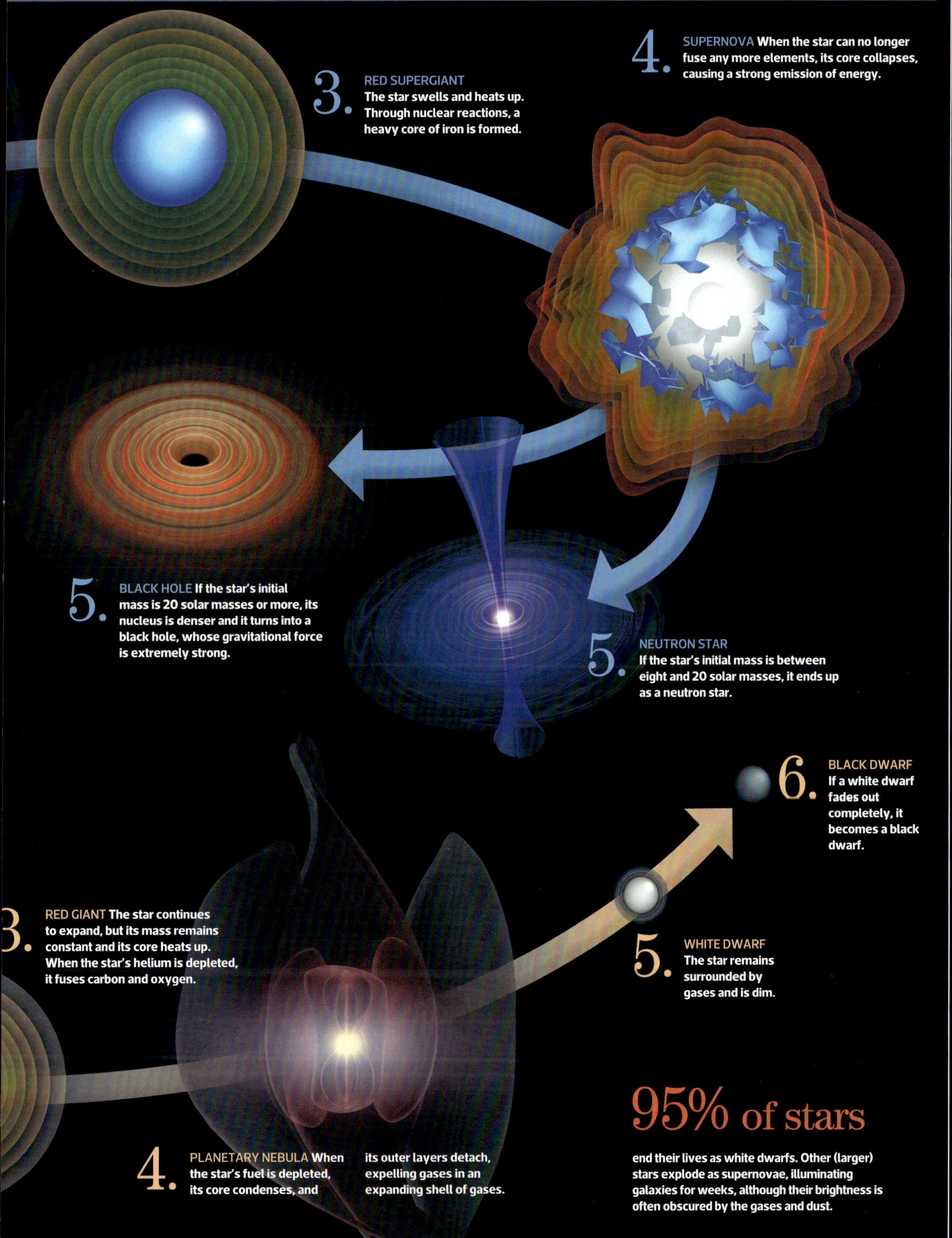

95% of stars

end their lives as white dwarfs. Other (larger) stars explode as supernovae, illuminating galaxies for weeks, although their brightness is often obscured by the gases and dust.

Red, Danger, and Death

When a star exhausts its hydrogen, it begins to die. The helium that now makes up the star's core begins to undergo nuclear reactions, and the star remains bright. When the star's helium is depleted, fusion of carbon and oxygen begins, which causes the star's core to contract. The star continues to live, though its surface layers begin to expand and cool as the star turns into a red giant. Stars similar to the Sun (solar-type stars) follow this process. After billions of years, they end up as white dwarfs. When they are fully extinguished, they will be black dwarfs, invisible in space.

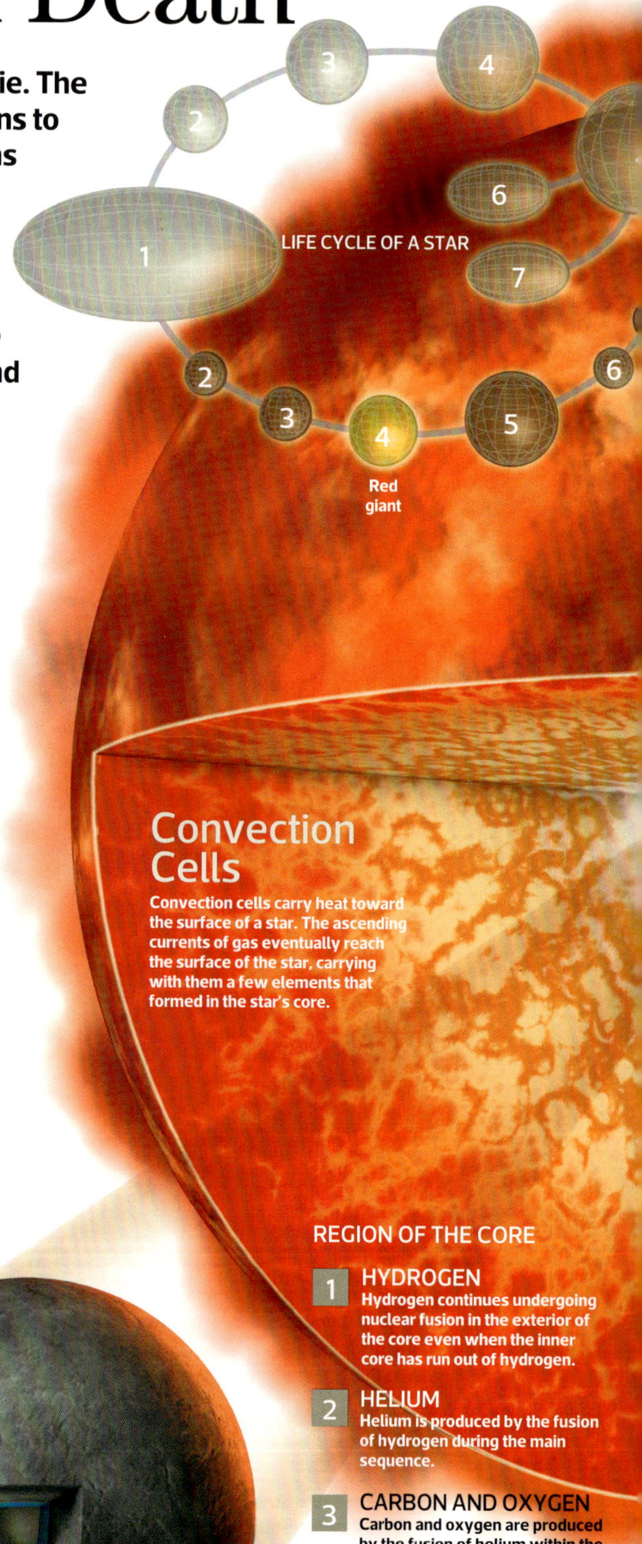

Red Giant

All stars go through a red-giant stage. Depending on a star's mass, it may collapse or it may simply die enveloped in gaseous layers. The core of a red giant is 10 times smaller than it was originally since it shrinks from a lack of hydrogen.

A supergiant star (one with an initial mass greater than eight solar masses) lives a much shorter life. Because of the high density attained by its core, it eventually collapses in on itself and explodes.

DIAMETER

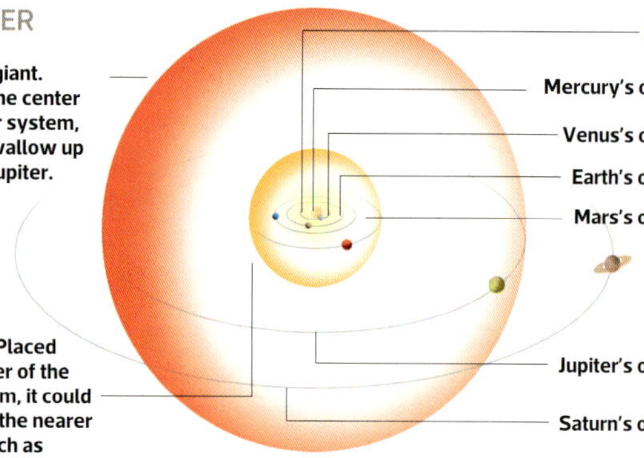

SPECTACULAR DIMENSIONS

On leaving the main sequence, the star enlarges to 200 times the size of the Sun. When the star begins to burn helium, its size decreases to between ten and one hundred times the size of the Sun. The star then remains stable until it becomes a white dwarf.

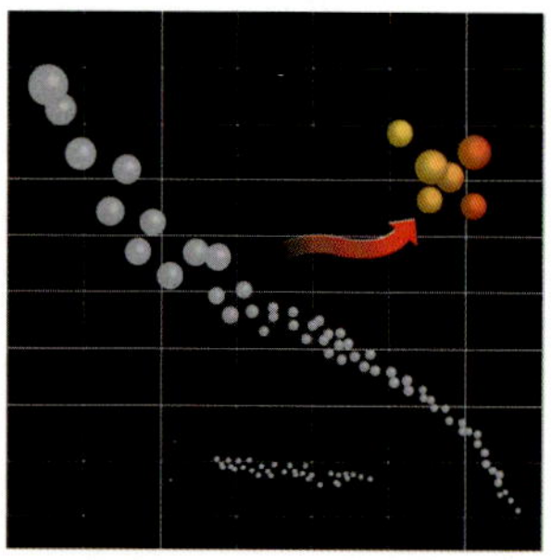

HERTZSPRUNG-RUSSELL

When the star exhausts its hydrogen, it leaves the main sequence and burns helium as a red giant (or a supergiant). The smallest stars take billions of years to leave the main sequences. The color of a red giant is caused by its relatively cool surface temperature of 3,600° F (2,000° C).

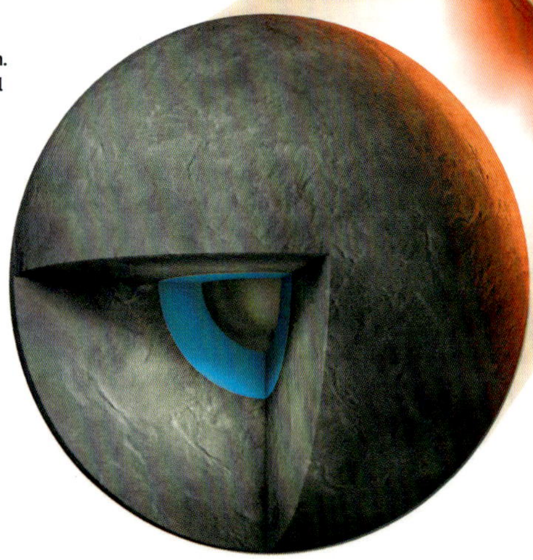

SUN

1%

The scale of the diameter of the Sun to the diameter of a typical red giant.

Hot Spots

Hot spots appear when large jets of incandescent gas reach the star's surface. They can be detected on the surface of red giants.

Dust Grains

Dust grains condense in the star's outer atmosphere and later disperse in the form of stellar winds. The dust acquires a dark appearance and is swept into interstellar space, where new generations of stars will form. The outer layer of the star may extend across several light-years of interstellar space.

White Dwarf

After going through the red-giant stage, a solar-type star loses its outer layers, giving rise to a planetary nebula. In its center remains a white dwarf—a relatively small, very hot (360,000° F [200,000° C]), dense star. After cooling for millions of years, it shuts down completely and becomes a black dwarf.

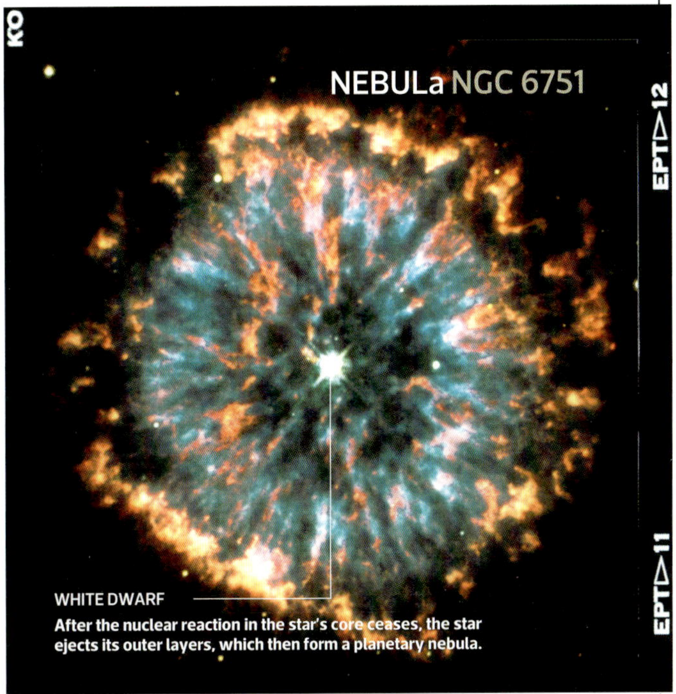

After the nuclear reaction in the star's core ceases, the star ejects its outer layers, which then form a planetary nebula.

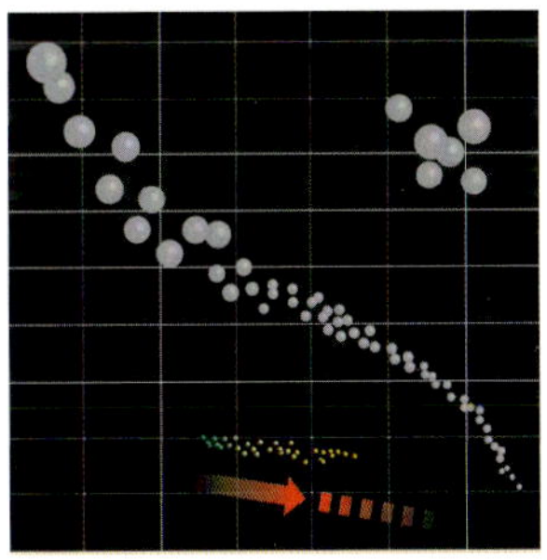

HERTZSPRUNG-RUSSELL

When a white dwarf leaves the red-giant stage, it occupies the lower-left corner of the H-R diagram. Its temperature may be double that of a typical red giant. A massive white dwarf can collapse in on itself and end its life as a neutron star.

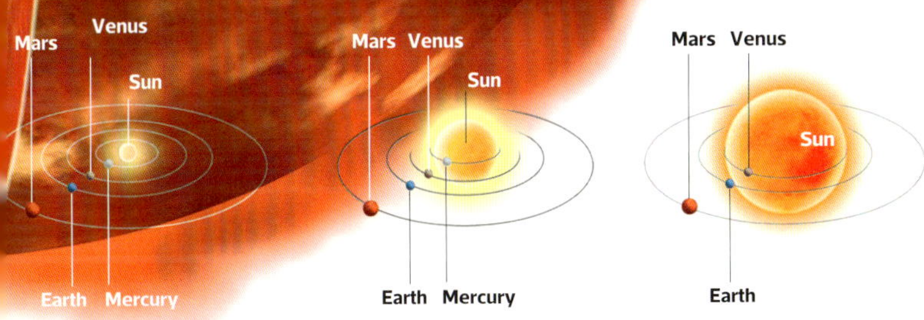

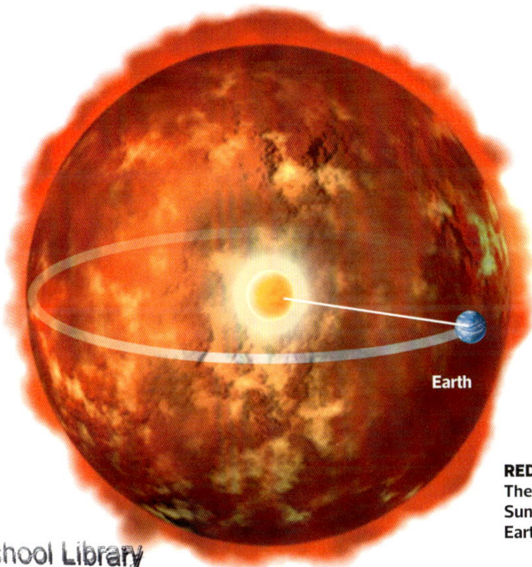

RED GIANT
The radius of the Sun reaches the Earth's orbit.

HE FUTURE OF THE SUN

ke any typical star, the Sun burns hydrogen uring its main sequence. After taking pproximately five billion years to exhaust s supply of hydrogen, it will begin its ansformation into a red giant, doubling in brightness and expanding until it swallows Mercury. At its maximum size, it may even envelop the Earth. Once it has stabilized, it will continue as a red giant for two billion years and then become a white dwarf.

Gas Shells

When a small star dies, all that remains is an expanding gas shell known as a planetary nebula, which has nothing to do with the planets. In general, planetary nebulae are symmetrical or spherical objects. Although it has not been possible to determine why they exist in such diversity, the reason may be related to the effects of the magnetic field of the dying central star. Viewed through a telescope, several nebulae can be seen to contain a central dwarf star, a mere remnant of its precursor star. ●

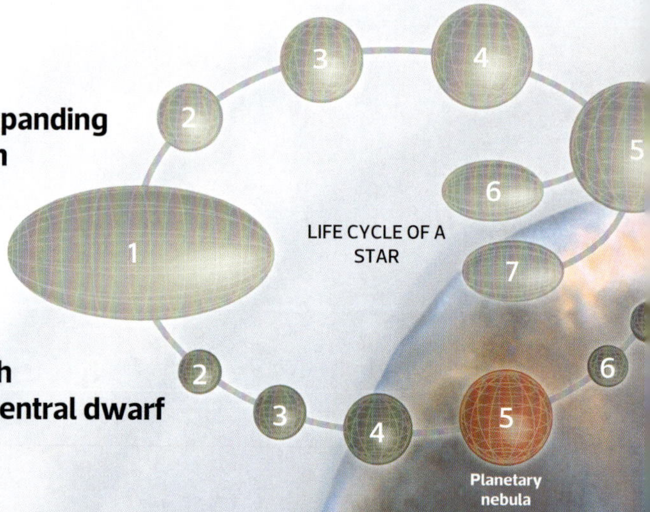

M2-9
The Butterfly Nebula contains a star in addition to a white dwarf. Each orbits the other inside a gas disk that is 10 times larger than Pluto's orbit. The Butterfly Nebula is located 2,100 light-years from Earth.

TWICE THE TEMPERATURE OF THE SUN
is reached at the surface of a white dwarf, causing it to appear white even though its luminosity is a thousand times less than that of the Sun.

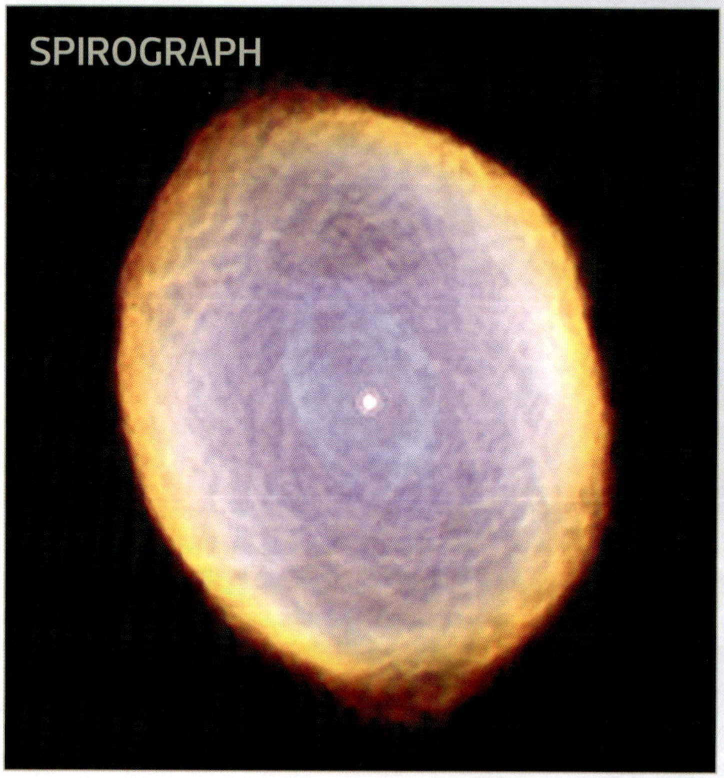

IC 418
The Spirograph Nebula has a hot, luminous core that excites nearby atoms, causing them to glow. The Spirograph Nebula is about 0.1 light-year wide and is located 2,000 light-years from Earth.

CHANDRASEKHAR LIMIT

The astrophysicist Subrahmanyan Chandrasekhar, winner of the Nobel Prize for Physics in 1983, calculated the maximum mass a star could have so that it would not eventually collapse on itself. If a star's mass exceeds this limit, the star will eventually explode in a supernova.

1.44 SOLAR MASSES
is the limit Chandrasekhar obtained. In excess of this value, a dwarf star cannot support its own gravity and collapses.

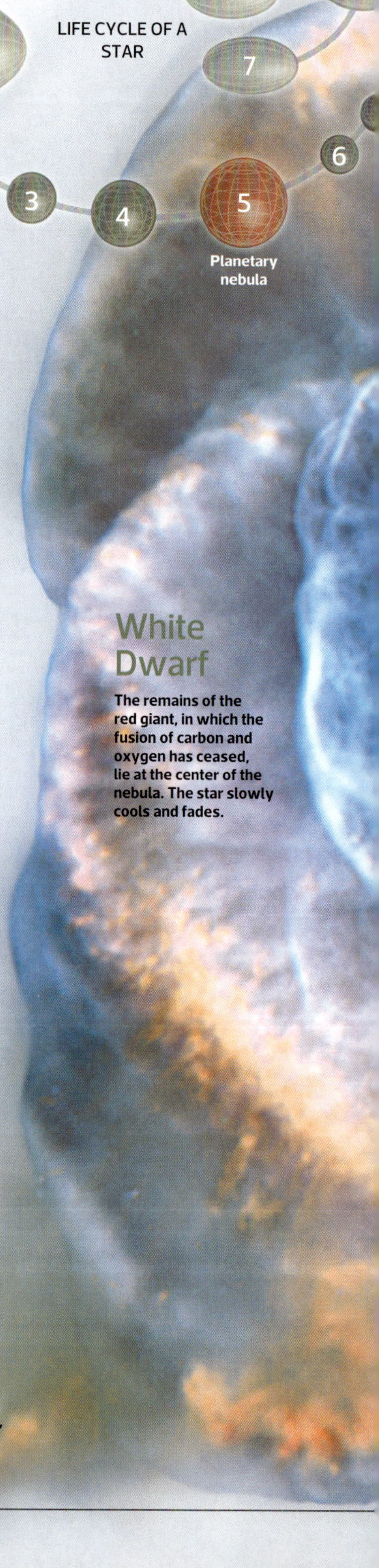

White Dwarf

The remains of the red giant, in which the fusion of carbon and oxygen has ceased, lie at the center of the nebula. The star slowly cools and fades.

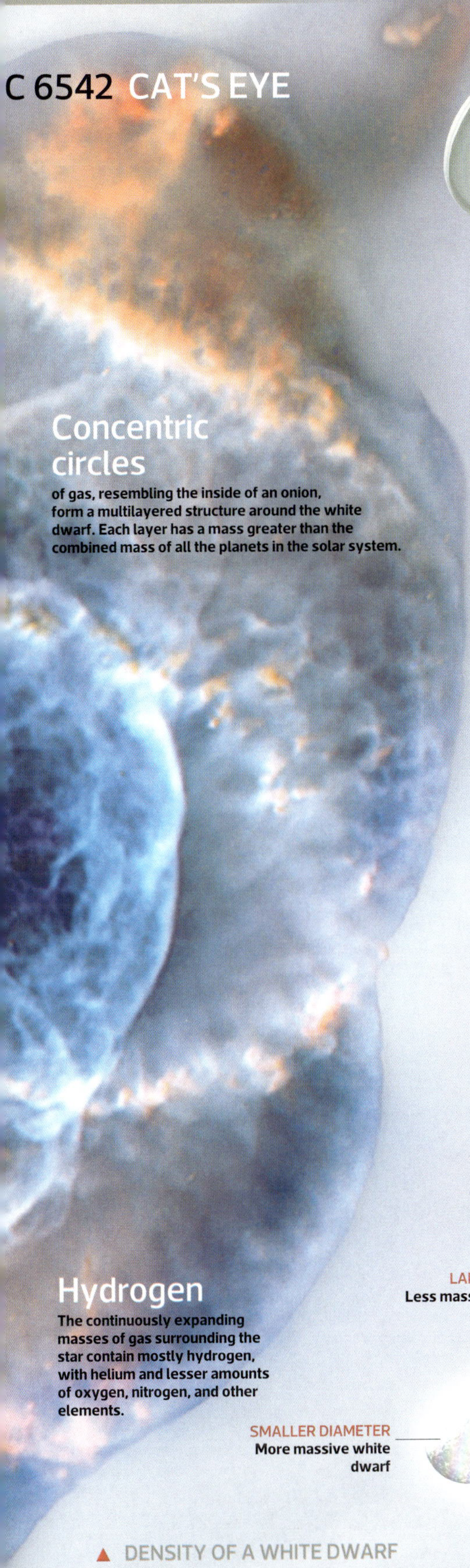

C 6542 CAT'S EYE

Concentric circles

of gas, resembling the inside of an onion, form a multilayered structure around the white dwarf. Each layer has a mass greater than the combined mass of all the planets in the solar system.

Hydrogen

The continuously expanding masses of gas surrounding the star contain mostly hydrogen, with helium and lesser amounts of oxygen, nitrogen, and other elements.

3 tons

is the weight of a single tablespoon of a white dwarf. A white dwarf is very massive in spite of the fact that its diameter of 9,300 miles (15,000 km) is comparable to the Earth's.

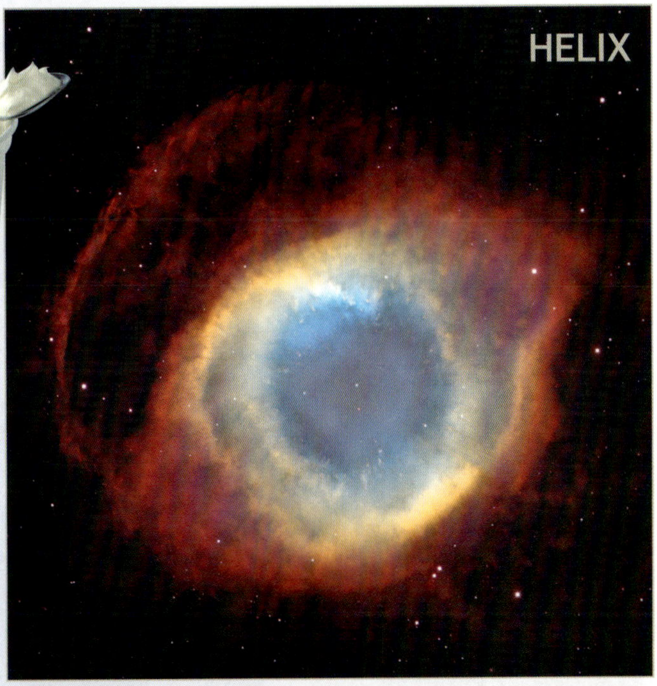

NGC 7293 ▶

The Helix is a planetary nebula that was created at the end of the life of a solar-type star. It is 650 light-years from the Earth and is located in the constellation Aquarius.

MYCN 18 ▶

The two rings of colored gas form the silhouette of this hourglass-shaped nebula. The red in the photograph corresponds to nitrogen, and the green corresponds to hydrogen. This nebula is 8,000 light-years from the Earth.

▲ DENSITY OF A WHITE DWARF

The density of a white dwarf is a million times greater than the density of water. In other words, each cubic meter of a white dwarf star weighs a million tons. The mass of a star is indirectly proportional to its diameter. A white dwarf with a diameter 100 times smaller than the Sun has a mass 70 times greater.

Supernovae

A supernova is an extraordinary explosion of a giant star at the end of its life, accompanied by a sudden increase in brightness and the release of a great amount of energy. In 10 seconds, a supernova releases 100 times more energy than the Sun will release in its entire life. After the explosion of the star that gives rise to a supernova, the gaseous remnant expands and shines for millions of years. It is estimated that, in our Milky Way galaxy, two supernovae occur per century.

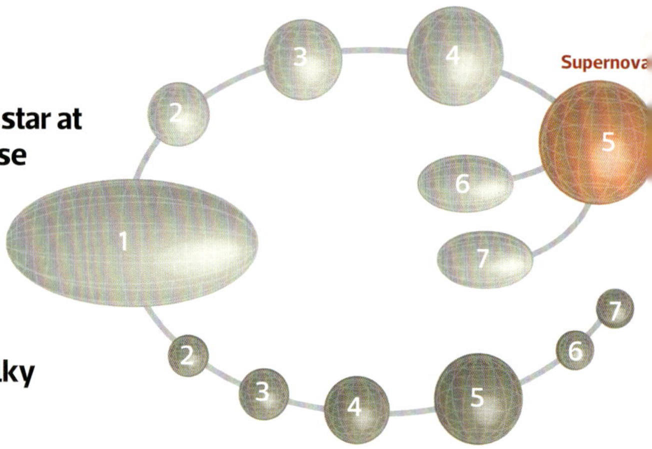

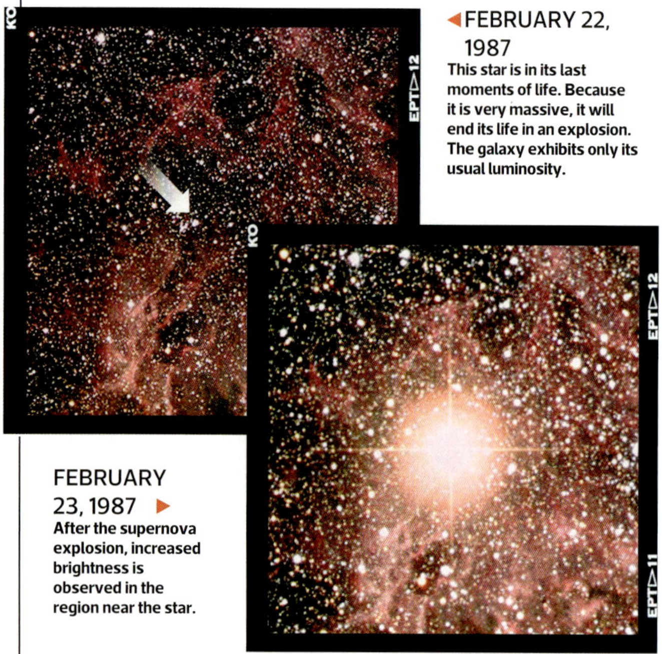

◄FEBRUARY 22, 1987
This star is in its last moments of life. Because it is very massive, it will end its life in an explosion. The galaxy exhibits only its usual luminosity.

FEBRUARY 23, 1987 ►
After the supernova explosion, increased brightness is observed in the region near the star.

BEFORE AND AFTER
The image at left shows a sector of the Large Magellanic Cloud, an irregular galaxy located 170,000 light-years from the Earth, depicted before the explosion of supernova 1987A. The image at right shows the supernova.

The Twilight of a Star

The explosion that marks the end of a supergiant's life occurs because the star's extremely heavy core has become incapable of supporting its own gravity any longer. In the absence of fusion in its interior, the star falls in upon itself, expelling its remaining gases, which will expand and shine for hundreds—or even thousands—of years. The explosion of the star injects new material into interstellar space and contributes heavy atoms that can give rise to new generations of stars.

Core

A star's core can be seen to be separated into distinct layers that correspond to the different elements created during nuclear fusion. The last element created before the star's collapse is iron.

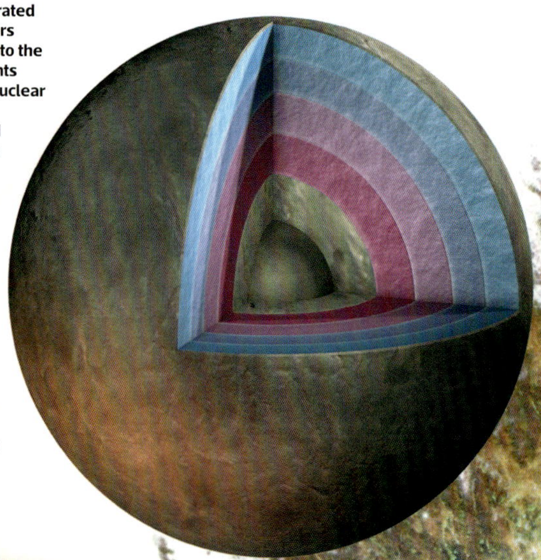

FUSION
The nuclear reactions in a dying star occur at a faster rate than they do in a red giant.

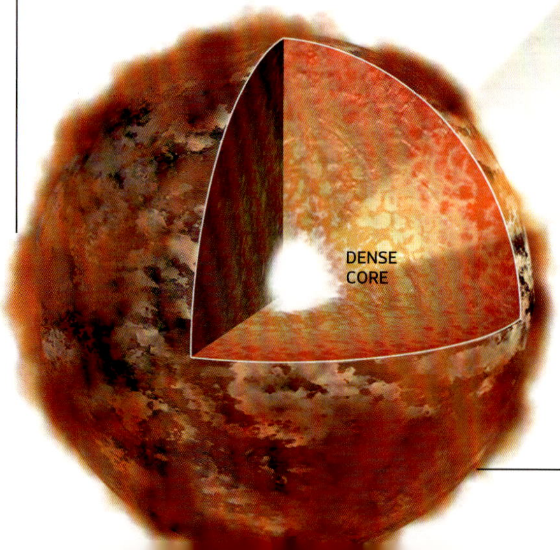

Supergiant

The diameter of the star may increase to more than one thousand times that of the Sun. Through nuclear fusion, the star can produce elements even heavier than carbon and oxygen.

Other Elements

hen a star's iron core creases in density to 1.44 olar masses, the star can o longer support its own eight and it collapses upon itself. The resulting explosion causes the formation of elements that are heavier than iron, such as gold and uranium.

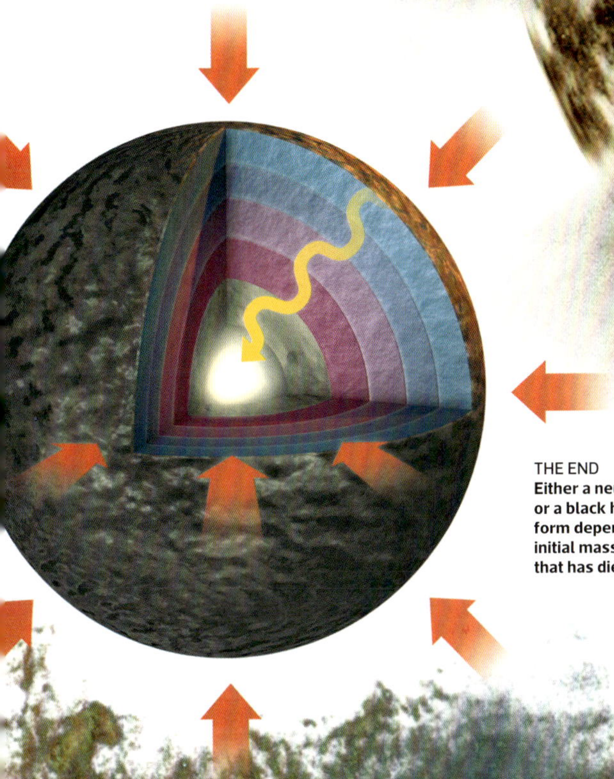

Explosion

The star's life ends in an immense explosion. During the weeks following the explosion, great quantities of energy are radiated that are sometimes greater than the energy emitted by the star's parent galaxy. A supernova may illuminate its galaxy for weeks.

THE END
Either a neutron star or a black hole may form depending on the initial mass of the star that has died.

SUPERMASSIVE
The mass of Eta Carinae is 100 times greater than that of the Sun. Astronomers believe that Eta Carinae is about to explode, but no one knows when.

GAS AND DUST
Gas and dust that have accumulated in the two visible lobes absorb the blue light and ultraviolet rays emitted from its center.

GASEOUS FILAMENTS
Gaseous filaments are ejected by the supernova at 620 miles (1,000 km) per second.

Stellar Remnant

When the star explodes as a supernova, it leaves as a legacy in space the heavy elements (such as carbon, oxygen, and iron) that were in the star's nucleus before its collapse. The Crab Nebula (M1) was created by a supernova seen in 1054 by Chinese astronomers. The Crab Nebula is located 6,500 light-years from Earth and has a diameter of twelve light-years. The star that gave rise to the Crab Nebula may have had an initial mass close to 10 solar masses. In 1969, a pulsar radiating X-rays and rotating 33 times per second was discovered at the center of the nebula, making the Crab Nebula a very powerful source of radiation.

The Final Darkness

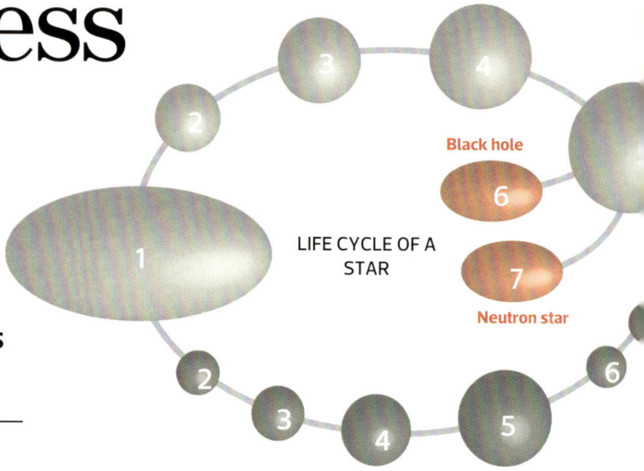

The last stage in the evolution of a star's core is its transformation into a very dense, compact stellar body. Its particulars depend upon the amount of mass involved in its collapse. The largest stars become black holes, their density so great that their gravitational forces capture even light. The only way to detect these dead stars is by searching for the effects of their gravitation.

Discovery of Black Holes

The only way of detecting the presence of a black hole in space is by its effect on neighboring stars. Since the gravitational force exerted by a black hole is so powerful, the gases of nearby stars are absorbed at great speed, spiraling toward the black hole and forming a structure called an accretion disk. The friction of the gases heats them until they shine brightly. The hottest parts of the accretion disk may reach 100,000,000° C and are a source of X-rays. The black hole, by exerting such powerful gravitational force, attracts everything that passes close to it, letting nothing escape. Since even light is not exempt from this phenomenon, black holes are opaque and invisible to even the most advanced telescopes. Some astronomers believe that supermassive black holes might have a mass of millions, or even billions, of solar masses.

Accretion Disk

An accretion disk is a gaseous accumulation of matter that the black hole draws from nearby stars. In the regions of the disk very close to the black hole, X-rays are emitted. The gas that accumulates rotates at very high speeds. When the gases from other stars collide with the disk, they create bright, hot spots.

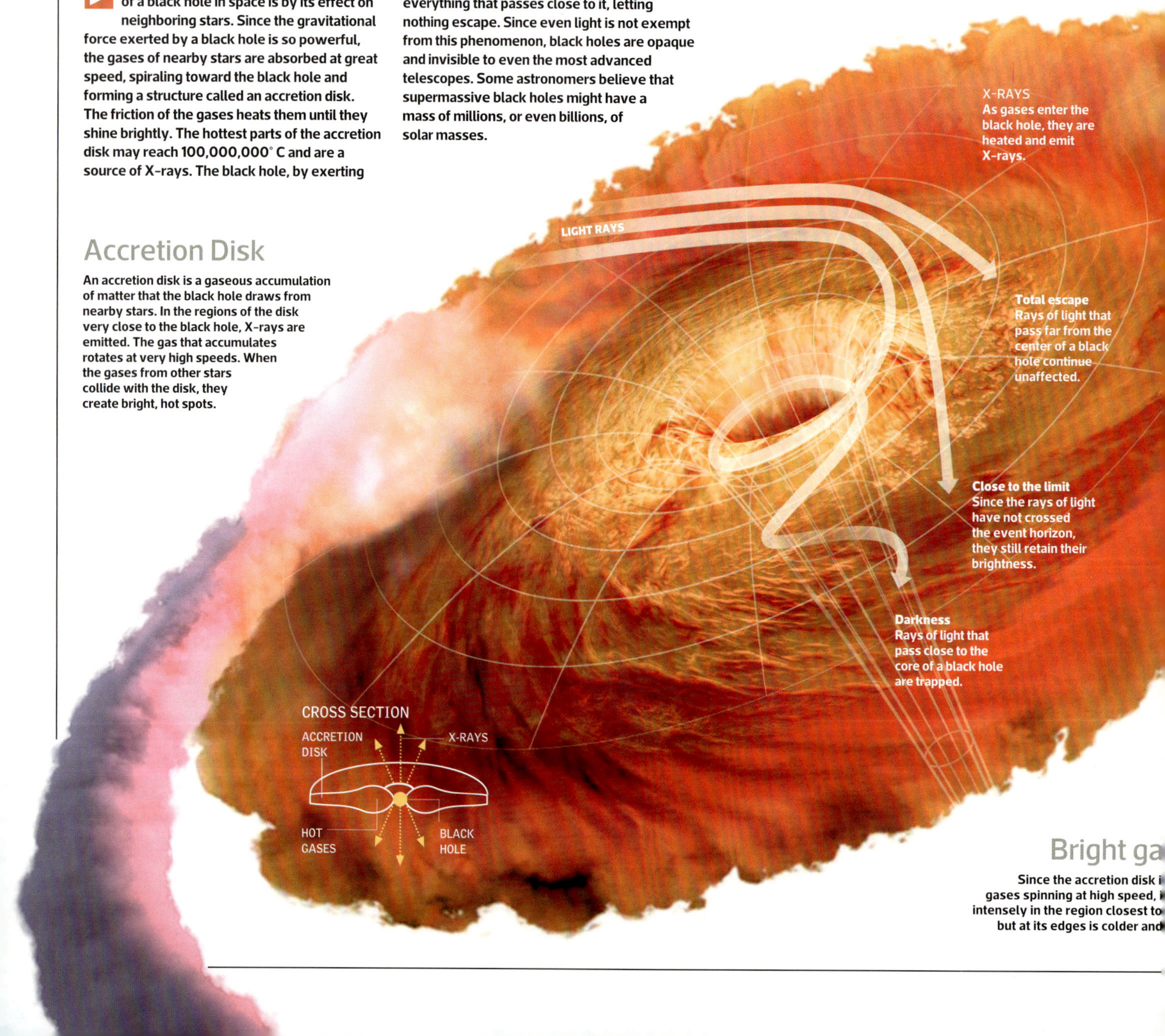

Bright ga

Since the accretion disk i
gases spinning at high speed, i
intensely in the region closest to
but at its edges is colder and

leutron Star

When a star's initial mass is between 10 and 20 solar masses, its final mass will be larger than the mass of the Sun. ›spite losing great quantities of matter ›ring nuclear reactions, the star finishes ›th a very dense core. Because of its ›ense magnetic and gravitational fields, a ›utron star can end up as a pulsar. A pulsar ›a rapidly spinning neutron star that gives ›f a beam of radio waves or other radiation. › the beam sweeps around the object, the ›diation is observed in very regular pulses.

trong Gravitational ›ttraction

›e gravitational force of the black hole attracts ›ses from a neighboring star. This gas forms a ›ge spiral that swirls faster and faster as it gets ›ser to the black hole. The gravitation field that ›enerates is so strong that it traps objects that pass close to it.

1 RED GIANT
A red giant leaves the main sequence. Its diameter is one hundred times greater than the Sun's.

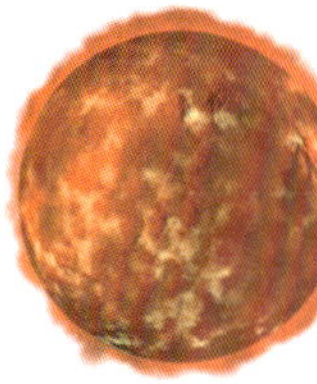

2 SUPERGIANT
A supergiant grows and rapidly fuses heavier chemical elements, forming carbon, oxygen, and finally iron.

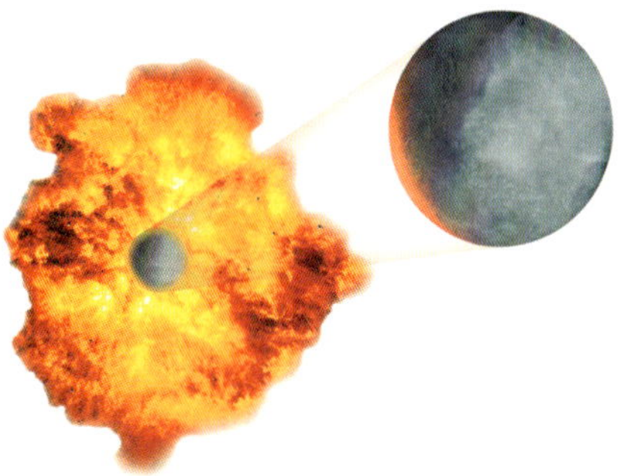

3 EXPLOSION
The star's iron core collapses. Protons and electrons annihilate each other and form neutrons.

LOSS OF MASS
Toward the end of its life, a neutron star loses more than 90 percent of its initial mass.

4 DENSE CORE
The core's exact composition is presently unknown. Most of its interacting particles are neutrons.

1 billion

tons is what one tablespoon of a neutron star would weigh. Its small diameter causes the star to have a compact, dense core accompanied by intense gravitational effects.

CURVED SPACE

The theory of relativity suggests that gravity is not a force but a distortion of space. This distortion creates a gravitational well, the depth of which depends on the mass of the object. Objects are attracted to other objects through the curvature of space.

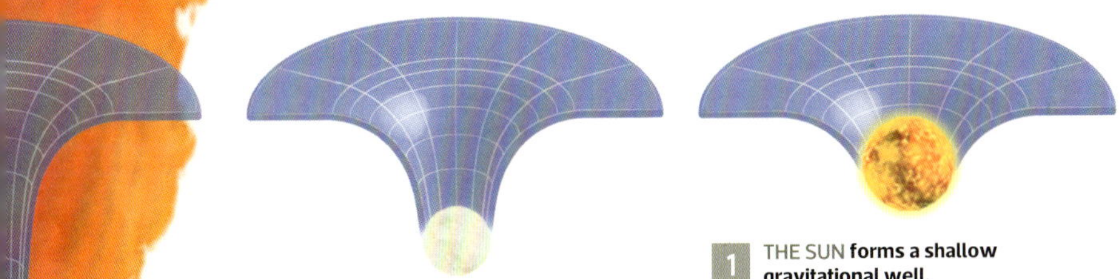

1 THE SUN forms a shallow gravitational well.

2 A WHITE DWARF generates a deeper gravitational well, drawing in objects at a higher speed.

3 A NEUTRON STAR attracts objects at speeds approaching half the speed of light. The gravitational well is even more pronounced.

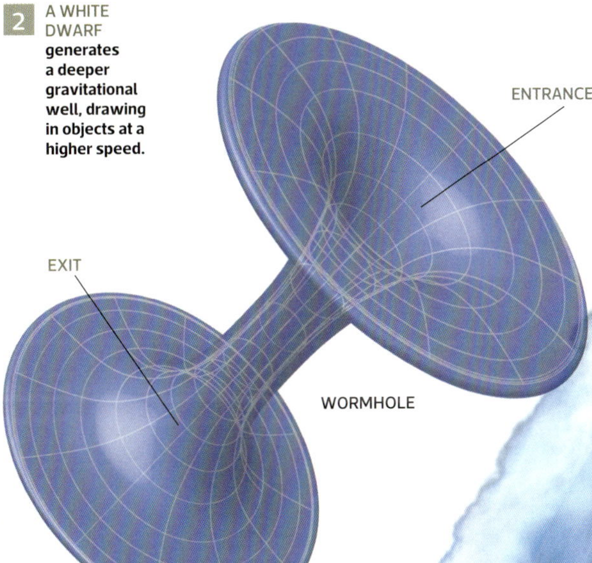

4 BLACK HOLE
The objects that approach the black hole too closely are swallowed by it. The black ›le's gravitational well is infinite and ›ps matter and light forever. The event ›rizon describes the limit of what is, ›d is not, absorbed. Any object that ›sses the event horizon follows a ›iral path into the gravitational well. ›me scientists believe in the existence of ›-called wormholes—antigravity tunnels, ›rough which travel across the universe ›hypothesized to be possible. By taking ›vantage of the curvature of space, scientists ›ink it could be possible to travel from the Earth ›the Moon in a matter of seconds.

Pulsars

The first pulsar (a neutron star radiating radio waves) was discovered in 1967. Pulsars rotate approximately 30 times per second and have very intense magnetic fields. Pulsars emit radio waves from their two magnetic poles when they rotate. If a pulsar absorbs gas from a neighboring star, a hot spot that radiates X-rays is produced on the pulsar's surface.

STRUCTURE OF A PULSAR

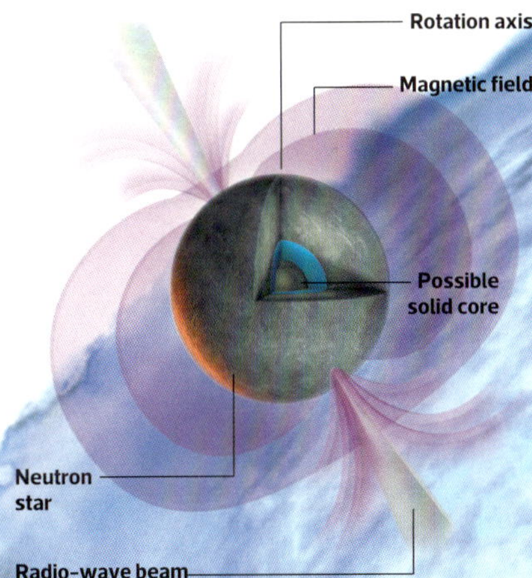

Devouring gas from a supergiant

Located within a binary system, the pulsar can follow the same process as a black hole. The pulsar's gravitational force causes it to absorb the gas of smaller, neighboring stars, heating up the pulsar's surface and causing it to emit X-rays.

Anatomy of Galaxies

Galaxies are rotating groups of stars, gas, and dust. More than 200 years ago, philosopher Immanuel Kant postulated that nebulae were island-universes of distant stars. Even though astronomers now know that galaxies are held together by gravitational force, they have not been able to decipher what reasons might be behind galaxies' many shapes. The various types of galaxies range from ovals of old stars to spirals with arms of young stars and bright gases. The center of a galaxy has the greatest accumulation of stars. The Milky Way Galaxy is now known to be so big that rays of light, which travel at 186,000 miles (300,000 km) per second, take 100,000 years to cross from one end to the other.

Star Cities

The first galaxies formed 100 million years after the big bang. Billions of these great conglomerates of stars can be found throughout space. The two most important discoveries concerning galaxies are attributed to the astronomer Edwin Hubble. In 1926, he pointed out that the spots, or patches, of light visible in the night sky were actually distant galaxies. Hubble's discovery put an end to the view held by astronomers at the time that the Milky Way constituted the universe. In 1929, as a result of various observations of the spectrum of light radiate by the stars in the galaxies, Hubble noted that the light from the galaxies showed a redshift (Doppler effect). This effect indicated that the galaxies were moving away from the Milky Way Galaxy. Hubble

COLLISION

300 million light-years from the Earth, these two colliding galaxies form a pair. Together they are called "The Mice" for the large tail of stars emanating from each galaxy. With time, these galaxies will fuse into a single, larger one. It is believed that in the future the universe will consist of a few giant stars.

1

1.2 BILLION YEARS ago, the Antennae (NGC 4038 and NGC 4039) were two separate spiral galaxies.

2

300 MILLION YEARS later, the galaxies collided at great speed.

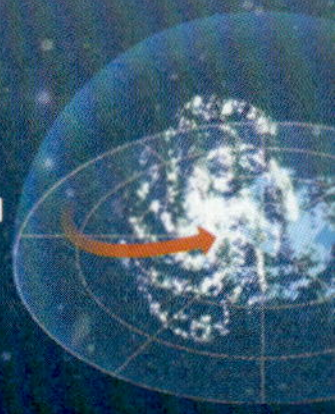

ILKY WAY

een from its side, the Milky Way looks e a flattened disk, swollen at the center. round the disk is a spherical region, called halo, containing dark matter and globular usters of stars. From June to September, e Milky Way is especially bright, something at would make it more visible viewed from bove than from the side.

CLASSIFYING GALAXIES ACCORDING TO HUBBLE

LLIPTICAL

hese galaxies are elliptical in hape and have little dust and as. Their masses fall within a ide range.

SPIRAL

In a spiral galaxy, a nucleus of old stars is surrounded by a flat disk of stars and two or more spiral arms.

IRREGULAR

Irregular galaxies have no defined shape and cannot be classified. They contain a large amount of gases and dust clouds.

UBCLASSIFICATIONS

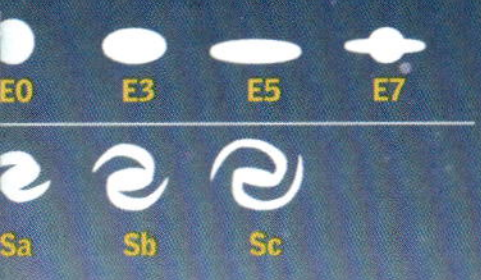

SUBCLASSIFICATIONS

Galaxies are subdivided into different categories according to their tendency toward round shape (in the case of elliptical galaxies), as well as by the presence of an axis and the length of their arms (in the case of spiral and barred spiral galaxies). An E0 galaxy is elliptical but almost circular, and an E7 galaxy is a flattened oval. An Sa galaxy has a large central axis and coiled arms, and an Sc galaxy has a thinner axis and more extended arms.

Galactic Clusters

Galaxies are objects that tend to form groups or clusters. Acting in response to gravitational force, they can form clusters of galaxies of anywhere from two to thousands of galaxies. These clusters have various shapes and are thought to expand when they join together. Abell 2151 (The Hercules cluster), shown here, is located approximately 500 million light-years from Earth. Each dot represents a galaxy that includes billions of stars.

concluded that the universe is expanding. But the expansion of the universe does not imply that galaxies are growing in numbers. On the contrary, galaxies can collide and merge. When two galaxies collide, they can distort each other in various ways. Over time, there are fewer and fewer galaxies. Some galaxies exhibit very peculiar shapes. The Sombrero Galaxy, shown in the center of the page, has a bright white core surrounded by thin spiral arms.

3

300 MILLION YEARS go by until the collision takes place and the shapes of the galaxies are distorted.

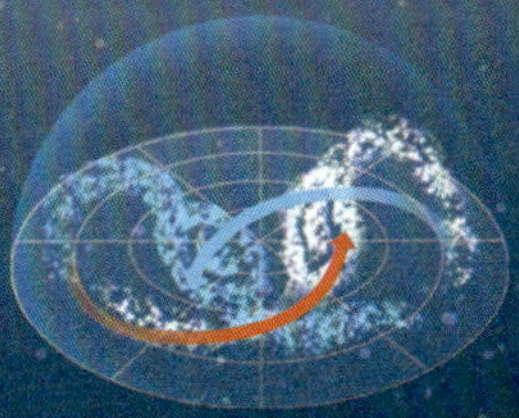

4

300 MILLION YEARS later, the stars in the spiral arms are expelled from both galaxies.

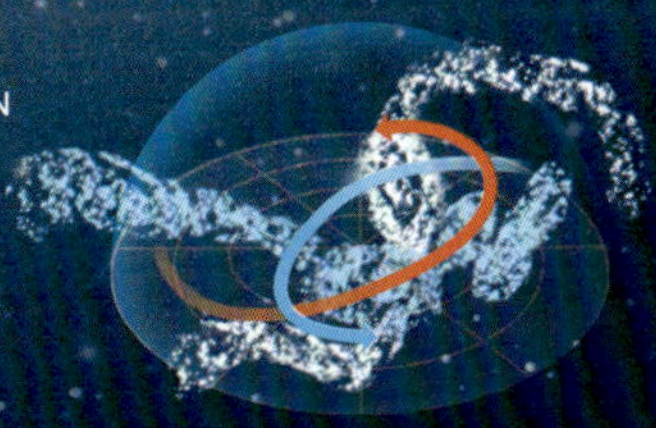

5

NOW two jets of expelled stars stretch far from the original galaxies.

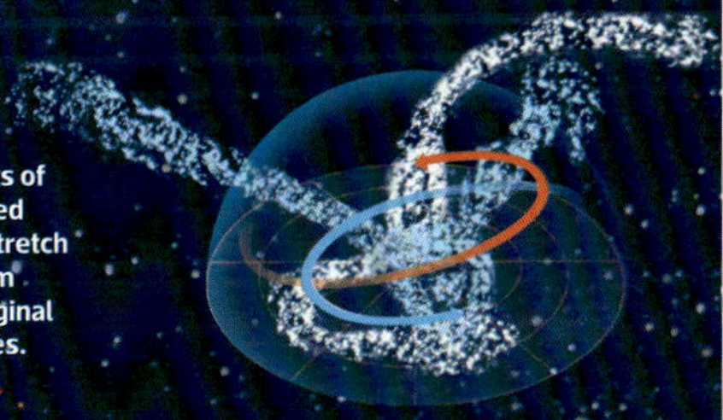

Active Galaxies

A small number of galaxies differ from the rest by emitting high amounts of energy. The energy emission might be caused by the presence of black holes in its core that were formed through the gravitational collapse accompanying the death of supermassive stars. During their first billion years, the galaxies might have accumulated surrounding gaseous disks with their corresponding emissions of radiation. It is possible that the cores of the first galaxies are the quasars that are now observed at very great distances.

Energetic Activity

Astronomers believe that active galaxies are a direct legacy from the beginning of the universe. After the big bang, these galaxies would have retained very energetic levels of radiation. Quasars, the brightest and most ancient objects in the universe, make up the core of this type of galaxy. In some cases, they emit X-rays or radio waves. The existence of this high-energy activity helps support the theory that galaxies could be born from a supermassive black hole with a quasar that became inactive as stars formed and it was left without gas to feed it. This process of formation might be common to many galaxies. Today quasars represent the limit of what it is possible to see, even with specialized telescopes. Quasars are small, dense, and bright.

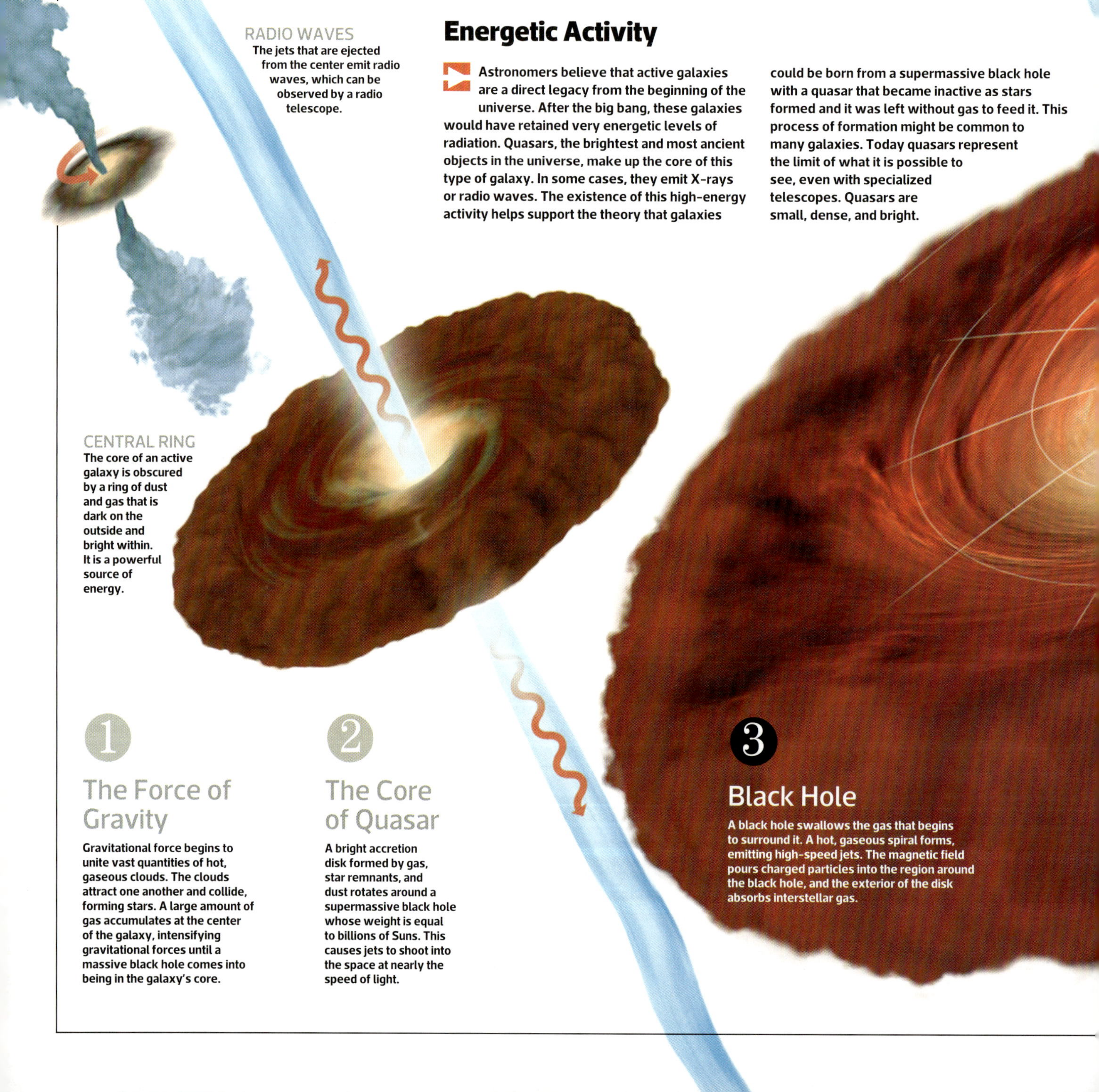

1 The Force of Gravity

Gravitational force begins to unite vast quantities of hot, gaseous clouds. The clouds attract one another and collide, forming stars. A large amount of gas accumulates at the center of the galaxy, intensifying gravitational forces until a massive black hole comes into being in the galaxy's core.

2 The Core of Quasar

A bright accretion disk formed by gas, star remnants, and dust rotates around a supermassive black hole whose weight is equal to billions of Suns. This causes jets to shoot into the space at nearly the speed of light.

3 Black Hole

A black hole swallows the gas that begins to surround it. A hot, gaseous spiral forms, emitting high-speed jets. The magnetic field pours charged particles into the region around the black hole, and the exterior of the disk absorbs interstellar gas.

Galaxy Formation

A theory of galaxy formation associated with active galaxies holds that many galaxies, possibly including the Milky Way, were formed from the gradual calming of a quasar at their core. As the surrounding gases consolidated in the formation of stars, the quasars, having no more gases to absorb, lost their energetic fury and became inactive. According to this theory, there is a natural progression from quasars to active galaxies to the common galaxies of today. In 1994, astronomers studying the center of the Milky Way discovered a region that may contain a black hole and could be left over from early galactic activity.

...ASSIFICATION

...e classification of an active galaxy depends ...on its distance from Earth and the perspective ...m which it is seen. Quasars, radio galaxies, and ...zars are members of the same family of objects ...d differ only in the way they are perceived.

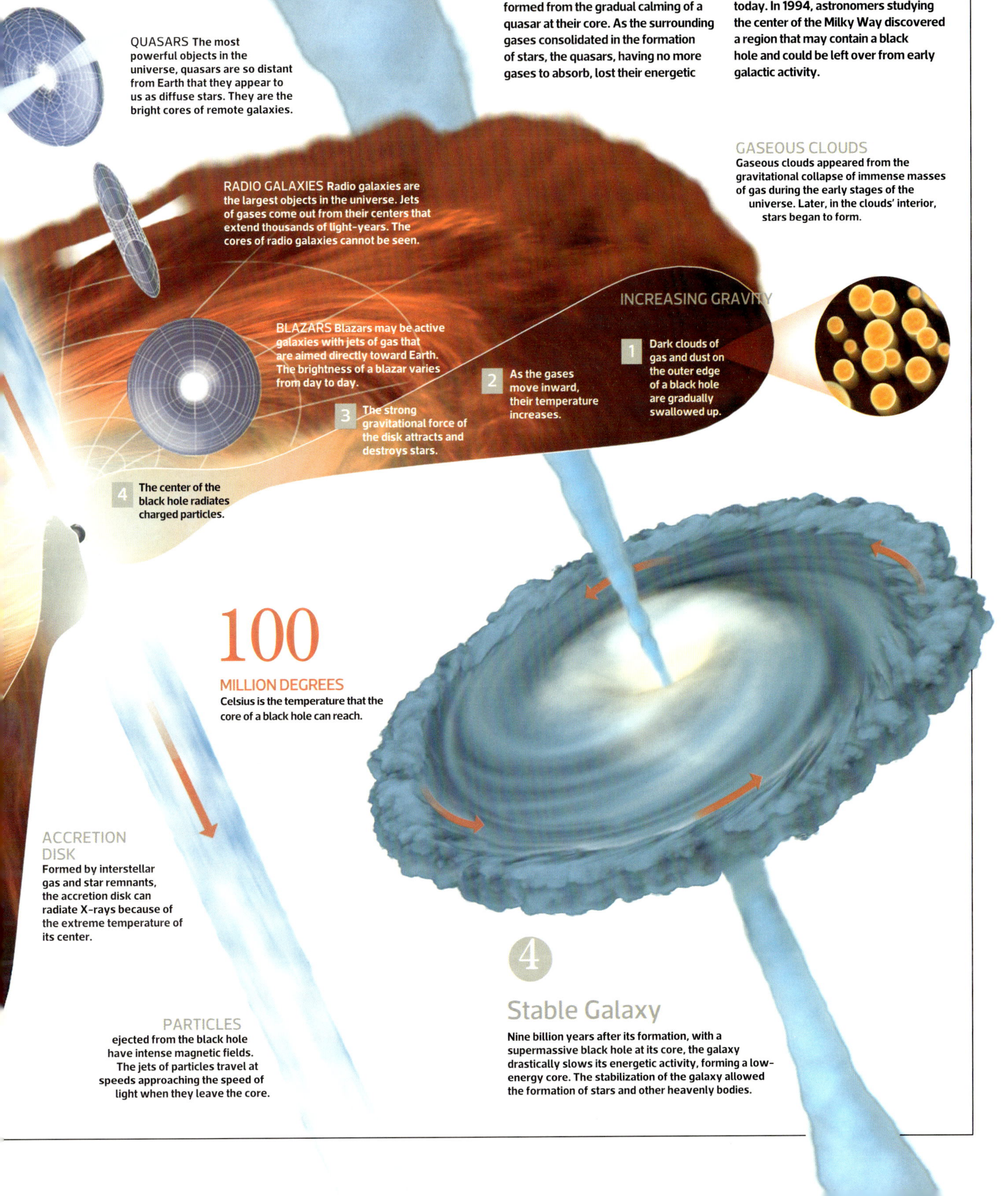

Stellar Metropolis

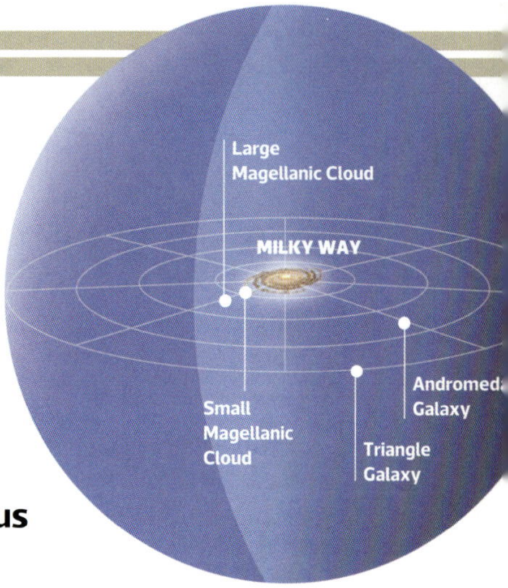

For a long time, our galaxy (called the Milky Way because of its resemblance to a stream of milk in the night sky) was a true enigma. It was Galileo Galilei who, in 1610, first pointed a telescope at the Milky Way and saw that the weak whitish strip was composed of thousands and thousands of stars that appeared to almost touch each other. Little by little, astronomers began to realize that all these stars, like our own Sun, were part of the enormous ensemble—the galaxy that is our stellar metropolis.

Structure of the Milky Way

The Milky Way, containing more than 100 billion stars, has two spiral arms rotating around its core. The Sagittarius arm, located between the Orion arm and the center of the Milky Way, holds one of the most luminous stars in the galaxy, Eta Carinae. The Perseus arm, the main outer arm of the Milky Way, contains young stars and nebulae. The Orion arm, extending between Perseus and Sagittarius, houses the solar system within its inner border. The Orion arm of the Milky Way is a veritable star factory, where gaseous interstellar material can give birth to billions of stars. Remnants of stars can also be found within it.

ROTATION

The speeds of the rotation of the various parts of the Milky Way vary according to those parts' distances from the core of the galaxy. The greatest number of stars is concentrated in the region between the Milky Way's core and its border. Here the speed of rotation is much greater because of the attraction that the objects in this region feel from the billions of stars within it.

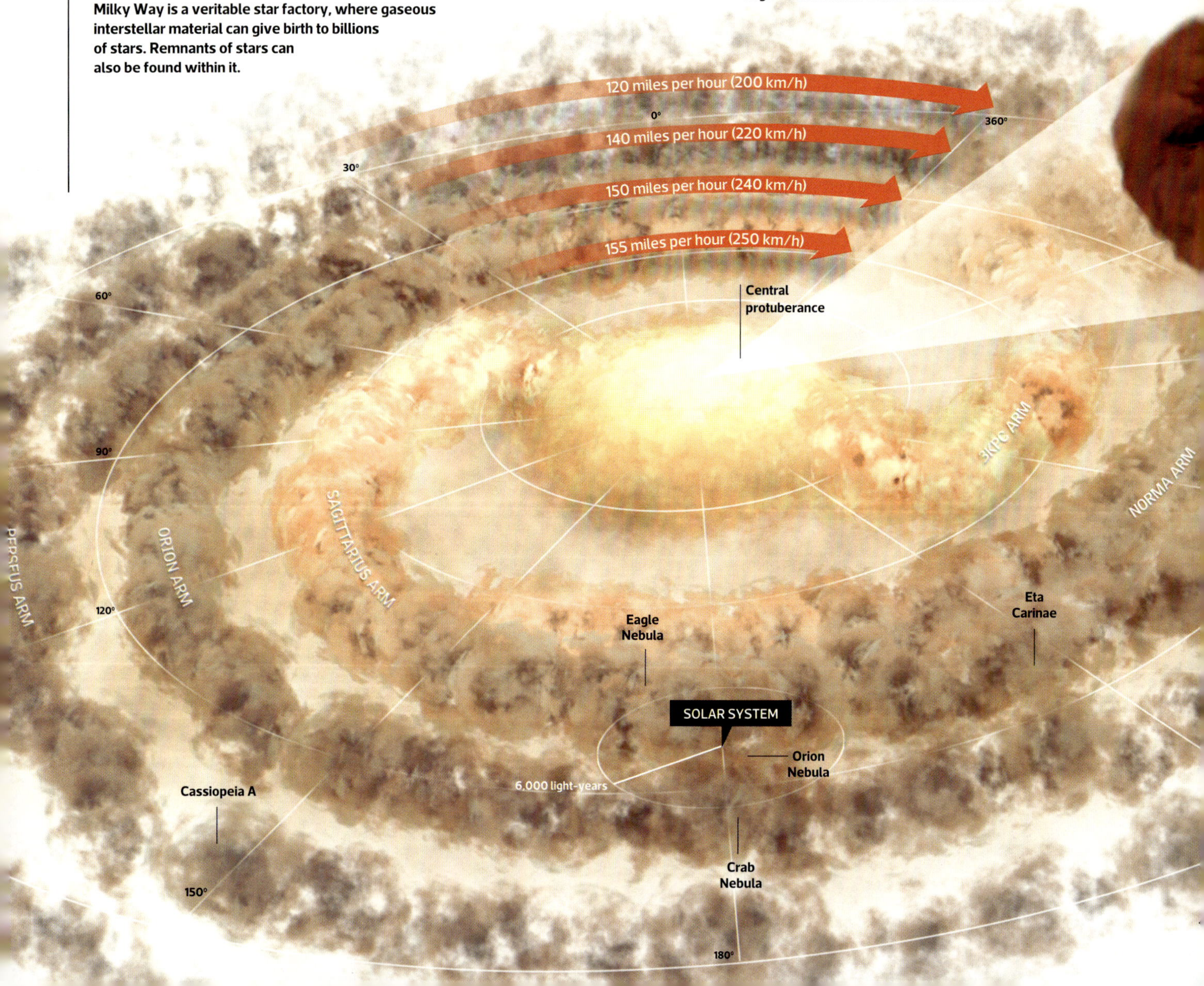

Central Region

Because the Milky Way is full of clouds of dust and rock particles, its center cannot be seen from outside the galaxy. The Milky Way's center can be seen only through telescopes that record infrared light, radio waves, or X-rays, which can pass through the material that blocks visible light. The central axis of the Milky Way contains ancient stars, some 14 billion years old, and exhibits intense activity within its interior, where two clouds of hot gas have been found: Sagittarius A and B. In the central region, but outside the core, a giant dark cloud contains 70 different types of molecules. These gas clouds are associated with violent activity in the center of our galaxy and contain the heart of the Milky Way within their depths. In general, the stars in this region are cold and range in color from red to orange.

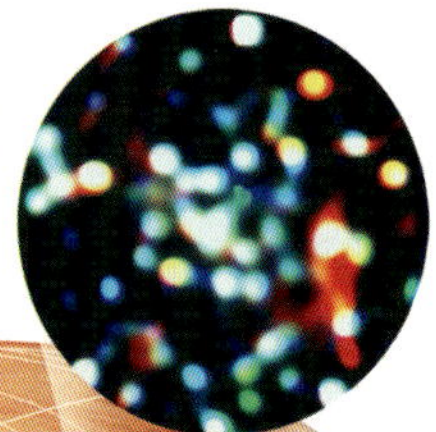

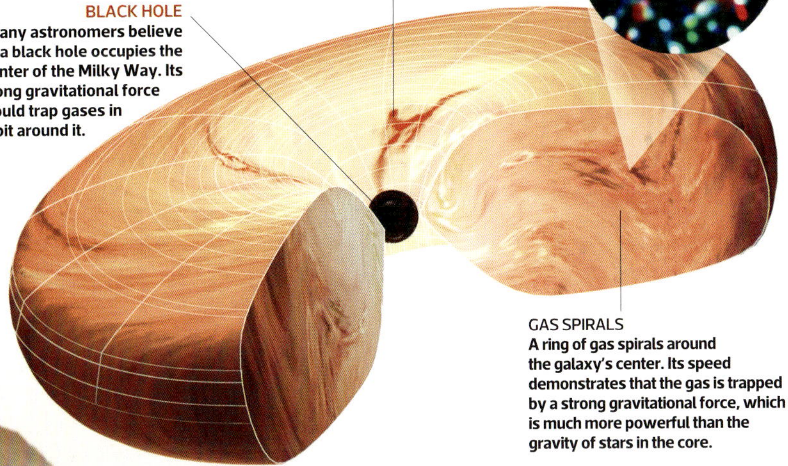

HOT GASES
The hot gases originating from the surface of the central region may be the result of violent explosions in the accretion disk.

BRIGHT STARS
Bright stars are born from gas that is not absorbed by the black hole. Most of them are young.

BLACK HOLE
Many astronomers believe that a black hole occupies the center of the Milky Way. Its strong gravitational force would trap gases in orbit around it.

GAS SPIRALS
A ring of gas spirals around the galaxy's center. Its speed demonstrates that the gas is trapped by a strong gravitational force, which is much more powerful than the gravity of stars in the core.

SAGITTARIUS B2
The largest dark cloud in the central region of the Milky Way, Sagittarius B2 contains enough alcohol to cover the entire Earth.

MAGNETISM
The center of the Milky Way is surrounded by strong magnetic fields, perhaps from a rotating black hole.

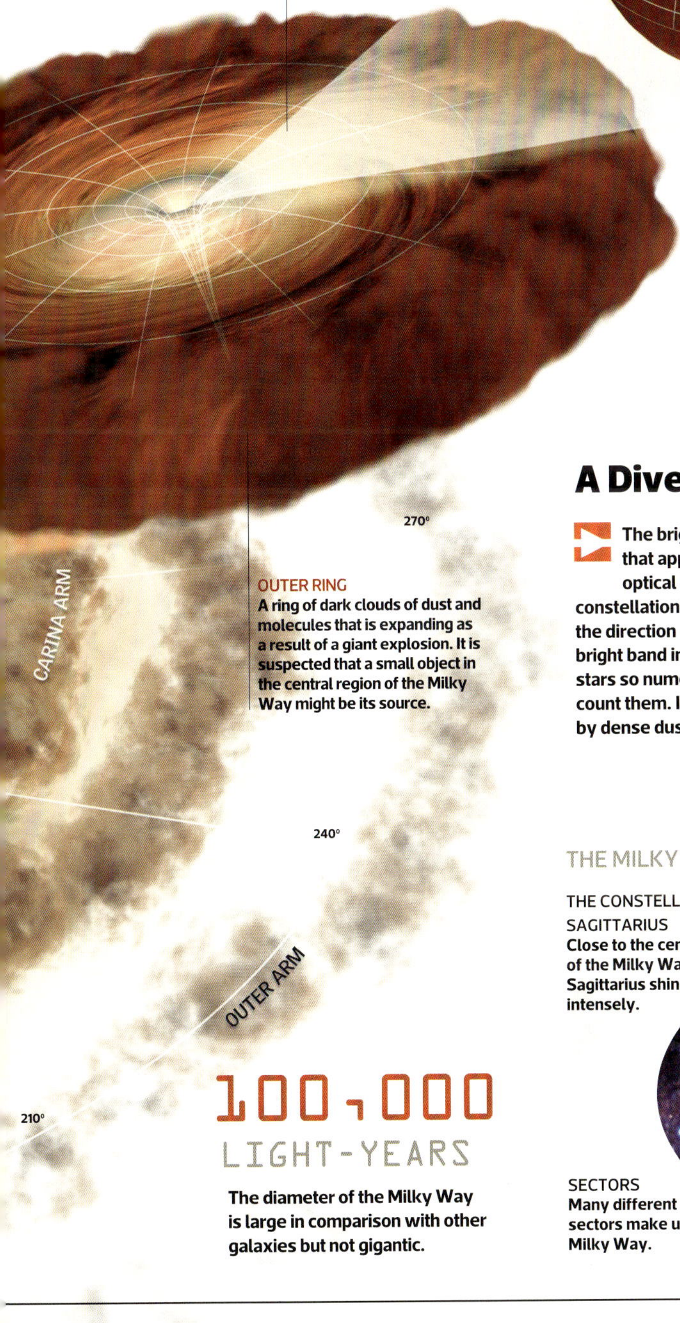

OUTER RING
A ring of dark clouds of dust and molecules that is expanding as a result of a giant explosion. It is suspected that a small object in the central region of the Milky Way might be its source.

The Exact Center

The core of the Milky Way galaxy is marked by very intense radio-wave activity that might be produced by an accretion disk made up of incandescent gas surrounding a massive black hole. The region of Sagittarius A, discovered in 1994, is a gas ring that rotates at very high speed, swirling within several light-years of the center of the galaxy. The speed of its rotation is an indication of the powerful gravitational force exerted from the center of the Milky Way, a force stronger than would be produced by the stars located in the region. The hot, blue stars that shine in the center of the Milky Way may have been born from gas not yet absorbed by the black hole.

A Diverse Galaxy

The brightest portion of the Milky Way that appears in photographs taken with optical lenses (using visible light) is in the constellation Sagittarius, which appears to lie in the direction of the center of the Milky Way. The bright band in the nighttime sky is made up of stars so numerous that it is almost impossible to count them. In some cases, stars are obscured by dense dust clouds that make some regions of the Milky Way seem truly dark. The objects that can be found in the Milky Way are not all of one type. Some, such as those known as the halo population, are old and are distributed within a sphere around the galaxy. Other objects form a more flattened structure called the disk population. In the spiral arm population, we find the youngest objects in the Milky Way. In these arms, gas and interstellar dust abound.

100,000
LIGHT-YEARS

The diameter of the Milky Way is large in comparison with other galaxies but not gigantic.

THE MILKY WAY IN VISIBLE LIGHT

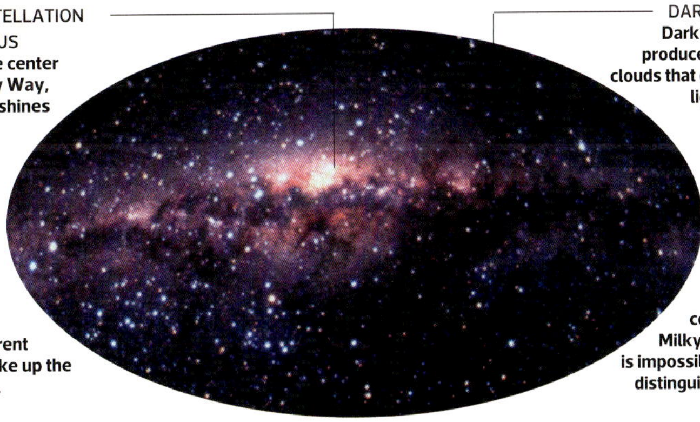

THE CONSTELLATION SAGITTARIUS
Close to the center of the Milky Way, Sagittarius shines intensely.

DARK REGIONS
Dark regions are produced by dense clouds that obscure the light of stars.

SECTORS
Many different sectors make up the Milky Way.

STARS
So many stars compose the Milky Way that it is impossible for us to distinguish them all.

The Solar System

Among the millions and millions of stars that form the Milky Way galaxy, there is a medium-sized one located in one of the galaxy's arms—the Sun. To ancient peoples, the Sun was a god; to us, it is the central source of energy that generates heat, helping life exist. This star, together with the planets and other bodies that spin in orbits around it

...LYMPUS MONS, ON MARS
...ympus Mons is the largest ...lcano of the solar system. It ... about two-and-a-half times ... high as Mount Everest.

...make up the solar system, which formed about 4.6 billion years ago. The planets that rotate around it do not produce their own light. Instead, they reflect sunlight. After the Earth, Mars is the most explored planet. Here we see a photo of Olympus Mons, the largest volcano in the entire solar system. It is almost two-and-a-half times as high as the tallest peak on the Earth, Mount Everest. ●

Attracted by a Star

Planets and their satellites, asteroids and other rocky objects, and an incalculable number of comet-like objects, some more than 1 trillion miles (1.6 trillion km) from the Sun, make up the solar system. In the 17th century, astronomer Johannes Kepler proposed a model to interpret the dynamic properties of the bodies of the solar system.

According to this interpretation, the planets complete elliptical trajectories, called orbits, around the Sun. In every case, the movement is produced by the influence of the gravitational field of the Sun. Today, as part of a rapidly developing field of astronomy, it is known that planet or planet-like bodies also orbit other stars.

Outer Planets

Planets located outside the asteroid belt. They are enormous gas spheres with small solid cores. They have very low temperatures because of their great distance from the Sun. The presence of ring systems is exclusive to these planets. The greatest of them is Jupiter: 1,300 Earths could fit inside of it. Its mass is 2.5 times as great as that of the rest of the planets combined.

NEPTUNE

DIAMETER 30,775 MILES (49,528 KM)
MOONS 14

Triton Proteus Nereid

URANUS

DIAMETER 31,763 MILES (51,118 KM)
MOONS 27

Titania Oberon Umbriel Ariel Miranda Puck

SATURN

DIAMETER 74,898 MILES (120,536 KM)
MOONS 62

Titan Rhea Iapetus Tethys

ORBITS

In general, the planets orbit in one common plane called the ecliptic.

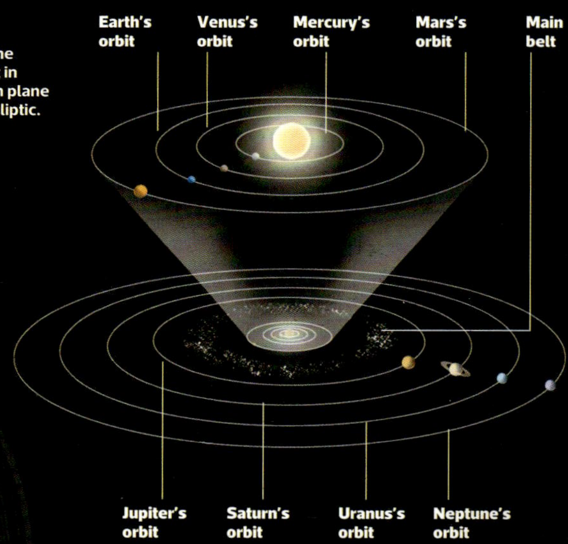

The rotation of most planets around their own axes is in counterclockwise direction. Venus and Uranus, however, revolve clockwise.

JUPITER

DIAMETER 88,846 MILES (142,984 KM)
MOONS 67

Ganymede Callisto Io Europa

Asteroid Belt

The border between the outer and inner planets is marked by millions of rocky fragments of various sizes that form a band called the asteroid belt. Their orbits are influenced by the gravitational pull exerted on them by the giant planet Jupiter. This effect also keeps them from merging and forming a planet.

Phobos Deimos

MARS

DIAMETER 4,217 MILES (6,786 KM)
MOONS 2

MOON

EARTH

DIAMETER 7,926 MILES (12,756 KM)
MOONS 1

VENUS

DIAMETER 7,520 MILES (12,103 KM)
MOONS 0

MERCURY

DIAMETER 3,031 MILES (4,878 KM)
MOONS 0

S U N

Inner Planets

Planets located inside the asteroid belt. They are solid bodies in which internal geologic phenomena, such as volcanism, which can modify their surfaces, are produced. Almost all of them have an appreciable atmosphere of some degree of thickness, according to individual circumstances, which plays a key role in the surface temperatures of each planet.

BUILDING PLANETS

Early ideas suggested that the planets formed gradually, beginning with the binding of hot dust particles. Today scientists suggest that the planets originated from the collision and melding of larger-sized bodies called planetesimals.

1 ORIGIN
Remains from the formation of the Sun created a disk of gas and dust around it, from which the planetesimals formed.

2 COLLISION
Through collisions among themselves, planetesimals of different sizes joined together to become more massive objects.

3 HEAT
The collisions produced a large amount of heat that accumulated in the interior of the planets, according to their distance from the Sun.

SOLAR GRAVITY

The gravitational pull of the Sun upon the planets not only keeps them inside the solar system but also influences the speed with which they revolve in their orbits around the Sun. Those closest to the Sun revolve in their orbits much faster than those farther from it.

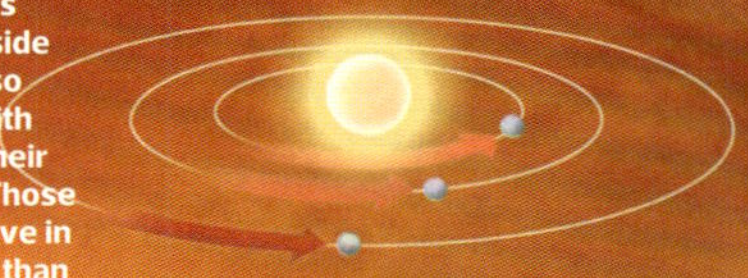

A Very Warm Heart

The Sun at the center of the solar system is a source of light and heat. This energy is produced by the fusion of atomic hydrogen nuclei, which generate helium nuclei. The energy that emanates from the Sun travels through space and initially encounters the bodies that populate the solar system. The Sun shines thanks to thermonuclear fusion, and it will continue to shine until its supply of hydrogen runs out in about six or seven billion years.

Very Gassy

The Sun is a giant ball of gases with very high density and temperature. Its main components are hydrogen (90%) and helium (9%). The balance of its mass is made up of trace elements, such as carbon, nitrogen, and oxygen, among others. Because of the conditions of extreme temperature and pressure on the Sun, these elements are in a plasma state.

CHARACTERISTICS

CONVENTIONAL PLANET SYMBOL ☉

ESSENTIAL DATA

Average distance from Earth	93 million miles (150 million km)
Equatorial diameter	864,000 miles (1,391,000 km)
Mass*	332,900
Gravity*	28
Density	0.81 ounce per cubic inch (1.4 g per cu cm)
Average temperature	9,932° F (5,500° C)
Atmosphere	Dense
Moons	None

*In both cases, Earth = 1

CONVECTIVE ZONE
extends from the base of the photosphere down to a depth of 15 percent of the solar radius. Here energy is transported up toward the surface by gas currents (through convection).

RADIATIVE ZONE
This portion of the Sun is traversed by particles coming from the core. A proton can take a million years to cross this zone.

14,400,000° F
(8,000,000° C)

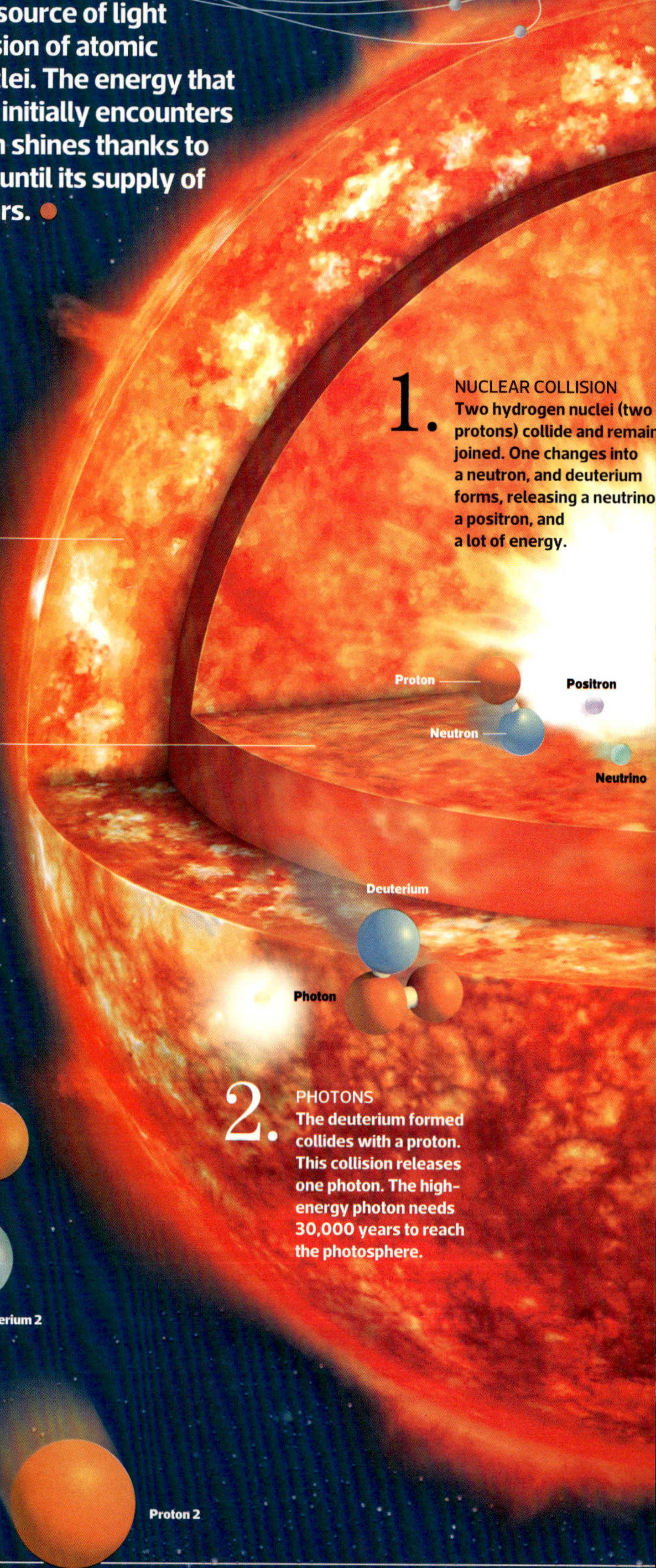

1. NUCLEAR COLLISION
Two hydrogen nuclei (two protons) collide and remain joined. One changes into a neutron, and deuterium forms, releasing a neutrino, a positron, and a lot of energy.

2. PHOTONS
The deuterium formed collides with a proton. This collision releases one photon. The high-energy photon needs 30,000 years to reach the photosphere.

NUCLEAR FUSION OF HYDROGEN

The extraordinary temperature of the nuclear core helps the hydrogen nuclei join. Under conditions of lower energy, they repel each other, but the conditions at the center of the Sun can overcome the repulsive forces, and nuclear fusion occurs. For every four hydrogen nuclei, a series of nuclear reactions produce one helium nucleus.

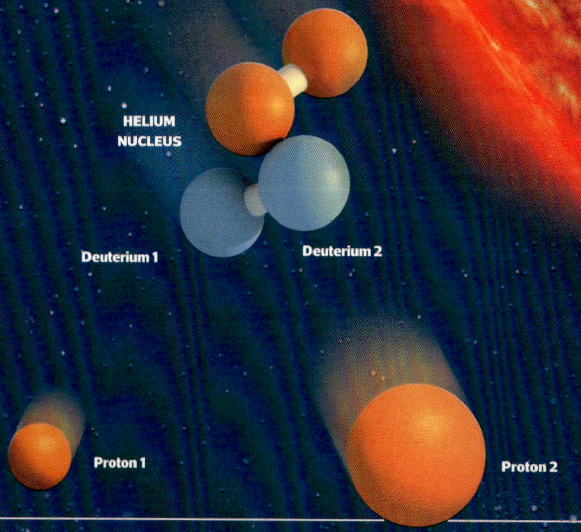

3. HELIUM NUCLEI
The group of two protons and a neutron collides with another such group. A helium nucleus forms, and a pair of protons is released.

Surface and Atmosphere

The visible portion of the Sun is a sphere of light, or photosphere, made of boiling gases emanating from the solar core. The gas flares form plasma, which passes through this layer. Later the gas flares enter a vast gas layer called the solar atmosphere. The density of this layer decreases toward its outermost region. Above the photosphere lies the solar atmosphere—the chromosphere and the corona. The energy generated at the core moves through the surface of the photosphere and solar atmosphere for thousands of years in search of an exit into space.

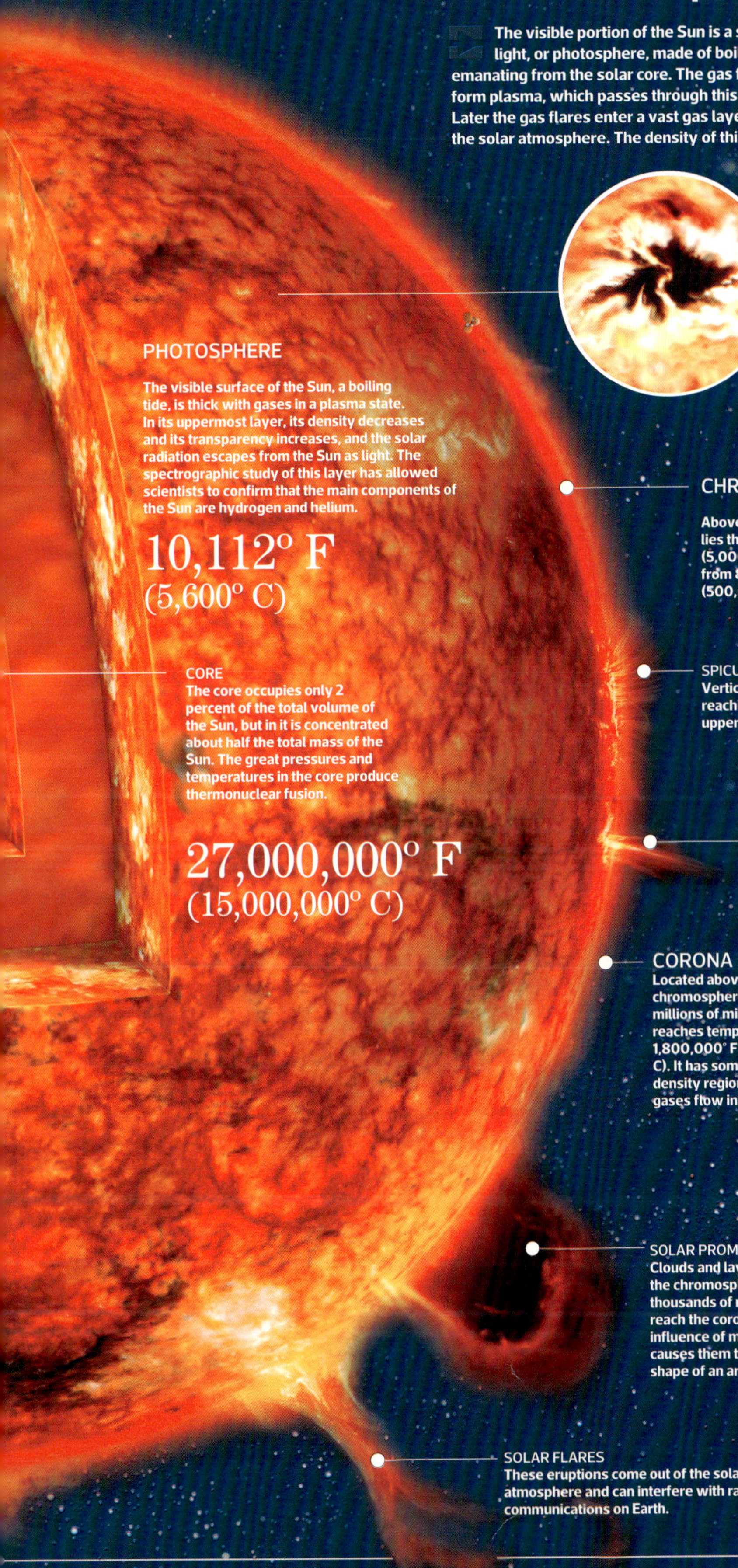

SUNSPOTS
are regions of gases that are generally colder (7,232° F [4,000° C]) than the photosphere (10,112° F [5,600° C]). For that reason, they appear dark.

PENUMBRA
Peripheral region. It is hotter and brighter than the umbra.

UMBRA
Central region. It is the coldest and darkest part.

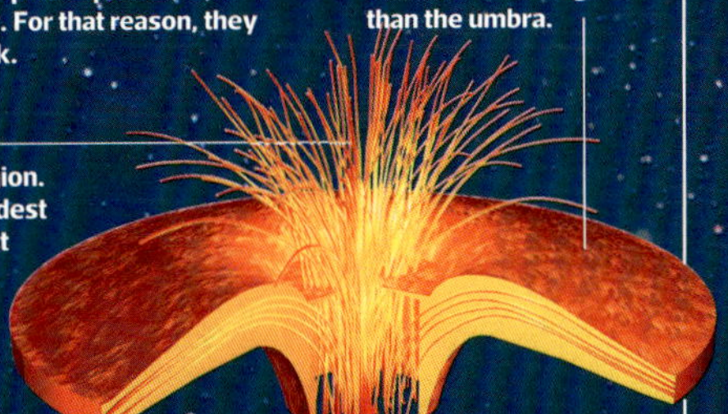

PHOTOSPHERE
The visible surface of the Sun, a boiling tide, is thick with gases in a plasma state. In its uppermost layer, its density decreases and its transparency increases, and the solar radiation escapes from the Sun as light. The spectrographic study of this layer has allowed scientists to confirm that the main components of the Sun are hydrogen and helium.

10,112° F
(5,600° C)

CORE
The core occupies only 2 percent of the total volume of the Sun, but in it is concentrated about half the total mass of the Sun. The great pressures and temperatures in the core produce thermonuclear fusion.

27,000,000° F
(15,000,000° C)

CHROMOSPHERE
Above the photosphere, and of less density, lies the chromosphere, a layer 3,110 miles (5,000 km) thick. Its temperature ranges from 8,100° F (4,500° C) to 900,000° F (500,000° C) with increasing altitude.

900,000° F
(500,000° C)

MAXIMUM TEMPERATURE OF THE CHROMOSPHERE

SPICULES
Vertical jets of gas that spew from the chromosphere, usually reaching 6,200 miles (10,000 km) in height. They originate in upper convection cells and can rise as high as the corona.

MACROSPICULES
This type of vertical eruption is similar to a spicule, but it usually reaches up to 25,000 miles (40,000 km) in height.

CORONA
Located above the chromosphere, it extends millions of miles into space and reaches temperatures nearing 1,800,000° F (1,000,000° C). It has some holes, or low-density regions, through which gases flow into the solar wind.

1,800,000° F
(1,000,000° C)

THE TEMPERATURE IN THE CORONA

SOLAR WIND
Consists of a flux of ions emitted by the solar atmosphere. The composition is similar to that of the corona. The Sun loses approximately 1,800 pounds (800 kg) of matter per second in the form of solar wind.

SOLAR PROMINENCES
Clouds and layers of gas from the chromosphere travel thousands of miles until they reach the corona, where the influence of magnetic fields causes them to take on the shape of an arc or wave.

SOLAR FLARES
These eruptions come out of the solar atmosphere and can interfere with radio communications on Earth.

Mercury, an Inferno

Mercury is the planet nearest to the Sun and is therefore the one that has to withstand the harshest of the Sun's effects. Due to its proximity to the Sun, Mercury moves at great speed in its solar orbit, completing an orbit every 88 days. It has almost no atmosphere, and its surface is dry and rugged, covered with craters caused by the impact of numerous meteorites; this makes it resemble the Moon. Numerous faults, formed during the cooling of the planet when it was young, are also visible on the surface. Constantly baked by its neighbor, the Sun, Mercury has an average surface temperature of 333° F (167° C).

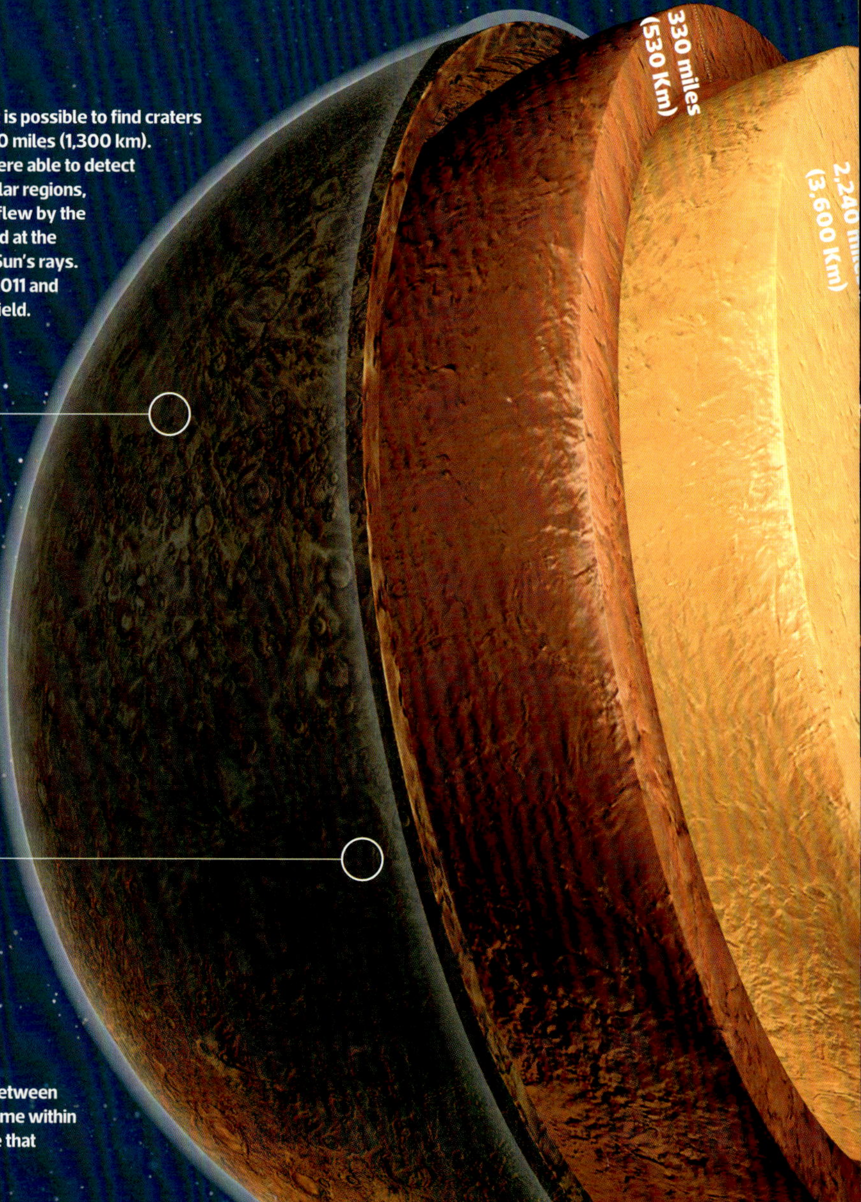

A Scar-Covered Surface

The surface of Mercury is very similar to that of the Moon. It is possible to find craters of varying sizes. The largest one has a diameter of some 810 miles (1,300 km). There are also hills and valleys. In 1991, radio telescopes were able to detect possible evidence of the presence of frozen water in Mercury's polar regions, information that Mariner 10 had been unable to gather. Mariner 10 flew by the planet three times between 1974 and 1975. The polar ice was found at the bottom of very deep craters, which limit the ice's exposure to the Sun's rays. The spacecraft Messenger, launched in 2004, orbited Mercury in 2011 and provided new information about Mercury's surface and magnetic field.

CALORIS CRATER
The largest impact crater in the solar system, it has a diameter of 810 miles (1,300 km).

The crater was flooded with lava.

When the projectile that formed the crater struck, Mercury was still forming. The extensive waves that extended from the site of impact formed hills and mountains ranges.

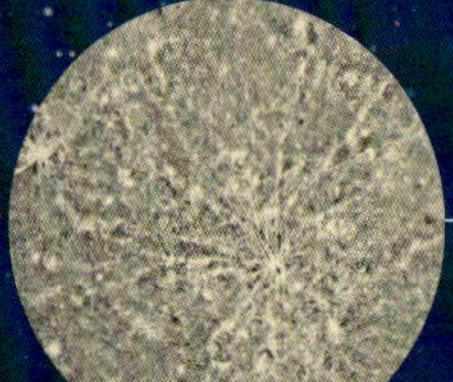

BEETHOVEN
is the second largest crater on Mercury. It is 400 miles (643 km) in diameter. Its floor was flooded by lava and later marked by meteorite impacts.

Missions to Mercury

The space probe Mariner 10 was the first to reach Mercury. Between 1974 and 1975, the craft flew by the planet three times and came within about 200 miles (320 km) of the surface. Messenger, a space probe that studied Mercury between 2008 and 2011, was launched in 2004.

Mariner 10

Messenger
The probe passed by Mercury twice in 2008 and once in 2009 before beginning to orbit the planet. On March 18, 2010 - starting at 12:45 a.m. UTC - Messenger transitioned from orbiting the Sun to being the first spacecraft ever to orbit the planet Mercury.

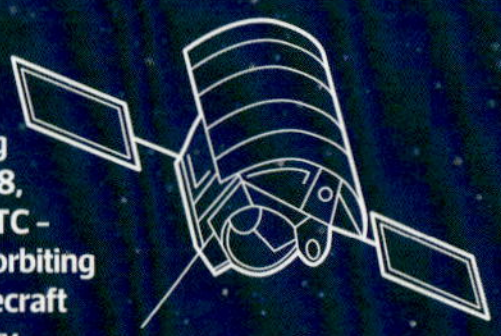

Composition and Magnetic Field

Like the Earth, Mercury has a magnetic field, although a much weaker one. The magnetism results from its enormous core ade of solid iron. The mantle that surrounds the core is believed to e a fine layer of iron and sulfur.

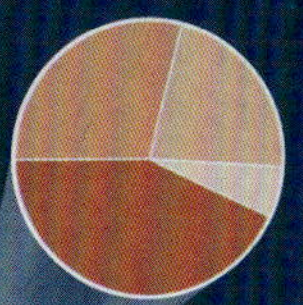

333° F (167° C)

Baked by its neighbor the Sun, Mercury is the planet with the greatest thermal fluctuations in the solar system. Its average temperature is 333° F (167° C), but when it gets closer to the Sun, the temperature can climb to 842° F (450° C). At night, it drops to -297° F (-183° C).

EXTREMELY THIN ATMOSPHERE

Mercury's atmosphere is almost nonexistent and consists of a very thin layer that cannot protect the planet either from the Sun or from meteorites. During the day, when Mercury is closer to the Sun, the planet's temperature can surpass 842° F (450° C). At night, temperatures can plummet to -297° F (-183° C).

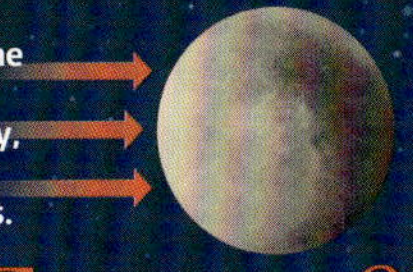

-297° F (-183° C)

883° F (473° C)

CHARACTERISTICS

CONVENTIONAL PLANET SYMBOL ☿

ESSENTIAL DATA

Average distance from the Sun	36,000,000 miles (57,900,000 km)
Solar orbit (Mercurian year)	88 days 00 hours
Equatorial diameter	3,032 miles (4,880 km)
Orbital speed	29.75 miles per second (47.87 km/s)
Mass*	0.06
Gravity*	0.38
Density	3.14 ounces per cubic inch (5.43 g/cu cm)
Average temperature	332° F (167° C)
Atmosphere	Almost nonexistent
Lunas	

*In both cases, Earth = 1

AXIS INCLINATION

0.1°

One rotation lasts 59 days.

Rotation and Orbit

Mercury rotates slowly on its axis and takes approximately 59 Earth days to complete a turn, but it only needs 88 days to travel in its orbit. To an observer in Mercury, these two combined motions would give a combined interval of 176 days between two sunrises. A person observing the sunrise from position 1 would have to wait for the planet to make two orbits around the Sun and make three rotations on its own axis before seeing the next sunrise.

ORBIT OF MERCURY AROUND THE SUN

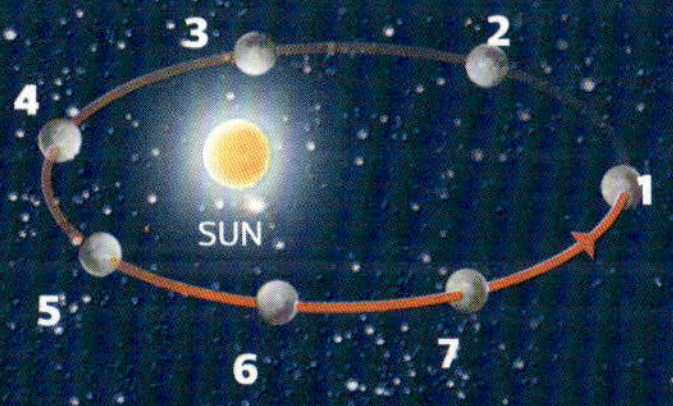

Each number corresponds to a position of the Sun in the sky as seen from Mercury.

VIEW FROM MERCURY

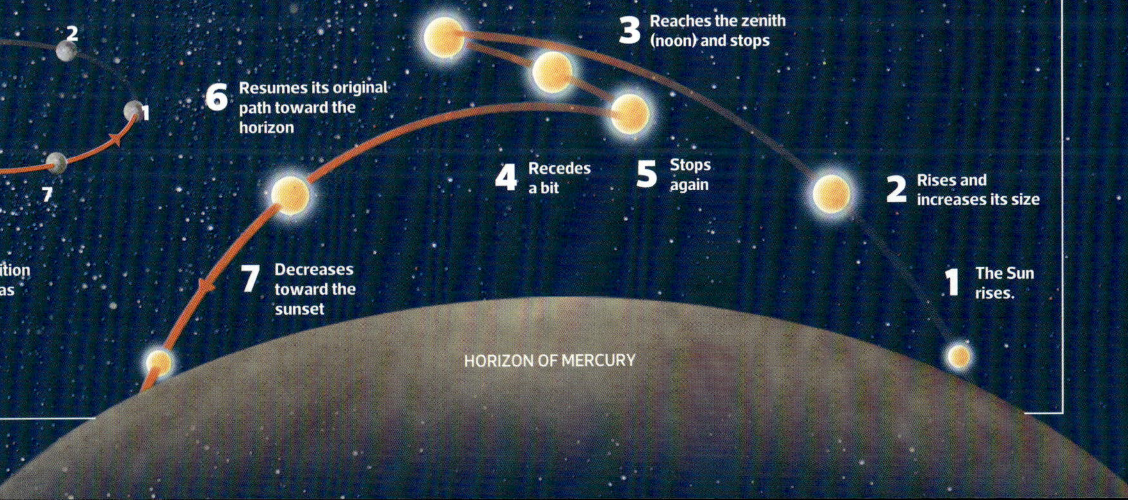

Venus, Our Neighbor

Venus is the second-closest planet to the Sun. Similar in size to the Earth, it has a volcanic surface, as well as a hostile atmosphere governed by the effects of carbon dioxide. Although about four billion years ago the atmospheres of the Earth and Venus were similar, the mass of Venus's atmosphere today is 100 times greater than the Earth's. Its thick clouds of sulfuric acid and dust are so dense that stars are invisible from the planet's surface. Viewed from the Earth, Venus can be bright enough to be visible during day and second only to the moon in brightness at night. Because of this, the movements of Venus were well-known by most ancient civilizations.

CHARACTERISTICS

CONVENTIONAL PLANET SYMBOL ♀

ESSENTIAL DATA	
Average distance from the Sun	67,000,000 miles (108,000,000 km)
Solar orbit (Venusian year)	224 days 17 hours
Equatorial diameter	7,520 miles (12,100 km)
Orbital speed	22 miles per second (35 km/s)
Mass*	0.8
Gravity*	0.9
Density	3.03 ounces per cubic inch (5.25 g/cu cm)
Average temperature	860° F (460° C)
Atmosphere	Very thick
Moons	None

*In both cases, Earth = 1

AXIS INCLINATION

177°

Rotates on its own axis every 243 days

Composition

The overwhelming presence of carbon dioxide in the Venusian atmosphere induces a greenhouse effect, increasing the surface temperature to 864° F (462° C). Because of this, Venus is hotter than Mercury, even though Venus is farther from the Sun and reflects all but 20 percent of the Sun's light. The surface temperature of Venus is relatively constant, averaging 860° F (460° C). The atmospheric pressure on Venus is 90 times greater than that on the Earth.

ATMOSPHERE
Venus's glowing appearance is caused by the planet's thick, suffocating atmosphere, which is made up of carbon dioxide and sulfuric clouds that reflect sunlight.

60 miles (100 km)

IS THE THICKNESS OF THE ATMOSPHERE.

Carbon dioxide	Nitrogen and traces of other gases
97%	3%

MANTLE
Made of molten rock, it constitutes most of the planet. It traps the solar radiation and is 1,860 miles (3,000 km) thick.

14,400° F (8,000° C)

CORE
It is believed that Venus's core i similar to the Earth's, containing metallic elements (iron and nickel) and silicates. Venus has no magnetic field—possibly because of its slow axial rotatio

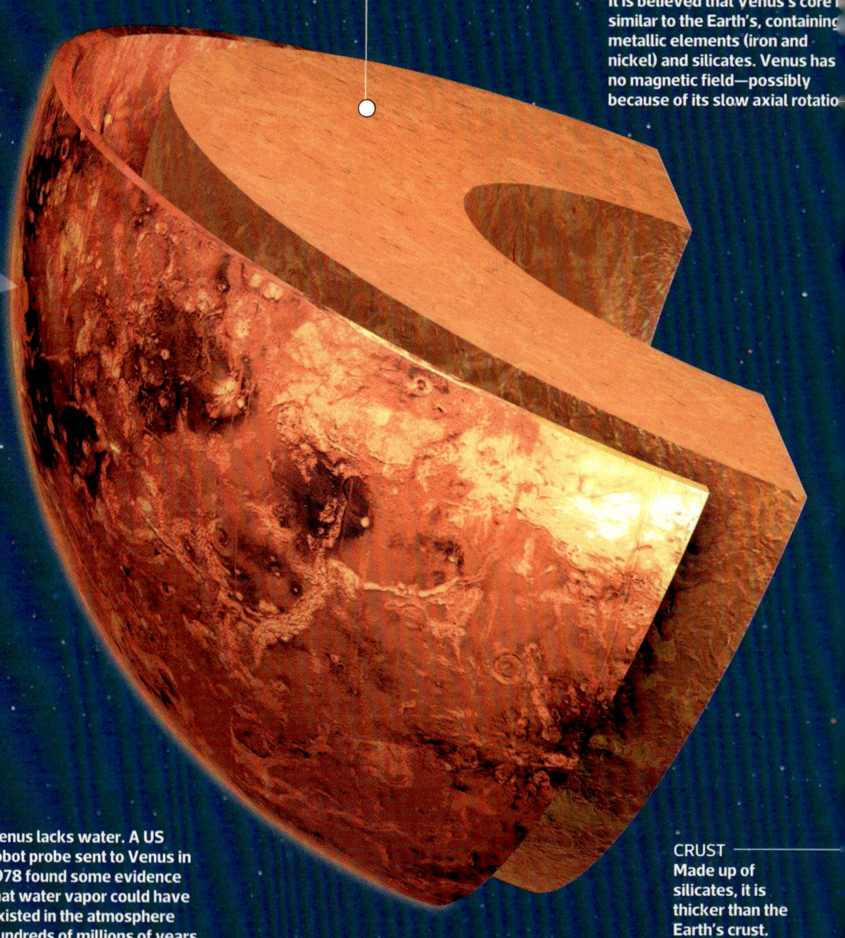

CRUST
Made up of silicates, it is thicker than the Earth's crust.

Venus lacks water. A US robot probe sent to Venus in 1978 found some evidence that water vapor could have existed in the atmosphere hundreds of millions of years ago, but today no trace of water remains.

GREENHOUSE EFFECT
Only 20 percent of the Sun's light reaches the surface of Venus. The thick clouds of dust, sulfuric acid, and carbon dioxide that constitute Venus's atmosphere reflect the remaining light, leaving Venus in permanent darkness.

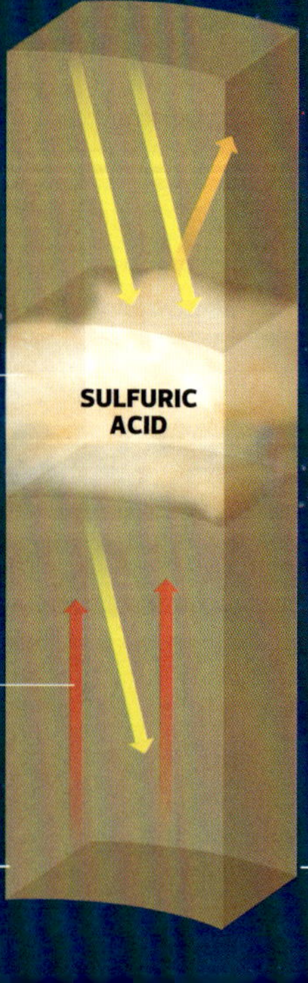

SOLAR RADIATION
Venus is kept hot by its thick atmosphere, which retains the energy of the Sun's rays.

864° F (462° C)

INFRARED RAYS
The surface of Venus radiates infrared radiation. Only 20 percent of the Sun's rays pass through Venus's thick clouds of sulfuric acid.

ENUS'S PHASES

Venus revolves around
e Sun, its solar illumination
ries as is seen from the Earth
pending upon its position
elation to the Sun and the
rth. Thus Venus has phases
nilar to the Moon's. During
elongations, when Venus is
thest from the Sun in the sky,
nus appears at its brightest.

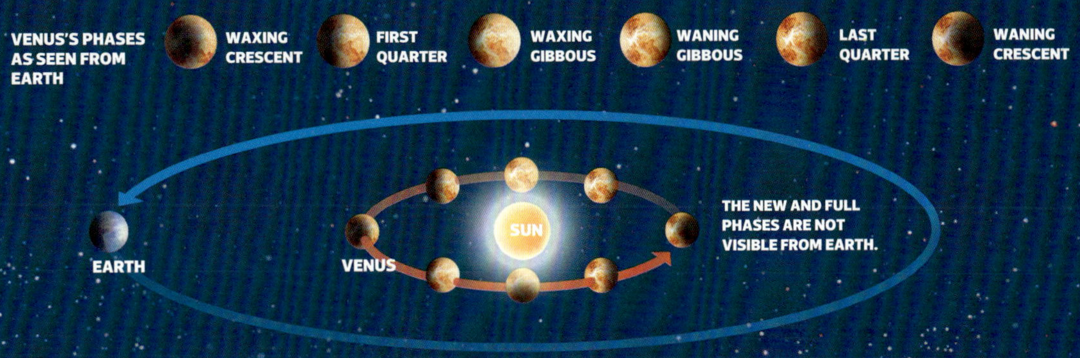

e surface of Venus
ocky and dry. Most
the planet is formed
volcanic plains and
er, elevated regions.

Surface

The Venusian surface has not remained the same throughout its life. The current one is some 500 hundred million years old, but the rocky landscape visible today was formed by intense volcanic activity. Volcanic rock covers 85 percent of the planet. The entire planet is crisscrossed by vast plains and enormous rivers of lava, as well as a number of mountains. The lava flows have created a great number of grooves, some of which are very wide. The brightness of Venus's surface is the result of metallic compounds.

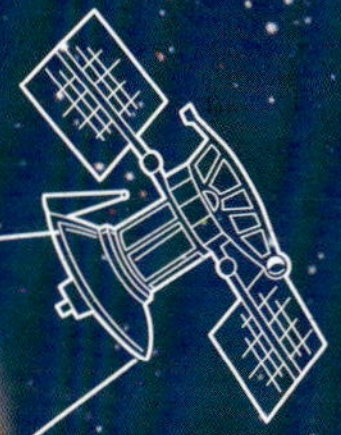

MAGELLAN
Venus was explored by the Magellan spacecraft between 1990 and 1994. The probe was equipped with a radar system to observe the surface through its dense atmosphere.

ISHTAR TERRA
One of the raised plateaus of Venus, it is similar in size to Australia and is located close to Venus's north pole. It has four main rocky mountain ranges called Maxwell Montes, Freyja Montes, Akna Montes, and Danu Montes.

APHRODITE TERRA
Larger than Ishtar Terra, it is the size of South America. Aphrodite Terra lies near the equator and consists mostly of mountainous regions to the east and west, which are separated by a low-lying region.

Red and Fascinating

Mars is the fourth planet from the Sun. Of all the planets, Mars most closely resembles the Earth. It has polar ice caps, and the tilt of its axis, period of rotation, and internal structure are similar to those of the Earth. Known as the Red Planet because of the reddish iron oxide that covers its surface, Mars has a thin atmosphere composed essentially of carbon dioxide. Mars does not have water, though it did in the past, and there is evidence some water might exist underground. Many spacecraft have been sent to explore Mars, in part because it is the planet other than Earth most likely to have developed some form of life, and it will probably be the first planet humans leave the Earth to visit. ●

Martian Orbit

Because Mars's orbit is more elliptical than that of Earth, Mars's distance from the Sun varies widely. At its perihelion, or closest approach to the Sun, Mars receives 45 percent more solar radiation than at its aphelion, or farthest point. Temperatures on Mars range from -220° F to 62° F (-140° C to 17° C).

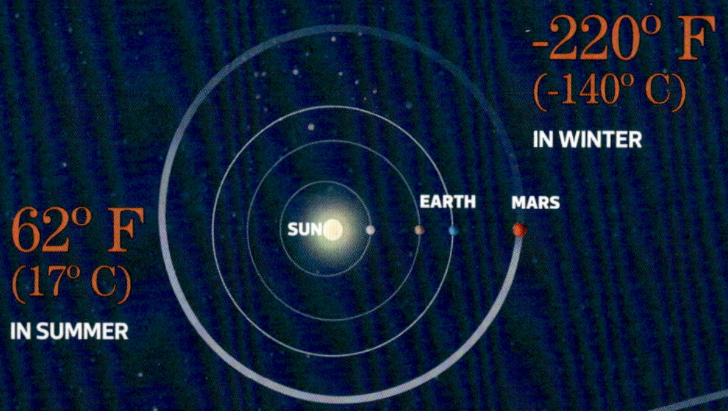

Composition

Mars, a rocky planet, has an iron-rich core. Mars is almost half the size of the Earth and has a similar period of rotation, as well as clearly evident clouds, winds, and other weather phenomena. Its thin atmosphere is made up of carbon dioxide, and its red color comes from its soil, which is rich in iron oxide.

CRUST
is thin and made up of solid rock. It is 31 miles (50 km) thick.

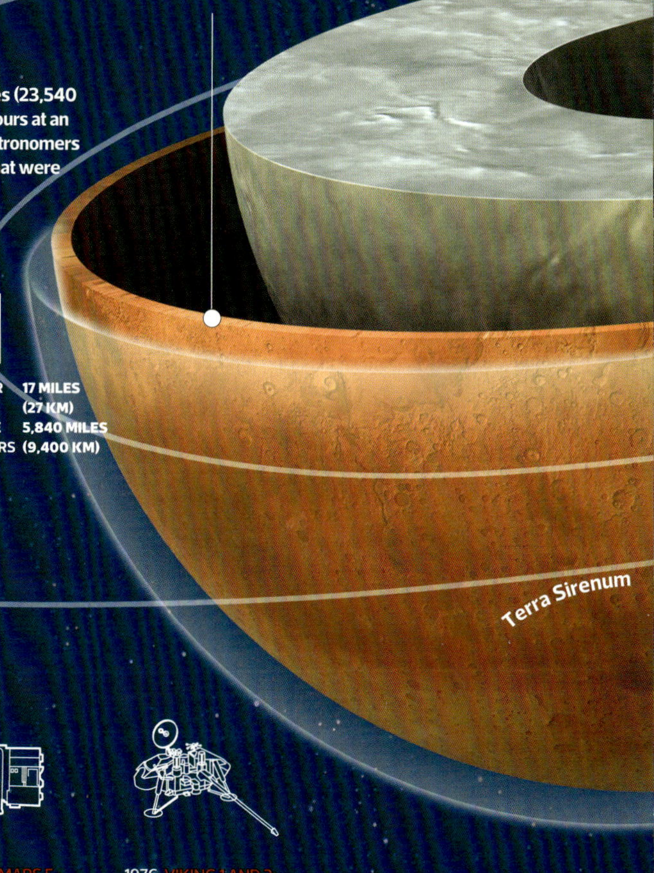

Moons

Mars has two moons, Phobos and Deimos. Both have a lower density than Mars and are pitted with craters. Phobos has a diameter of 17 miles (27 km), and Deimos has a diameter of nine miles (15 km). Deimos orbits Mars in 30 hours at an altitude of 14,627 miles (23,540 km), and Phobos orbits Mars in eight hours at an altitude of 5,840 miles (9,400 km). Astronomers believe that the moons are asteroids that were captured by Mars's gravity.

DEIMOS

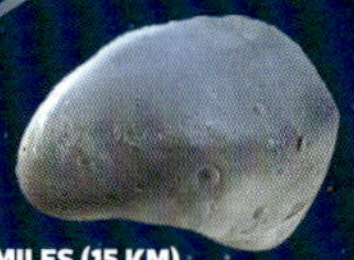

DIAMETER 9 MILES (15 KM)
DISTANCE FROM MARS 14,627 MILES (23,540 KM)

PHOBOS

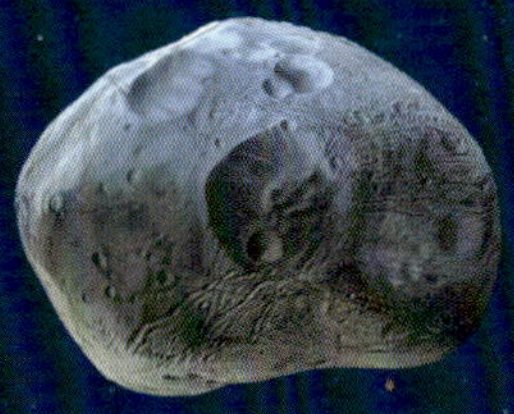

DIAMETER 17 MILES (27 KM)
DISTANCE FROM MARS 5,840 MILES (9,400 KM)

MISSIONS TO MARS
After our own Moon, Mars has been a more attractive target for exploratory missions than any other object in the solar system.

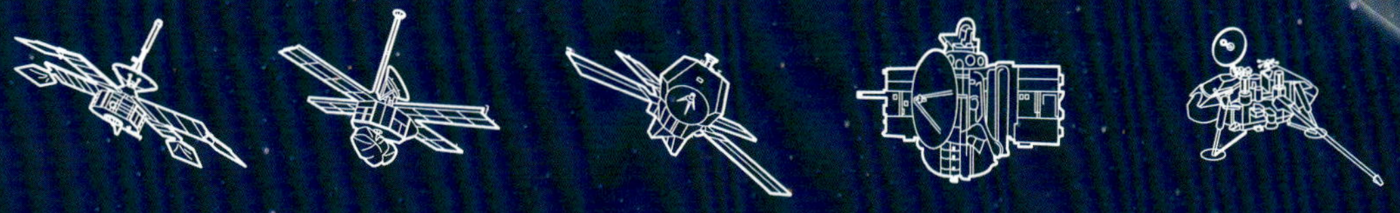

1965 MARINER 4
The first mission sent to Mars, it made only brief flyovers.

1969 MARINER 6 AND 7 studied the southern hemisphere and equator of Mars.

1971 MARINER 9
photographed the Olympus volcano for the first time.

1973 MARS 4, MARS 5, MARS 6, AND MARS 7
Russian spacecraft successfully sent to Mars

1976 VIKING 1 AND 2
searched for traces of life. They were the first spacecraft to land on Martian soil.

Surface

It is a place of geologic extremes, shaped by volcanic activity, meteorite bombardment, windstorms, and floods (though there is little or o water on Mars today). Mountains dominate the outhern hemisphere, but lowlands are common the northern hemisphere.

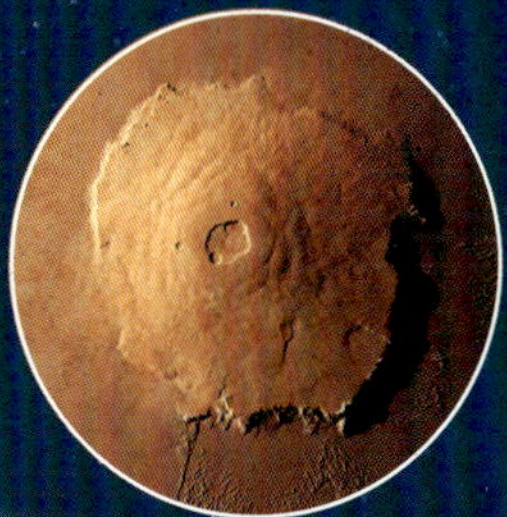

OLYMPUS MONS

This gigantic, inactive volcano is not only the largest on Mars but also in the solar system.

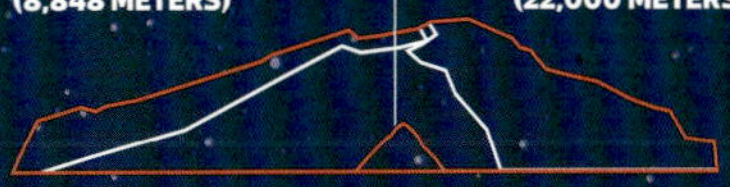

VALLES MARINERIS

The canyon system of the Valles Marineris was likely caused naturally, primarily by water erosion.

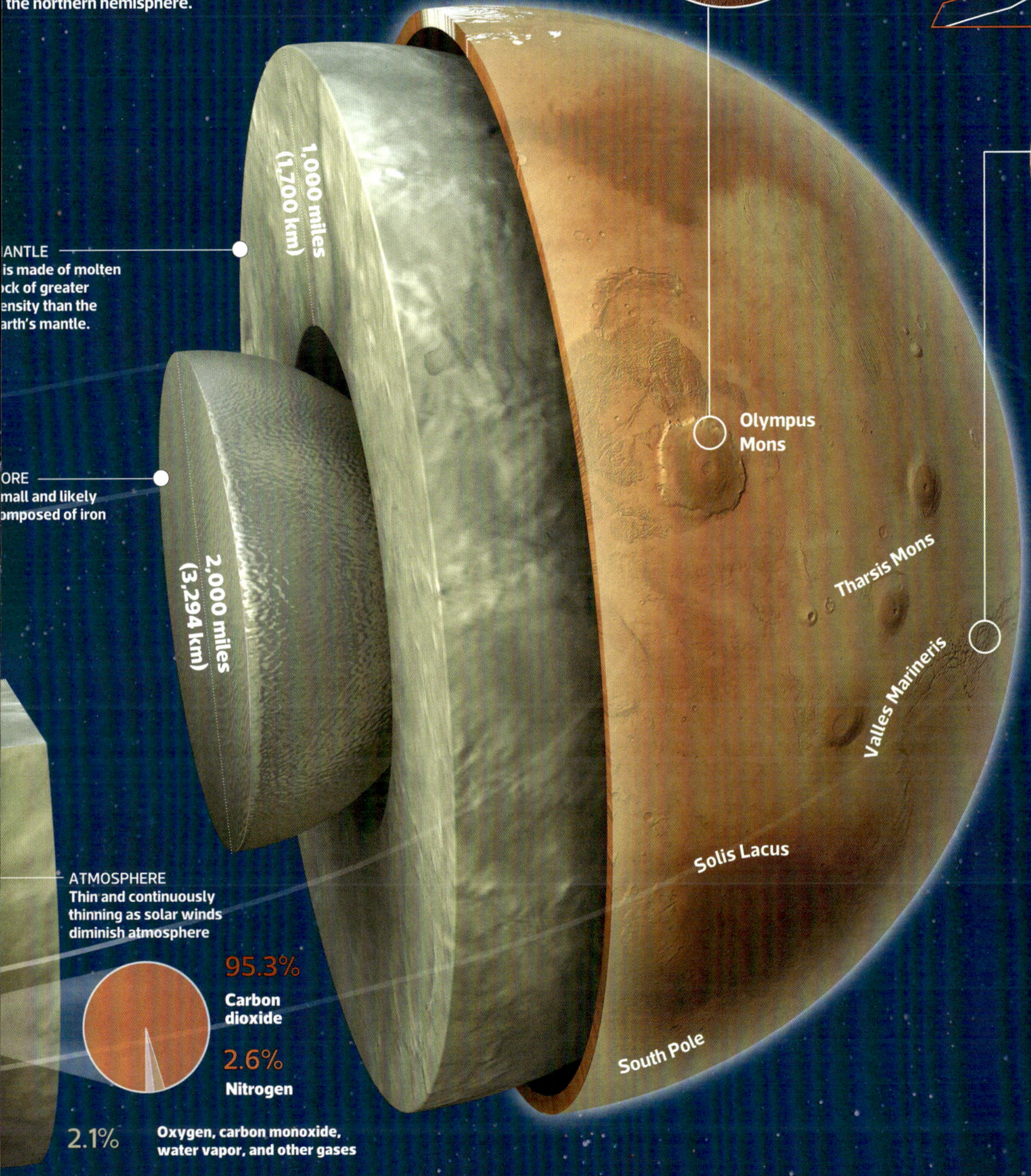

ANTLE
is made of molten ock of greater ensity than the arth's mantle.

ORE
mall and likely omposed of iron

ATMOSPHERE
Thin and continuously thinning as solar winds diminish atmosphere

95.3% Carbon dioxide

2.6% Nitrogen

2.1% Oxygen, carbon monoxide, water vapor, and other gases

CHARACTERISTICS

CONVENTIONAL PLANET SYMBOL ♂

ESSENTIAL DATA

Average distance from the Sun	141,600,000 miles (227,900,000 km)
Solar orbit (Martian year)	24 hours and 40 minutes
Equatorial diameter	4,222 miles (6,794 km)
Orbital speed	15 miles per second (24 km/s)
Mass*	0.107
Gravity*	0.38
Density	2.27 ounces per cubic inch (3.93 g/cu cm)
Average temperature	-81° F (-63° C)
Atmosphere	Very thin
Moons	2

*In both cases, Earth = 1

AXIS INCLINATION

25.2°

One rotation lasts 24 hours and 40 minutes.

997 MARS PATHFINDER was the hird successful Mars anding.

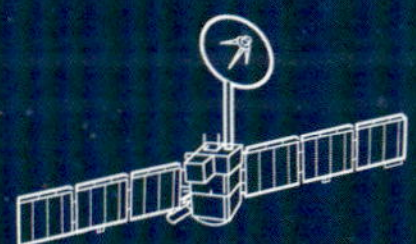

1997 MARS GLOBAL SURVEYOR took more than 100,000 photos of the planet.

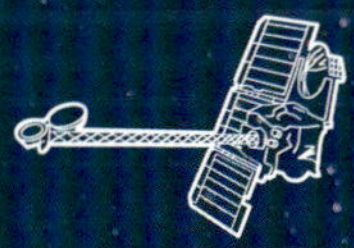

2001 MARS ODYSSEY mapped the mineralogy and morphology of Mars's surface.

2003 MARS EXPRESS Orbiting probe. First spacecraft sent by the European Space Agency.

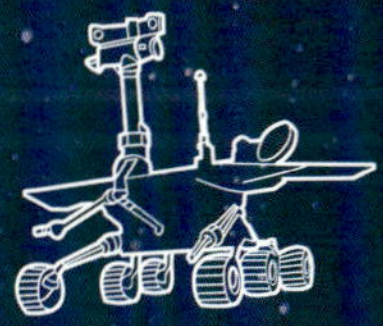

2004 SPIRIT AND OPPORTUNITY surveyed many square miles of the surface.

2006 MARS RECONNAISSANCE ORBITER made a detailed study of the Martian surface while orbiting the planet.

Jupiter, Gas Giant

Jupiter is the largest planet in the solar system. Its diameter is 11 times that of the Earth, and its mass is 300 times as great. Because the speed of Jupiter's rotation flattens the planet at its poles, its equatorial diameter is greater than its polar diameter. Jupiter rotates at 25,000 miles per hour (40,000 km/hr). One of the most distinctive elements of Jupiter's atmosphere is its Great Red Spot, a giant high-pressure region of turbulence that has been observed from the Earth for more than 300 years. The planet is orbited by numerous satellites and has a wide, faint ring of particles.

Composition

Jupiter is a giant ball of hydrogen and helium that have been compressed into liquid in the planet's interior and into metallic rock in its core. Not much is known about Jupiter's core, but it is believed to be bigger than the Earth's core.

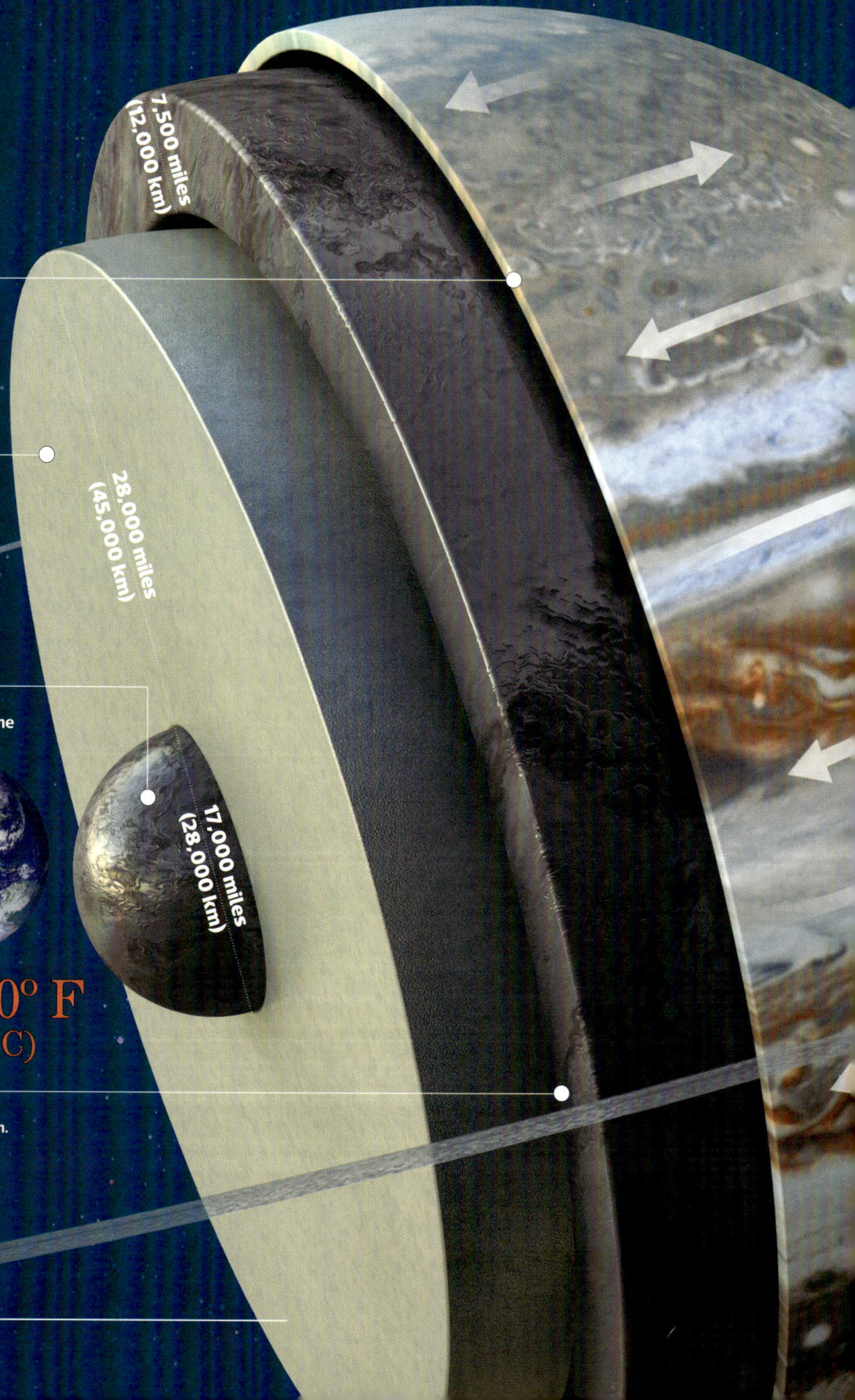

ATMOSPHERE measures 620 miles (1,000 km).

INNER MANTLE Surrounds the core. It is made of liquid metallic hydrogen, an element only found under hot, high-pressure conditions. The inner mantle is a soup of electrons and nuclei.

CORE Its size is about ten times larger than the Earth's core.

54,000° F (30,000° C)

OUTER MANTLE Made of liquid molecular hydrogen. The outer mantle merges with the atmosphere.

CHARACTERISTICS

CONVENTIONAL PLANET SYMBOL ♃

ESSENTIAL DATA

Average distance from the Sun	483,000,000 miles (778,000,000 km)
Solar orbit (Jovian year)	11 years 312 days
Equatorial diameter	88,700 miles (142,800 km)
Orbital speed	8 miles per second (13 km/s)
Mass*	318
Gravity*	2.36
Density	0.77 ounce per cubic inch (1.33 g/cu cm)
Average temperature	-184° F (-120° C)
Atmosphere	Very dense
Moons	67

*In both cases, Earth = 1

AXIS INCLINATION

3.1°

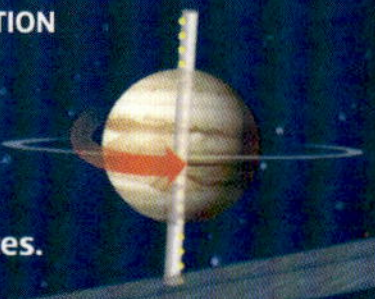

One rotation lasts 9 hours and 55 minutes.

The Moons of Jupiter

Jupiter has 67 moons. Many of them have not been officially confirmed and do not even have names. Jupiter's rotation is gradually slowing because of the moons' tidal effects.

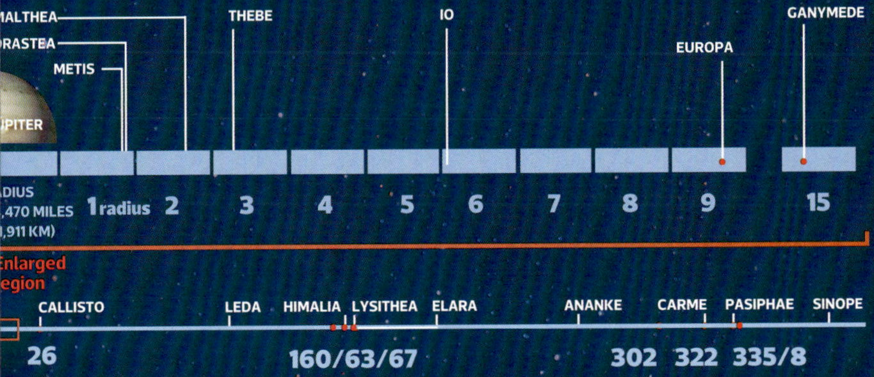

GALILEAN MOONS

Of Jupiter's 67 moons, four are visible from Earth with binoculars. These are called the Galilean moons in honor of their discoverer, Galileo Galilei. Astronomers believe that Io has active volcanoes and that Europa has an ocean underneath its icy crust.

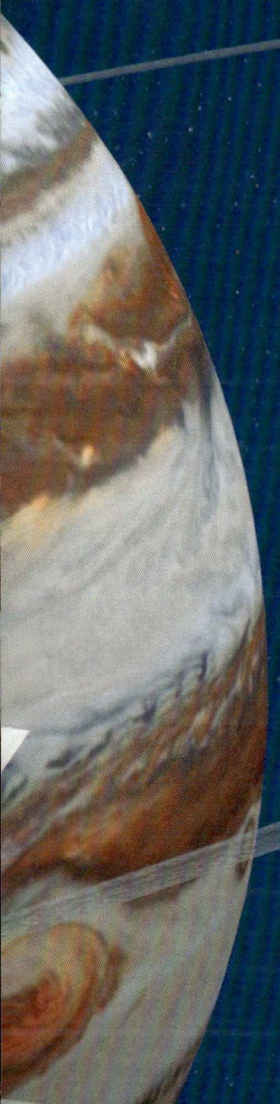

Winds

The winds on Jupiter blow in contiguous bands and opposing directions. The bands' small differences in temperature and chemical composition give the planet its multicolored appearance. Jupiter's inclement environment, in which winds blow at more than 370 miles per hour (600 km/h), can cause large storms, such as the Great Red Spot in the southern hemisphere of the planet. The Great Red Spot, which is 16,155 miles (26,000 km) long, is believed to be composed mainly of ammonia gas and clouds of ice.

16,160 miles *(26,000 km)*

GREAT RED SPOT

RINGS

Jupiter's rings are made of dust from the planet's four inner moons. These rings were first seen in 1979 by the space probe Voyager 1 and later by Voyager 2.

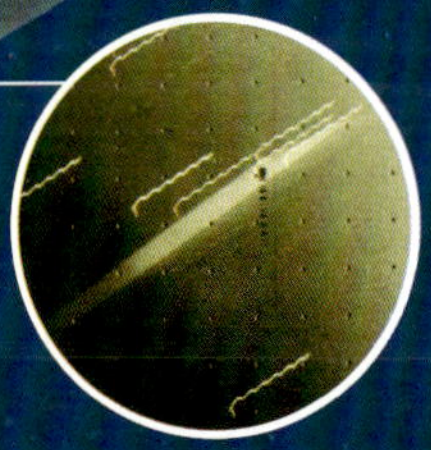

RING MATERIAL

JUPITER'S MAGNETISM

Jupiter's magnetic field is 20,000 times stronger than the Earth's. Astronomers believe the field is caused by the electrical currents that are created by the rapid rotation of metallic hydrogen. Jupiter is surrounded by a huge magnetic bubble, the magnetosphere. The magnetosphere's tail reaches more than 370,000,000 miles (600,000,000 km)—beyond the orbit of Saturn.

Jupiter's magnetosphere is the largest object in the solar system. It varies in size and shape in response to the solar wind, which is composed of the particles continuously radiated from the Sun.

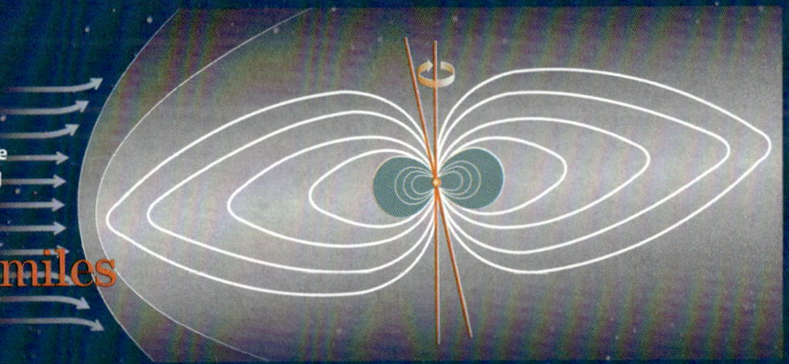

400,000,000 miles
(650,000,000 km)

ATMOSPHERE

surrounds the inner liquid layers and the solid core. It is 620 miles thick (1,000 km).

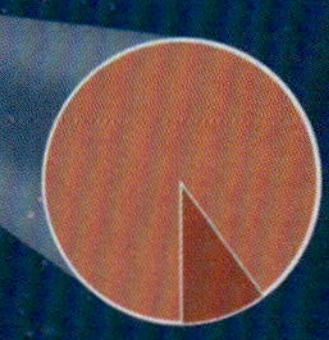

89.8%
Hydrogen

10.2%
Helium With traces of methane and ammonia

The Lord of the Rings

Saturn is the solar system's second-largest planet. Like Jupiter, it is a large ball of gas surrounding a small, solid core. Saturn was the most distant planet discovered before the invention of the telescope. To the naked eye, it looks like a yellowish star, with the help of a telescope, its rings are clearly visible. Ten times farther from the Sun than the Earth, S is the least dense planet. If an ocean could be found large enough to hold it, Saturn would float.

Rings

Saturn's rings, the brightest rings in the solar system, are made of rock and ice and orbit Saturn's equator. The rings are probably remains of destroyed comets that were trapped by Saturn's gravitational field.

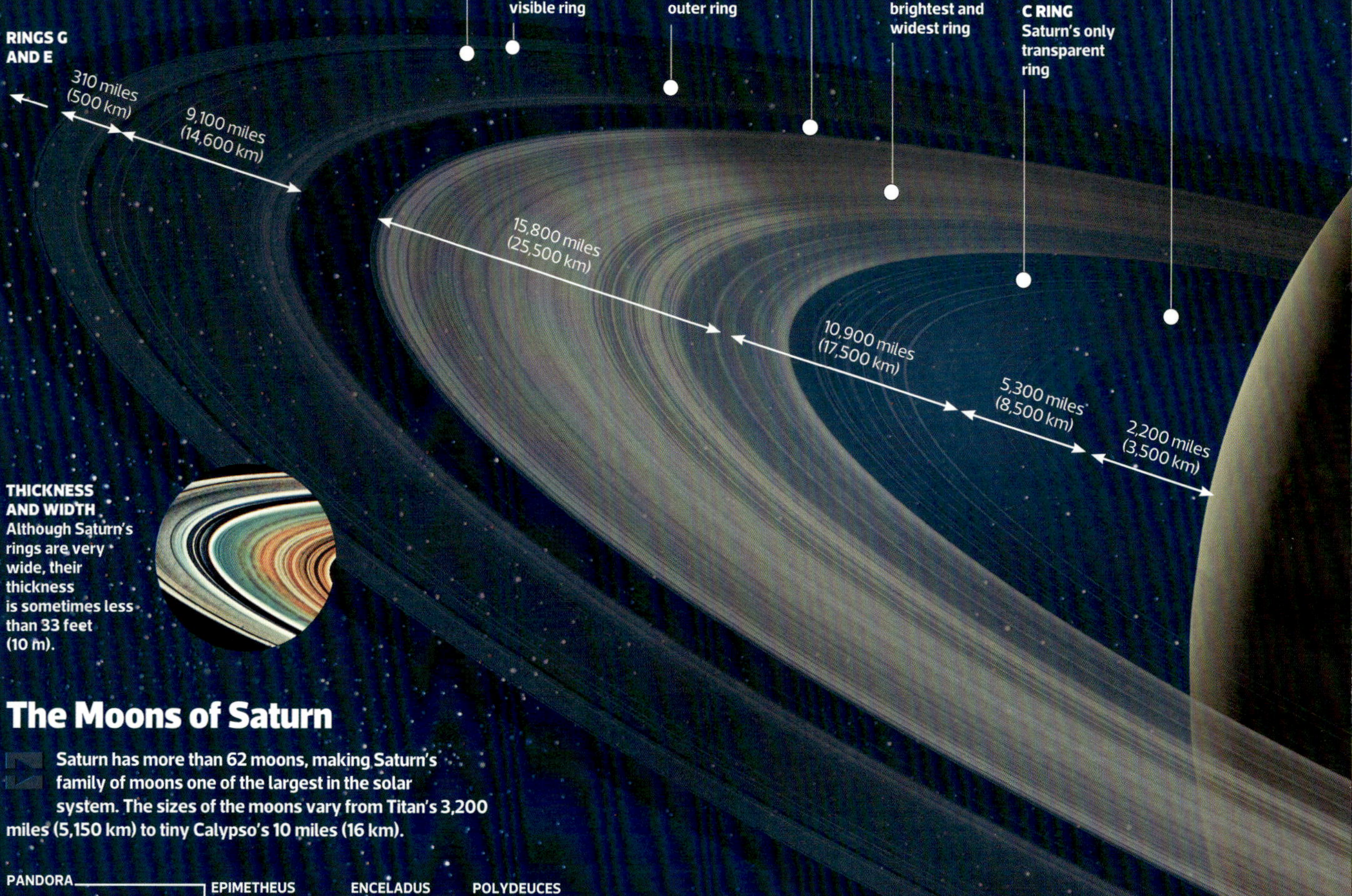

THICKNESS AND WIDTH
Although Saturn's rings are very wide, their thickness is sometimes less than 33 feet (10 m).

The Moons of Saturn

Saturn has more than 62 moons, making Saturn's family of moons one of the largest in the solar system. The sizes of the moons vary from Titan's 3,200 miles (5,150 km) to tiny Calypso's 10 miles (16 km).

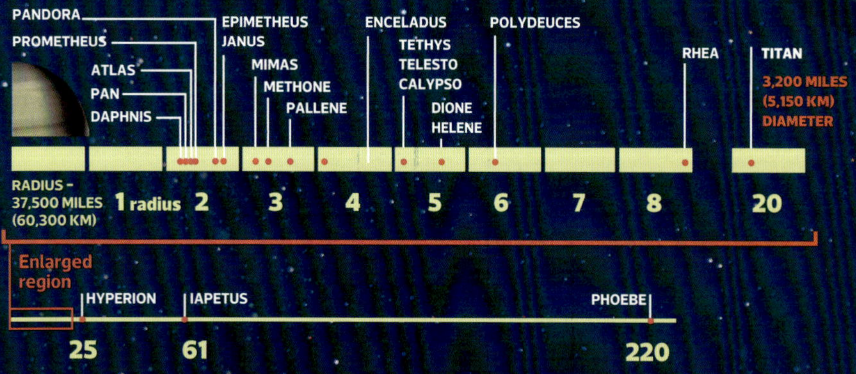

Titan's diameter is larger than Mercury's. It has an atmosphere that is mostly made of nitrogen.

urface

Like Jupiter, Saturn has a surface of clouds that form ands because of the anet's rotation. Saturn's ouds are less turbulent and ss colorful than Jupiter's. he higher, white clouds ach temperatures of -220° -140° C). A layer of haze tends above the clouds.

Gaseous Exterior

Saturn and Jupiter differ very little in their composition. Both are gaseous balls surrounding solid cores. What sets Saturn apart are its rings, formed by clustered pieces of ice that range in size from small particles to large chunks. Each particle in a ring is a satellite orbiting Saturn. From the Earth, the massed debris seems to form large structures, but each discrete piece actually has its own orbit.

ATMOSPHERE

<1% Sulfur gives it a yellowish appearance.

2% Helium

97% Hydrogen

COMPONENTS

The main components of Saturn's atmosphere are hydrogen (97%) and helium (2%). The rest is composed of sulfur, methane, and other gases.

CHARACTERISTICS

CONVENTIONAL PLANET SYMBOL ♄

ESSENTIAL DATA

Average distance from the Sun	887,000,000 miles (1,427,000,000 km)
Solar orbit (Saturnine year)	29 years 154 days
Equatorial diameter	74,940 miles (120,600 km)
Orbital speed	6 miles per second (10 km/s)
Mass*	95
Gravity*	0.92
Density	0.4 ounce per cubic inch (0.7 g/cu cm)
Average temperature	-193° F (-125° C)
Atmosphere	Very dense
Moons	More than 62

*In both cases, Earth = 1

AXIS INCLINATION

26.7°

One rotation lasts 10 hours and 39 minutes.

INDS

aturn's winds generally ach speeds of about 220 iles per hour (360 km/h), ausing strong storms.

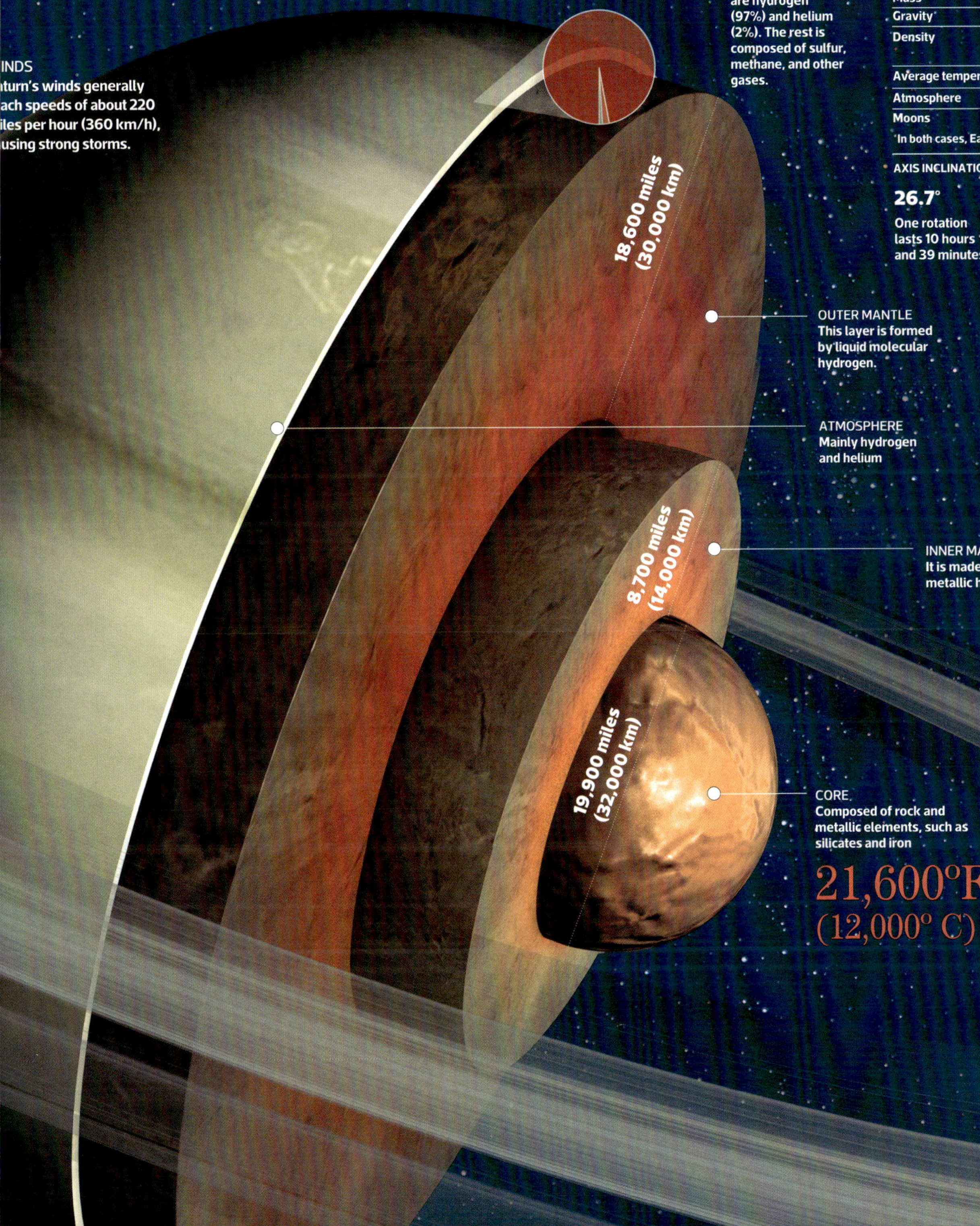

Uranus Without Secrets

To the unaided eye, Uranus looks like a star at the limit of visibility. It is the seventh-farthest planet from the Sun and the third-largest planet in the solar system. One peculiarity distinguishing it from the other planets is its anomalous axis of rotation, tilted nearly 98 degrees around the plane of its orbit, so that one or the other of Uranus's poles points toward the Sun. Astronomers speculate that, during its formation, Uranus may have suffered an impact with a protoplanet, which could have altered Uranus's tilt. Uranus's orbit is so large that the planet takes 84 years to completely orbit the Sun. Uranus's period of rotation is 17 hours and 14 minutes.

MAGNETIC FIELD

Uranus generates a magnetic field 50 times more powerful than Earth's. This field is not centered on the planet, but is offset and tilted 60 degrees from Uranus's axis. If this were the case on Earth, the magnetic north pole would be located in Morocco. Unlike other planets, Uranus's magnetic field originates in the planet's mantle, not its core.

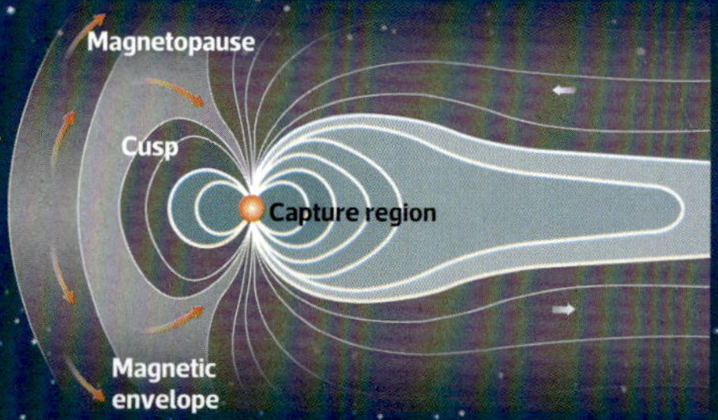

Some scientists suggest that Uranus's anomalous magnetic field may indicate that the convection of Uranus's core has stopped because of cooling—or, perhaps, that the planet is currently undergoing a magnetic inversion, as has happened on the Earth.

Composition

Uranus's core is made of abundant amounts of silicates and ice. The planet is almost four times larger than the Earth, and its atmosphere is made up of hydrogen, helium, and methane. Uranus has an almost horizontal tilt, causing it to have very long seasons.

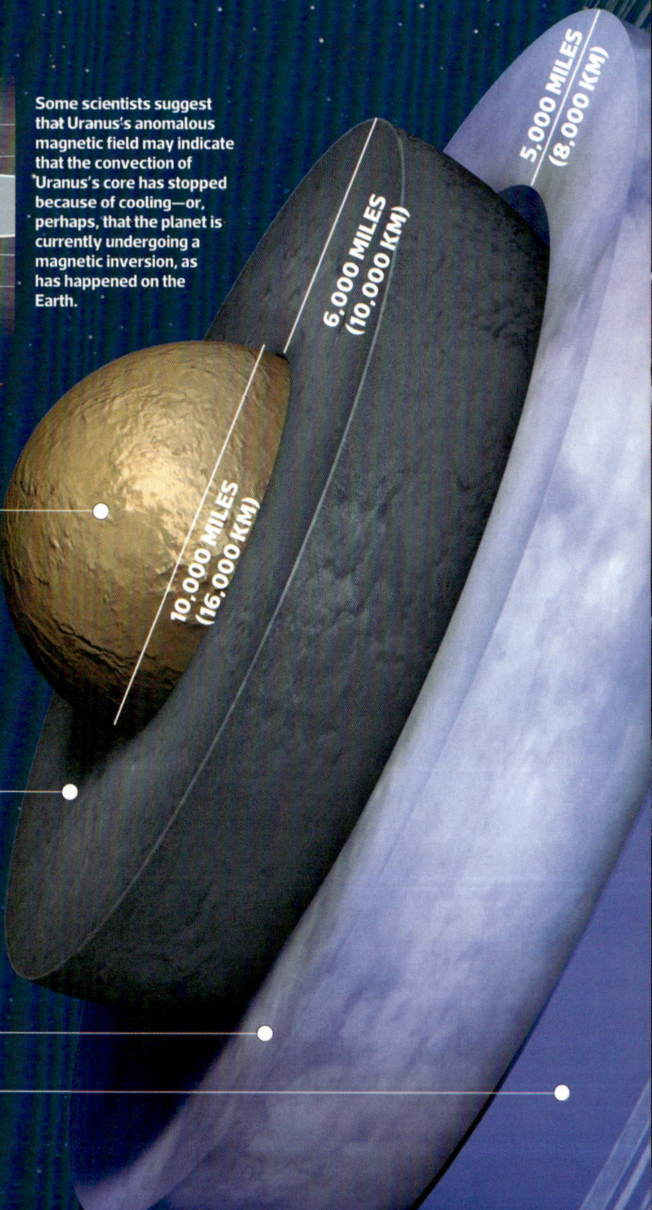

CORE
Made up of silicates and ice

INNER MANTLE
Probably icy water, methane, and ammonia. (According to some models, the materials of the mantle and core do not form layers.)

OUTER MANTLE
Composed primarily of hydrogen and helium, as well as a small amount of methane

ATMOSPHERE
Uranus's atmosphere is made up of hydrogen, methane, helium, and small amounts of acetylene and other hydrocarbons.

CHARACTERISTICS

CONVENTIONAL PLANET SYMBOL ♅

ESSENTIAL DATA	
Average distance from the Sun	1,780,000,000 miles (2,870,000,000 km)
Solar orbit (Uranian year)	84 years 4 days
Equatorial diameter	31,763 miles (51,118 km)
Orbital speed	4 miles per second (7 km/s)
Mass*	14.5
Gravity*	0.89
Density	0.8 ounce per cubic inch (1.3 g/cu cm)
Average temperature	-346° F (-210° C)
Atmosphere	Less dense
Moons	27

* In both cases, Earth = 1

AXIS INCLINATION

97.9°

One rotation lasts 17 hours and 14 minutes.

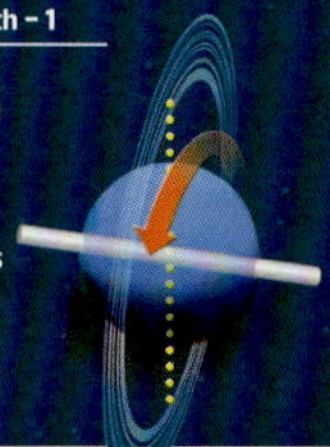

-346° F
(-210° C)
AVERAGE TEMPERATURE

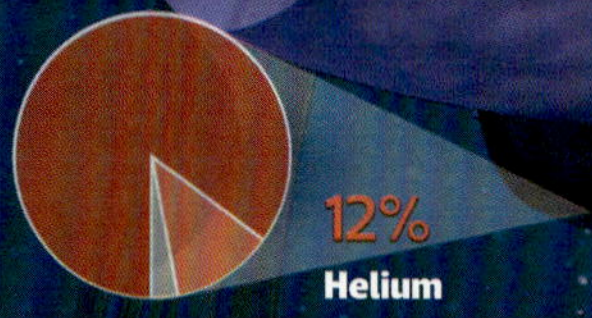

Rings

Like all giant planets of the solar system, Uranus has a ring system, but it is much darker than Saturn's and more difficult to see. The planet's 13 rings, which orbit the planet's equator, were discovered in 1977. In 1986, they were explored by Voyager 2.

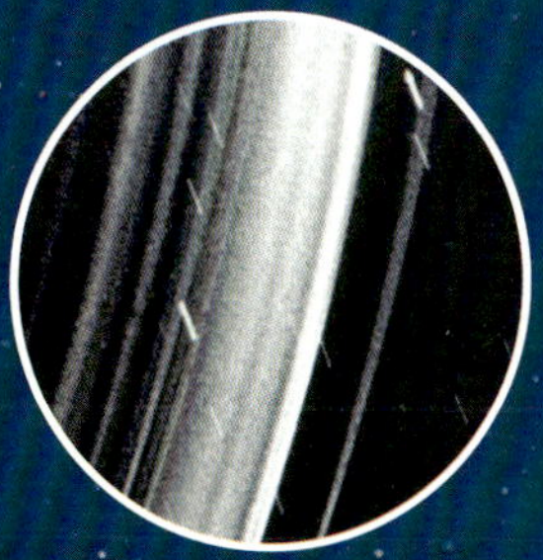

Satellites

Uranus has 27 moons. The first four were discovered in 1787, and another ten were identified in 1986 by the space probe Voyager 2. Uranus's moons were named in honor of characters from the works of William Shakespeare and Alexander Pope, a naming convention that distinguishes them from the other moons in the solar system. Some of Uranus's moons are large, but most measure only dozens of miles.

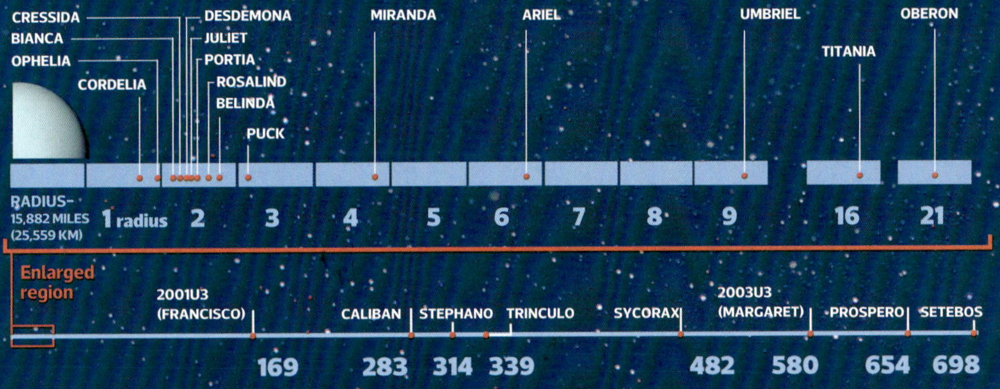

MOONS

Uranus has small, dark moons, discovered by Voyager 2, as well as bigger moons, such as Miranda, Ariel, Umbriel, Oberon, and Titania. These last two are approximately 930 miles (1,500 km) in diameter.

Miranda, only 293 miles (472 km) in diameter, is the smallest of Uranus's five main moons. It has an irregular surface with grooves and a bright mark.

Surface

For a long time, Uranus was believed to have a smooth surface. The Hubble Space Telescope, however, showed that Uranus is a dynamic planet that has the solar system's brightest clouds and a fragile ring system that wobbles like an unbalanced wheel.

REFRACTION OF RAYS

1. In Uranus, sunlight is reflected by a curtain of clouds that lie underneath a layer of methane.

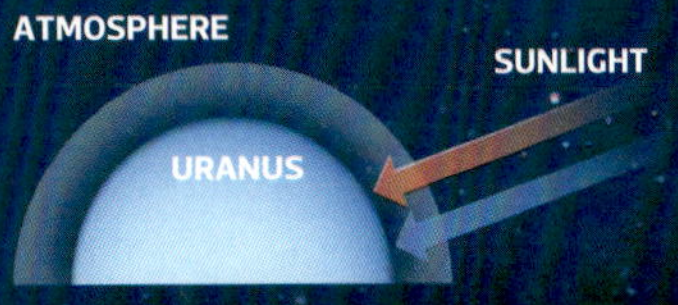

2. When sunlight passes through this layer, the methane absorbs the red light waves and lets the blue light waves pass through, producing the planet's hue.

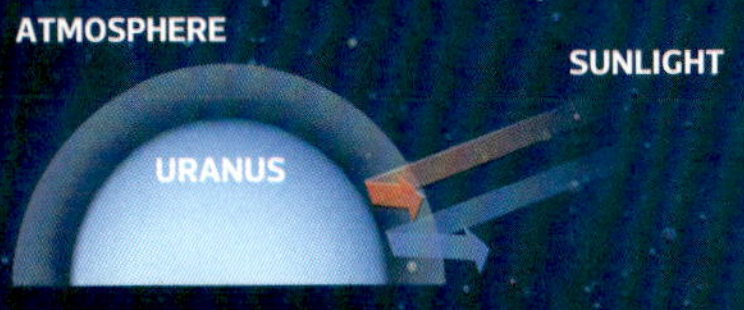

Neptune: Deep Blue

Seen from our planet, Neptune appears as a faint, blue point invisible to the naked eye. Images sent to Earth by Voyager 2 show the planet as a remarkably blue sphere, an effect produced by the presence of methane in the outer part of Neptune's atmosphere. The farthest of the gaseous planets, Neptune is 30 times farther from the Sun than the Earth is. Its rings and impressive clouds are noteworthy, as is its resemblance to Uranus. Neptune is of special interest to astronomers because, before its discovery, its existence and location were predicted on the basis of mathematical calculations.

Moons

Neptune has 14 natural satellites, all are named. Triton and Nereid were the first moons observed by telescope from Earth. The 12 remaining moons were observed from space by the US space probe Voyager 2. All the names of Neptune's satellites correspond to ancient Greek marine deities.

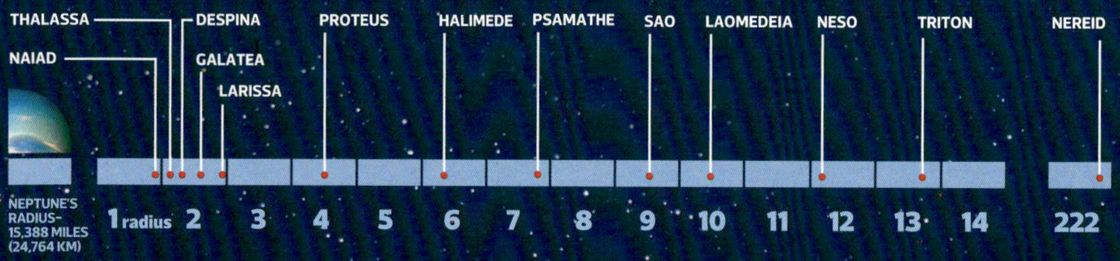

TRITON

Its diameter is 1,681 miles (2,706 km). Triton orbits Neptune in a direction opposite that of the other moons. Its surface has dark stripes formed by the material spewed from its geysers and volcanoes.

-391° F (-235° C)

is its temperature, making Triton one of the coldest bodies in the solar system.

1,200 miles per hour (2,000 km/h)

Rings

Uranus has faint rings of dust. When they were discovered from the Earth, astronomers thought the rings formed incomplete arcs. The ring names honor the first scientists to study Neptune.

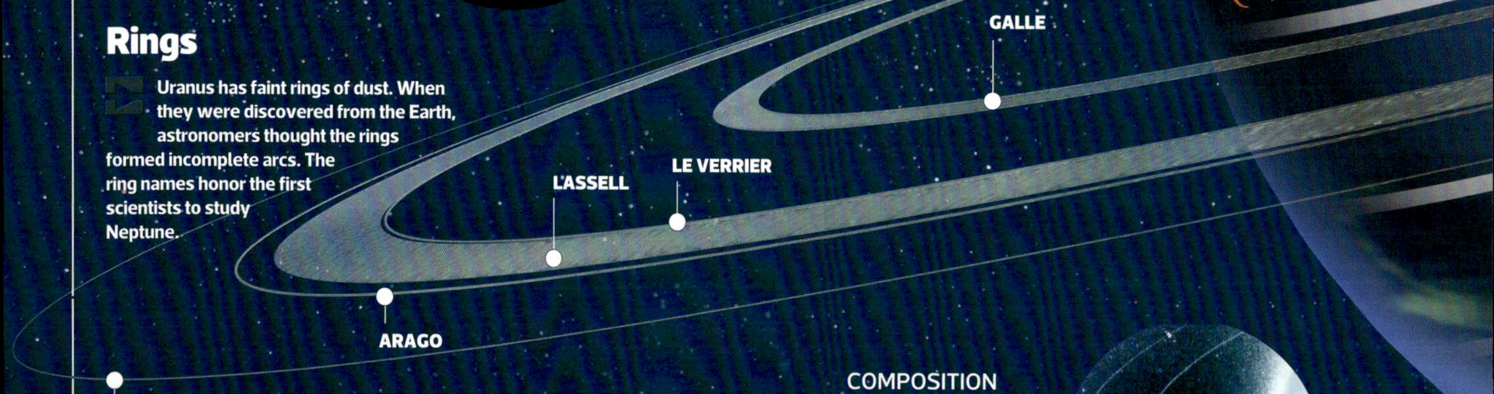

ADAMS

Located 39,000 miles (63,000 km) from the planet's core, this ring has three prominent arcs, or sections, named Liberty, Fraternity, and Equality.

COMPOSITION

Neptune's rings are dark, like those of Uranus and Jupiter. Their composition is unknown, and they are believed to be unstable. Liberty, which makes up part of the outer ring, could vanish before the 22nd century.

Surface

White methane clouds surround Neptune, circulating at some of the fastest speeds in the solar system. Neptune's winds reach 1,200 miles per hour (2,000 km/h) from east to west, swirling against the direction of the planet's rotation.

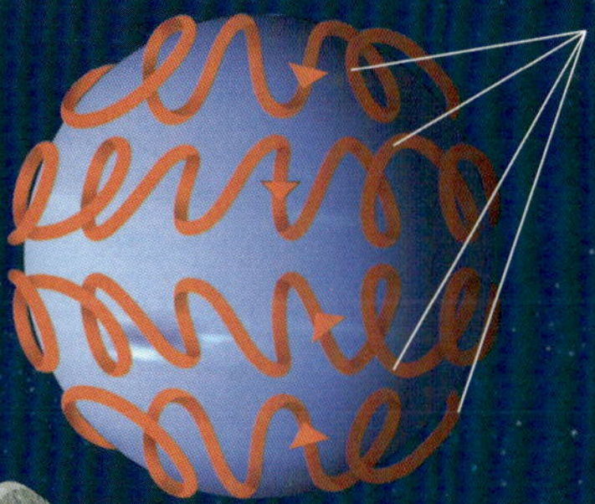

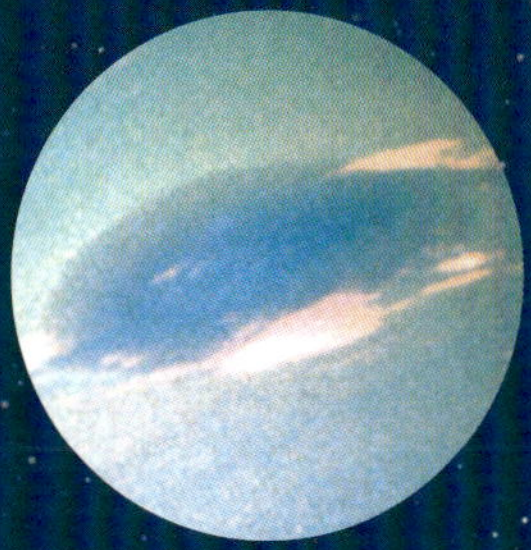

THE GREAT SPOT
This giant storm, called the Great Dark Spot, was first seen on the surface of Neptune in 1989 and was as large as the Earth. By 1994, it had disappeared.

Hard Heart

According to some models, Neptune has a rocky silicate core, covered by a mantle of icy water, ammonia, hydrogen, and methane. According to some models, however, the materials of the mantle and core do not form layers.

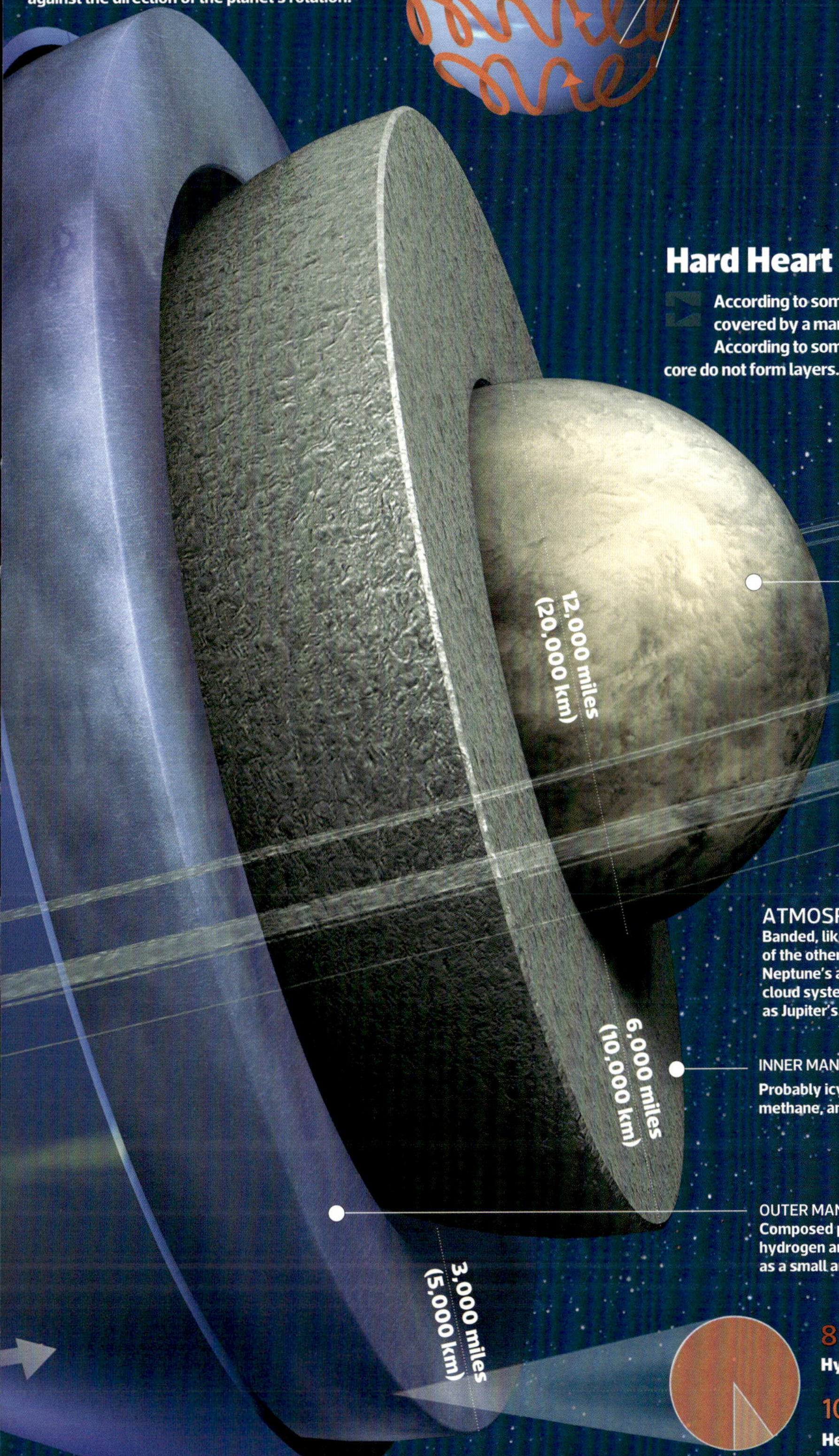

CHARACTERISTICS

CONVENTIONAL PLANET SYMBOL ♆

ESSENTIAL DATA	
Average distance from the Sun	2,800,000,000 miles (4,500,000,000 km)
Solar orbit (Neptunian year)	164 years 264 days
Equatorial diameter	30,800 miles (49,500 km)
Orbital speed	3.4 miles per second (5.5 km/s)
Mass*	17.2
Gravity*	1.12
Density	1 ounce per cubic inch (1.6 g/cu cm)
Average temperature	-330° F (-200° C)
Atmosphere	Dense
Moons	14

*In both cases, Earth = 1

AXIS INCLINATION
28.3°
One rotation lasts 16 hours and 36 minutes.

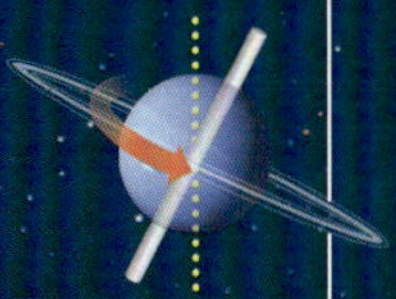

Pluto: Now a Dwarf

Pluto stopped being the ninth planet of the solar system in 2006 when the International Astronomical Union decided to change the classification of cold, distant Pluto to that of dwarf planet. This tiny body in our solar system has never had an imp profile, and it has not yet been possible to study it closely. All that is known about Pluto comes through observations made from the Earth or Earth orbit, such as those made by the Hubble Space Telescope. D the lack of information gathered about Pluto, it is notable for its unique orbit, the tilt of its axis, and its loc within the Kuiper belt. All these characteristics make Pluto especially intriguing.

A Double World

Pluto and its largest satellite, Charon, have a very special relationship. They have been called double planets—the diameter of Charon is about that of Pluto. One theory hypothesizes that Charon was formed from ice that was torn from Pluto when another object collided with the dwarf planet.

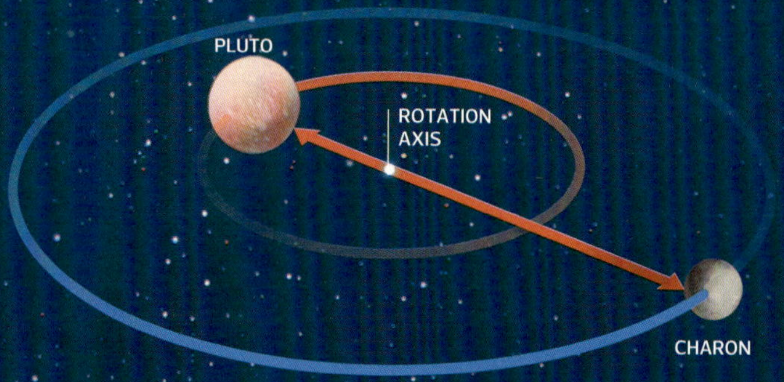

Surface

Only a little is known about Pluto, but the Hubble Space Telescope showed a surface covere by a frozen mixture of nitrogen and methane. The presence of solid methane indicates that its temperatur is less than -333° F (-203° C), but the dwarf planet's temperature varies according to its place in orbit, ranging between 30 and 50 astronomical uni from the Sun.

SYNCHRONIZED ORBITS

The orbital arrangement of Pluto and Charon is unique. Each always faces the other, making the two seem connected by an invisible bar. The synchronization of the two bodies is such that an observer on one side of Pluto would be able to see Charon, but another observer standing on the other side could not see this moon due to the curvature of Pluto.

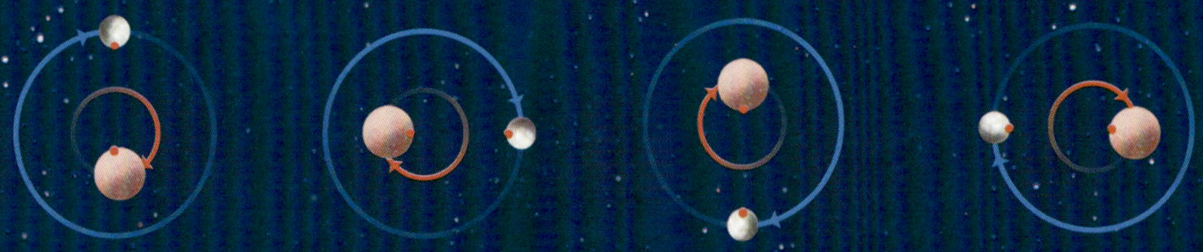

BEST VIEW OF PLUTO AVAILABLE

Moons

In addition to Charon, which was discovered in 1978, Pluto is orbited by four additional moons. Unlike the surface of Pluto, which is made of frozen nitrogen, methane, and carbon dioxide, Charon appears to be covered with ice, methane, and carbon dioxide. One theory holds that the matter that formed this satellite was ejected from Pluto as a result of a collision, an origin similar to that ascribed to Earth's moon.

DENSITY

Charon's density is between 0.7 and 0.8 ounce per cubic inch (1.2 and 1.3 g/cu cm), indicating that its composition does not include much rock.

730 miles (1,172 km)

Charon's diameter is half of Pluto's

Composition

Scientific calculations have deduced that 75 percent of Pluto consists of a mixture of rocks and ice. This frozen surface is made up of 98 percent nitrogen, as well as traces of solidified carbon monoxide and methane. Recently scientists have concluded that Pluto is an object that belongs to the Kuiper belt, a group of objects left over from the formation of the outer planets. In addition to large amounts of frozen nitrogen, Pluto has simple molecules containing hydrogen and oxygen, the building blocks of life.

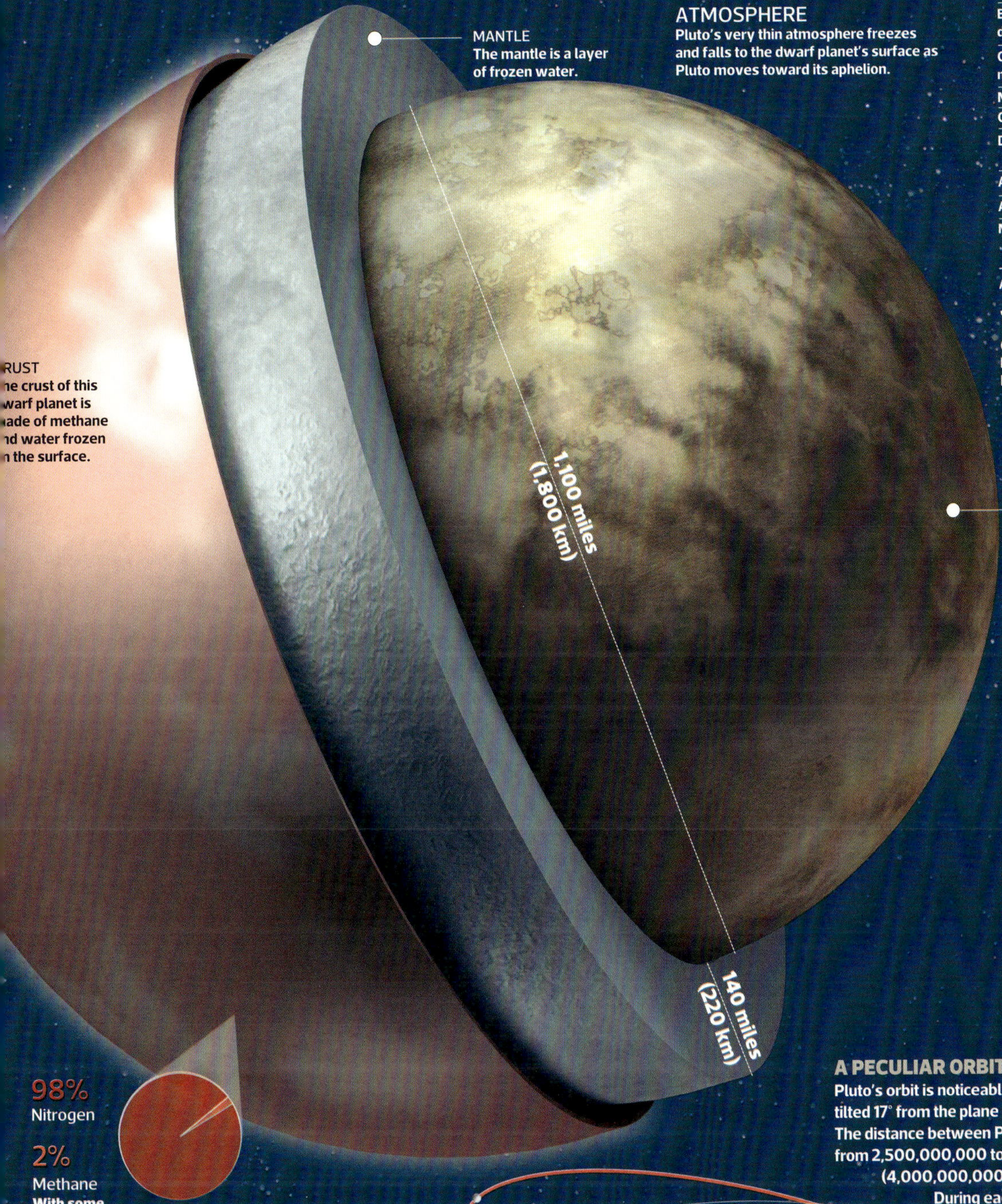

CHARACTERISTICS

CONVENTIONAL PLANET SYMBOL	♇
ESSENTIAL DATA	
Average distance from the Sun	3,700,000,000 miles (5,900,000,000 km)
Solar orbit (Plutonian year)	247.9 years
Equatorial diameter	1,400 miles (2,247 km)
Orbital speed 3 miles per second	(4.8 km/s)
Mass*	0.002
Gravity*	0.067
Density	1.2 ounces per cubic inch (2.05 g/cu cm)
Average temperature	-380° F (-230° C)
Atmosphere	Very thin
Moons	5

* In both cases, Earth = 1

AXIS INCLINATION

122°

One rotation lasts 6.387 Earth days.

6,387

terrestrial days is the time Pluto takes to complete one rotation.

A PECULIAR ORBIT

Pluto's orbit is noticeably elliptical, and it is tilted 17° from the plane of the planets' orbits. The distance between Pluto and the Sun varies from 2,500,000,000 to 4,300,000,000 miles (4,000,000,000 to 7,000,000,000 km). During each 248-year orbit, Pluto orbits closer to the Sun than Neptune for nearly 20 years. Although Pluto appears to cross paths with Neptune, it is impossible for them to collide.

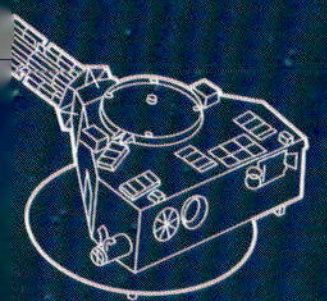

NEW HORIZONS MISSION
The first space probe to be sent to Pluto was launched on January 19, 2006. It reached the dwarf planet in July 2015 and achieved the first flyby of Pluto and Charon.

Distant Worlds

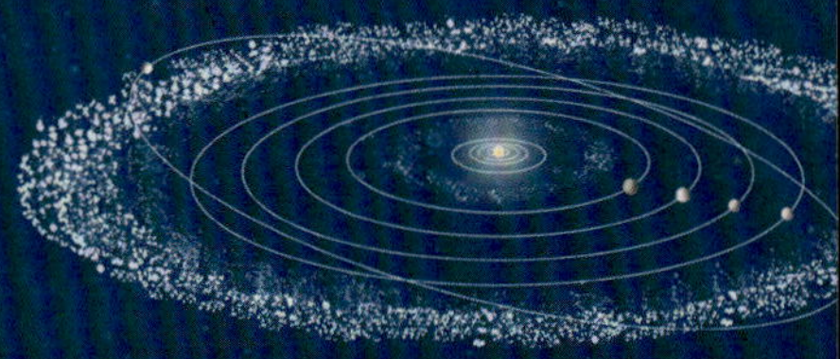

Farther even than Neptune, the eighth planet, we find frozen bodies smaller than the Earth's Moon—the more than 100,000 objects forming the Kuiper belt, the frozen boundary of our solar system. In 2006, astronomers of the International Astronomical Union decided to reclassify Pluto as a dwarf planet because of its size and eccentric orbit. Periodic comets (comets that appear at regular intervals) originate in the Kuiper belt. Nonperiodic comets, on the other hand, come from the Oort cloud, a gigantic sphere surrounding the entire solar system.

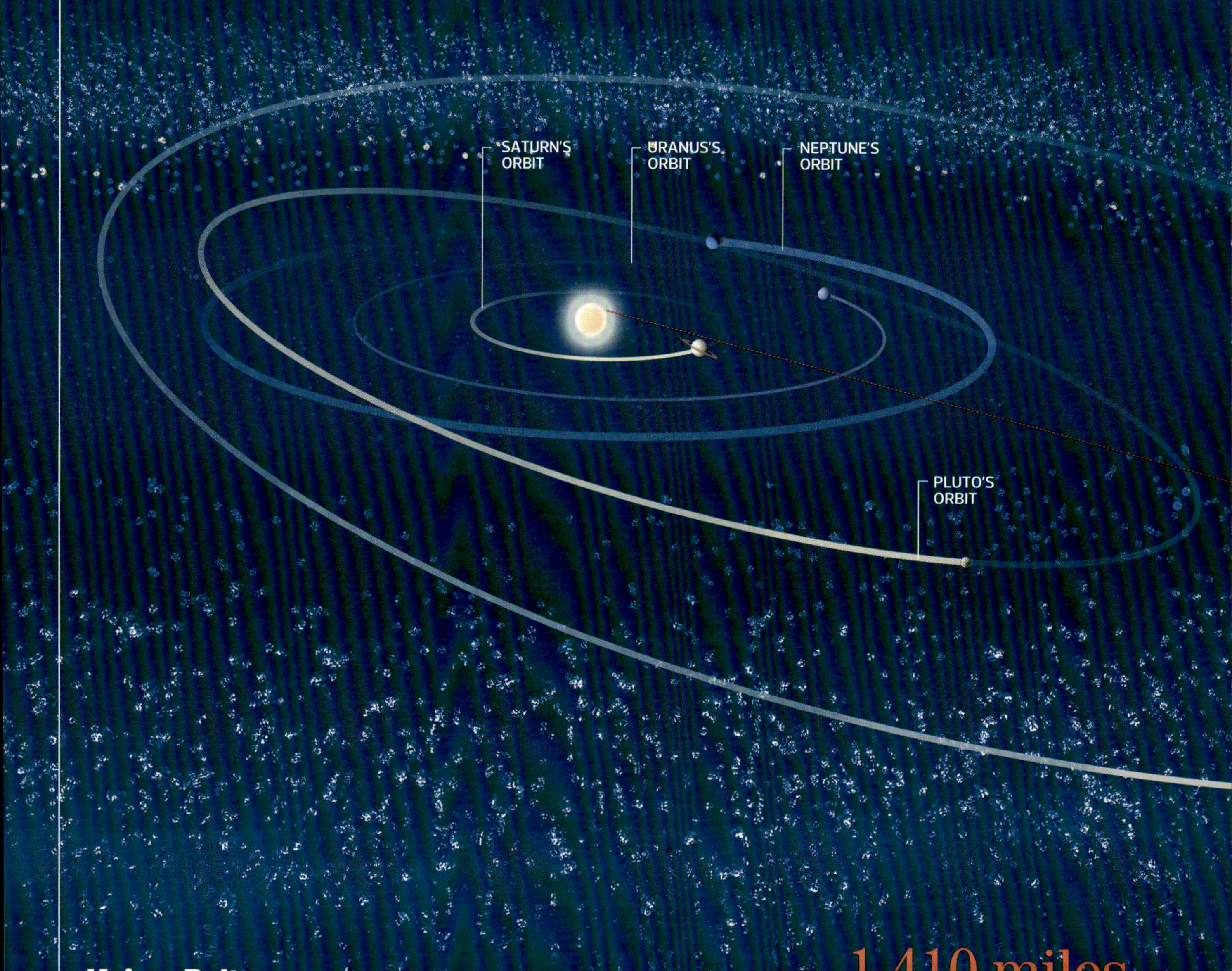

Kuiper Belt

Extending outward from the orbit of Neptune are many frozen worlds similar in some ways to planets but much smaller. They are located in the Kuiper belt, the frozen boundary of our solar system. So far, almost a thousand objects have been cataloged, including Quaoar, which has a diameter of 810 miles (1,300 km). The Kuiper belt, estimated to contain more than 100,000 bodies of ice and rock larger than 60 miles (100 km) in diameter (including Pluto), spreads out in the shape of a wide ring. Many of the comets that approach the Sun come from the Kuiper belt.

1,410 miles (2,274 km)

is the diameter of Pluto—750 miles (1,200 km) smaller than the Earth's Moon. Because of its size and orbit, Pluto is considered a dwarf planet instead of a planet.

Comparable Sizes

The discovery of Quaoar in 2002 allowed scientists to find the link they had long looked for between the Kuiper belt and the origin of the solar system. Quaoar's almost circular orbit helped prove that some objects both belong to the Kuiper belt and orbit the Sun. At the official meeting of the International Astronomical Union, on August 24, 2006, Pluto was reclassified from a planet to a dwarf planet. For the time being, any further objects discovered in the Kuiper belt will be classified in the same category.

QUAOAR
has a diameter of 810 miles (1,300 km).

SEDNA
Its diameter is estimated at 1,000 miles (1,600 km).

PLUTO
possesses a diameter of 1,400 miles (2,300 km).

ERIS
Larger than Pluto, its diameter is about 1,900 miles (3,000 km).

200 OR MORE, POSSIBLE EXTRASOLAR PLANETS HAVE BEEN DETECTED.

THE FARTHEST ONE

Eris is 97 astronomical units (9,040,000,000 miles [14,550,000,000 km]) from the Sun, making it the most distant object observed in the solar system. This dwarf planet follows an oval, eccentric orbit that takes 560 years to complete. The dwarf planet measures about 1,900 miles (3,000 km) in diameter, and traces of methane ice have been detected on its surface.

Construction Debris: Asteroids and Meteorites

Ever since the formation of the solar system, the melting, collision, and rupture of various materials played an essential role in the formation of the planets. Remnants of this process remain in the form of rock debris, which serve as witnesses to the formation of the solar system. These objects are also associated with episodes that influenced subsequent evolutionary processes on Earth. They are a possible cause of the mass extinction of dinosaurs more than 60 million years ago.

Extraterrestrial

One of the main goals of scientist who study meteorites is to understand their nature. Meteoric material holds extraterrestrial solids and gases. Scientific tests have confirmed that some meteorites are from the Moon or Mars, but most meteorites are associated with asteroids. The samples obtained from meteorites are analyzed and classified by their composition.

A HUGE METEORITE STRIKES

A meteorite is an object from space that does not completely vaporize as it penetrates the Earth's atmosphere. Larger meteorites can form a crater when they strike the Earth. Shown is the impact of an exceptionally large meteorite, such as the one that many scientists believed might have led to the extinction of dinosaurs and many other species about 65 million years ago.

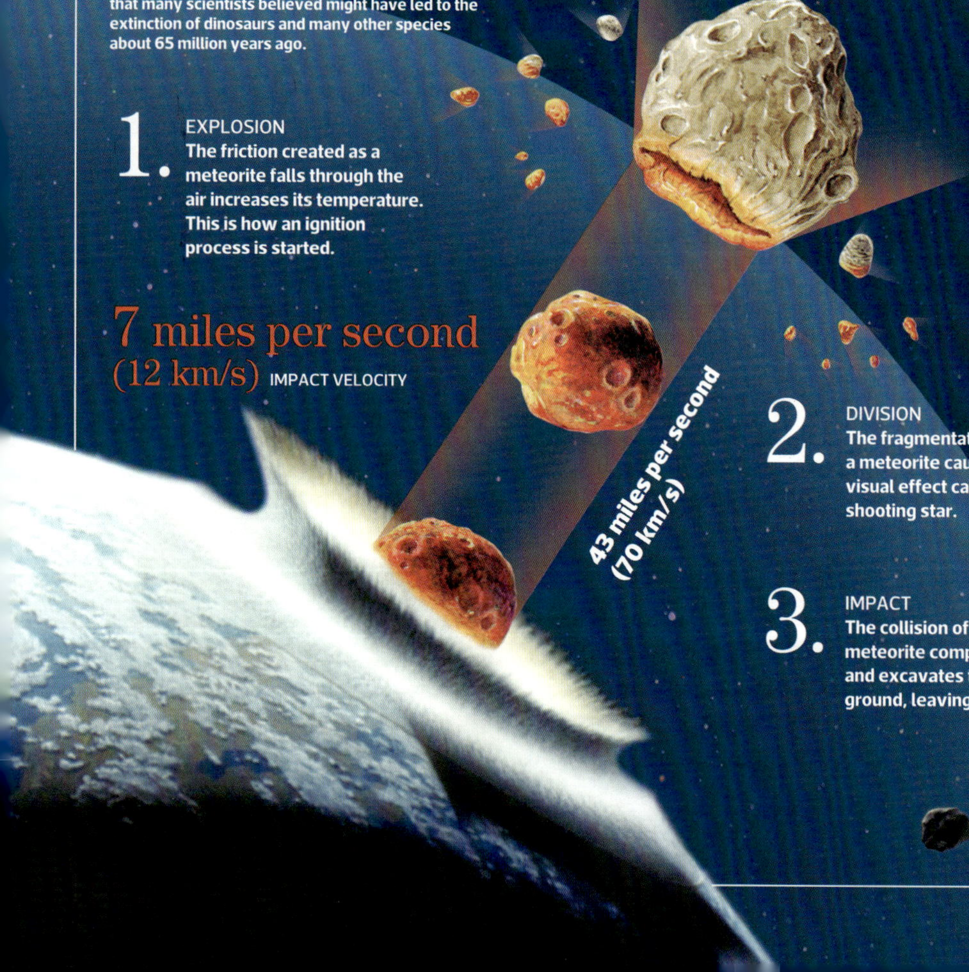

1. EXPLOSION
The friction created as a meteorite falls through the air increases its temperature. This is how an ignition process is started.

7 miles per second
(12 km/s) IMPACT VELOCITY

2. DIVISION
The fragmentation of a meteorite causes a visual effect called a shooting star.

3. IMPACT
The collision of the meteorite compresses and excavates the ground, leaving a crater.

TYPES OF METEORITES

STONY

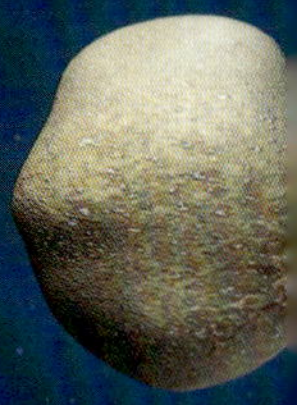

meteorites contain silicate minerals. They are subdivided into chondrites and achondrites.

IRON

meteorites contain a high percentage of iron and nickel compounds. They are created in the rupture of asteroids.

MESOSIDERITES

contain similar quantities of iron, nickel, and silicates.

Asteroids

Also called minor planets, they are the millions of rock and metal fragments of various shapes and sizes that orbit the Sun. They are mostly located in a belt between the orbits of Mars and Jupiter, but a few, such as those that belong to the Amor, Apollo, and Aten asteroid groups, orbit closer to Earth.

15%

The percentage of the total mass of the asteroids compared with the mass of the Moon

HIDALGO

completes a solar orbit every 14 Earth years.

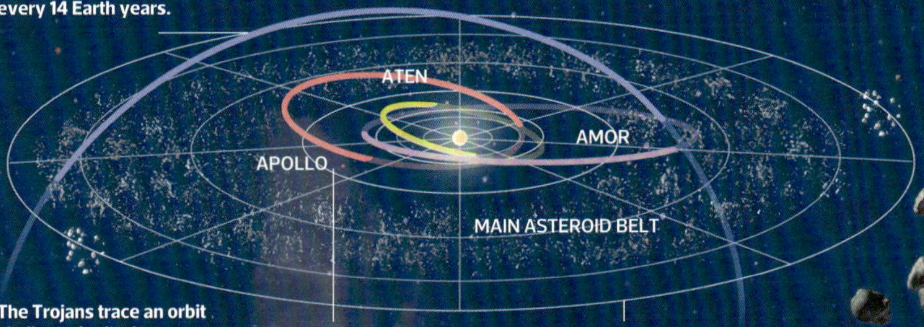

The Trojans trace an orbit similar to Jupiter's, one group in front of the planet and another behind it.

Tighten Your Belt

More than a million asteroids at least a mile in diameter are distributed in the main asteroid belt. Ceres was the first asteroid discovered (in 1801). It is the largest known asteroid, with a diameter of 580 miles (932 km).

KIRKWOOD

The Kirkwood gaps are the open areas in the main asteroid belt that are devoid of asteroids.

TYPES OF ASTEROIDS

Despite a great variety in size and shape, three types of minor planets, or asteroids, are known. Classified by their composition, they are grouped as siliceous, carbonaceous, and metallic.

IDA

An asteroid 35 miles (56 km) long, its surface is marked by collisions with other bodies.

Ferrous-type rocks dominate its composition.

Those with a Tail

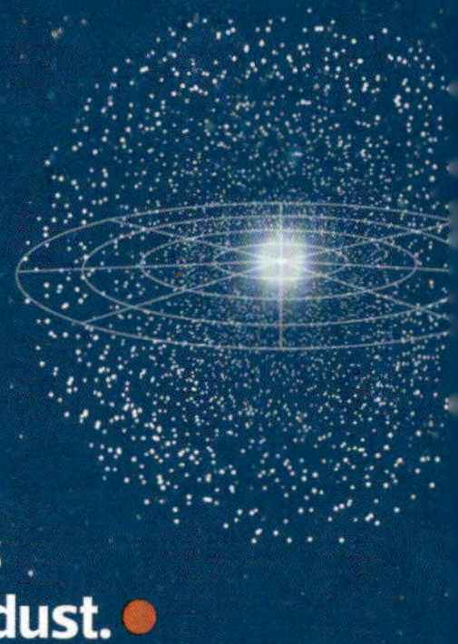

Comets are small, deformed objects a few miles in diameter that are normally frozen and dark. Made of dust, rock, gases, and organic molecules rich in carbon, comets are usually found in orbits beyond that of Neptune in the Kuiper belt or in the Oort cloud. Occasionally a comet, such as Halley's comet, veers toward the interior of the solar system, where its ice is heated and sublimates, forming a head and long, spectacular tails of gases and dust.

Types of Comets

Comets with short periods have orbits around the Sun that are shorter than 200 years. Those with a period of more than 200 years travel tens or hundreds of times farther from the Sun than Pluto.

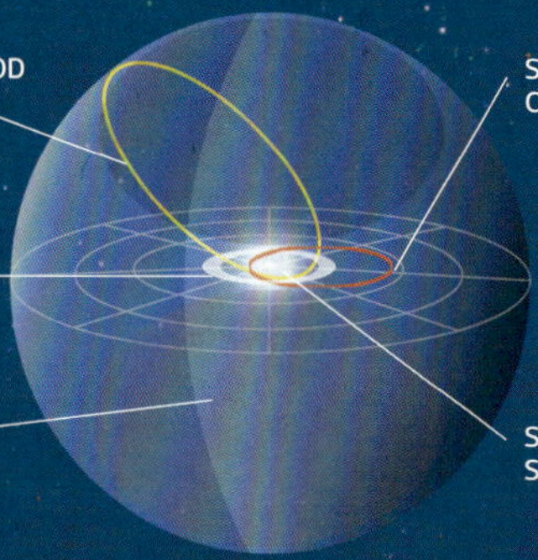

Periodic comets

Comets that leave their original orbits and approach the Sun generally settle into new trajectories. Halley's comet, for example, completes its elongated orbit in 76 years.

HEAD

Formed by the nucleus and the coma. The front part is called the impact front.

COMA

Envelops the nucleus. It is formed by the gases and dust that it releases.

Deep Impact Mission

On January 12, 2005, as part of the Discovery program, NASA launched the space probe Deep Impact, which, in turn, sent a projectile on a collision course toward the comet 9P/Tempel 1, where it obtained samples to be studied on Earth.

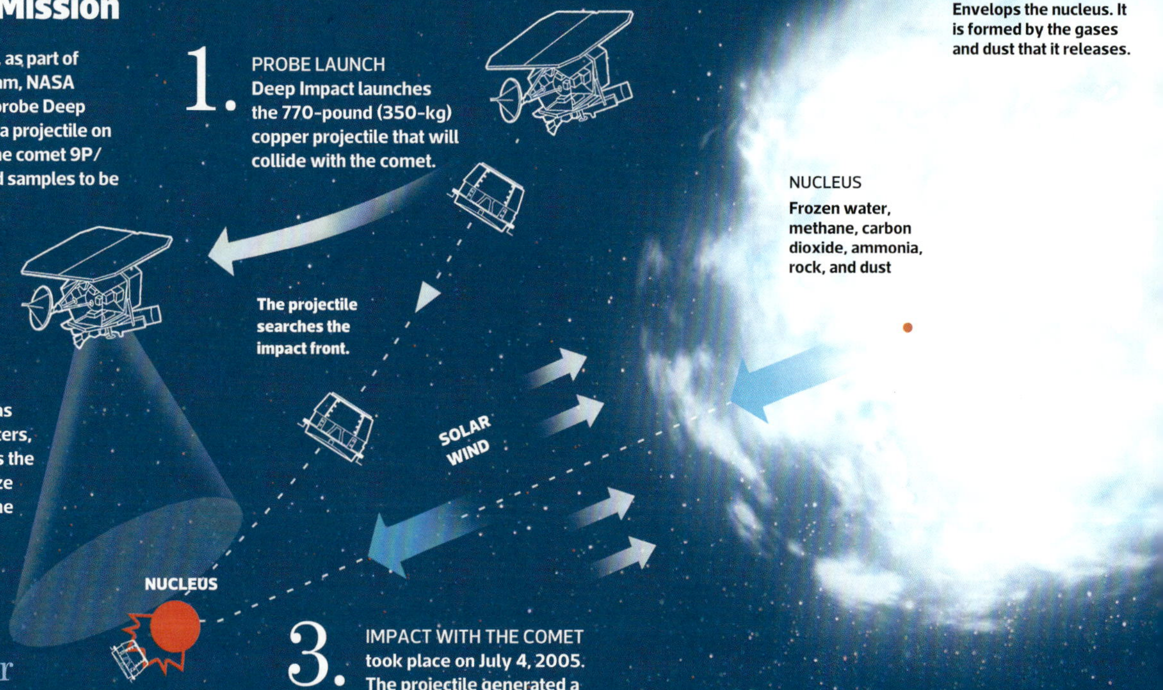

1. PROBE LAUNCH
Deep Impact launches the 770-pound (350-kg) copper projectile that will collide with the comet.

2. IN POSITION
By means of infrared cameras and spectrometers, the ship follows the comet to analyze the impact on the nucleus.

3. IMPACT WITH THE COMET
took place on July 4, 2005. The projectile generated a crater the size of a football field and seven stories deep.

22,370
miles per hour
(36,000 km/h)
VELOCITY OF THE COMET IMPACT

PREVIOUS MISSIONS

NASA has sent other unmanned missions to comets. The first was the international craft ISEE-3/ICE. Launched in 1978, its mission ended after crossing the tail of the Giacobini-Zinner comet in September 1985.

GIOTTO

Launched in 1986, it passed the nucleus of Halley's comet at a distance of 310 miles (500 km) in 1992.

DEEP SPACE

The NASA spacecraft approached the comet Borrelly in 2001.

STARDUST

In 2004, it took samples of the comet Wild 2 and sent them to Earth.

THE HEAD

The head of a comet can measure 62,000 miles (100,000 km) or more in diameter.

ION TAIL

The trail of suspended gases generates a low-intensity, luminous region with a bluish color. The gas molecules lose an electron and therefore have an electrical charge.

DUST TAIL

The suspended dust particles trail behind the comet, reflecting sunlight and making the luminous tail visible.

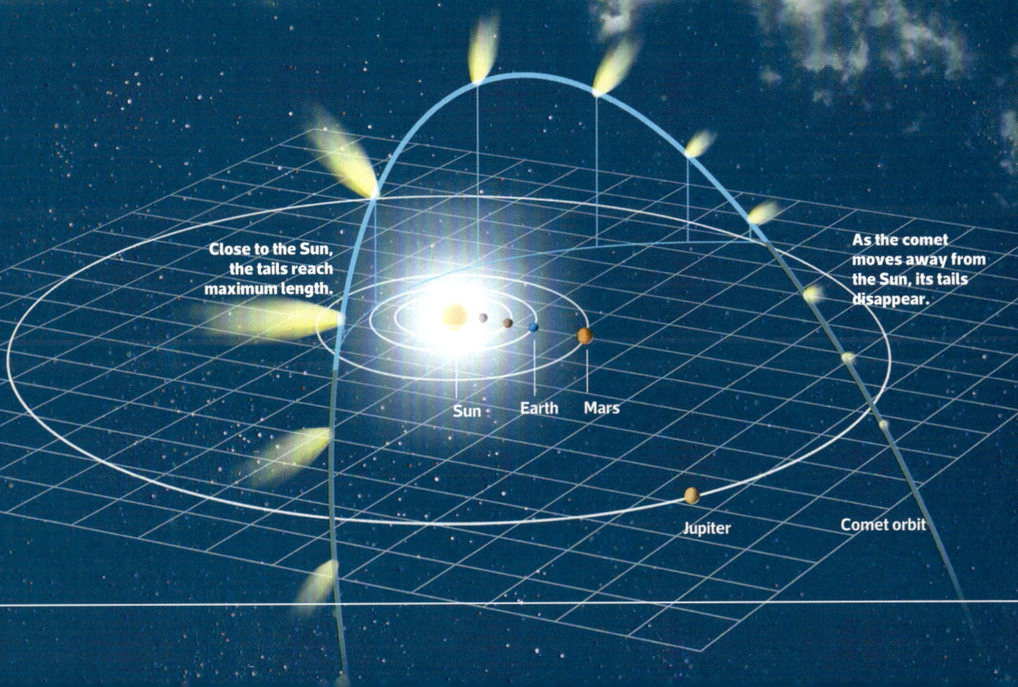

ORMATION OF THE TAIL ND HEAD

ecause of the effects of solar radiation and e solar wind, gases and dust are released om an accelerating comet. The dust articles tend to form a curving trail, which less sensitive to the pressure of the solar ind. As the comet leaves the confines f the solar system, its tails coincide once ore, but they disappear as the nucleus ools down and ceases releasing gases.

The Earth and the Moon

In the beginning, the Earth was an incandescent mass that slowly began to cool, allowing the continents to emerge and acquire their current form. Although many drastic changes took place during these early eras, our blue planet has still not stopped changing. It must be recognized that life on Earth would be impossible without the presence of the atmosphere—the

RIAL VIEW OF THE EARTH
this partial image of the Earth, we can
e Bora-Bora, an island that forms part
the Leeward Islands, located in French
lynesia.

olorless, odorless, invisible layer of ases that surrounds us, giving us air o breathe and protecting us from the un's harmful radiation. Although the tmosphere is approximately 435 miles (700 km) thick, it has no clear boundary and fades into space until it finally disappears. ●

The Blue Planet

The Earth is known as the blue planet because of the color of the oceans that cover two-thirds of its surface. This planet, the third planet from the Sun, is the only one where the right conditions exist to sustain life, something that makes the Earth special. It has liquid water in abundance, a mild temperature, and an atmosphere that protects it from objects that fall from outer space. The atmosphere also filters solar radiation thanks to its ozone layer. Slightly flattened at its poles and wider at its equator, the Earth takes 24 hours to revolve once on its axis.

The Phenomenon of Life

Water, in liquid form, makes it possible for life to exist on the Earth, the only planet where temperatures vary from 32° F to 212° F (0° C to 100° C), allowing water to exist as a liquid. The Earth's average distance from the Sun, along with certain other factors, allowed life to develop 3,8 billion years ago.

70%

of the Earth's surface is water. From space, the planet looks blue.

-76° F
(-60° C)

ONLY ICE
Mars is so far from the Sun that all its water is frozen.

32° to 212° F
(0° to 100° C)

3 STATES
On the Earth, water is found in all three of its possible states.

Above 212° F
(100° C)

ONLY STEAM
On Mercury or Venus, which are very close to the Sun, water would evaporate.

1. EVAPORATION
Because of the Sun's energy, the water evaporates, entering the atmosphere from oceans and, to a lesser extent, from lakes, rivers, and other sources on the continents.

EARTH MOVEMENTS

The Earth moves, orbiting the Sun and rotating on its own axis.

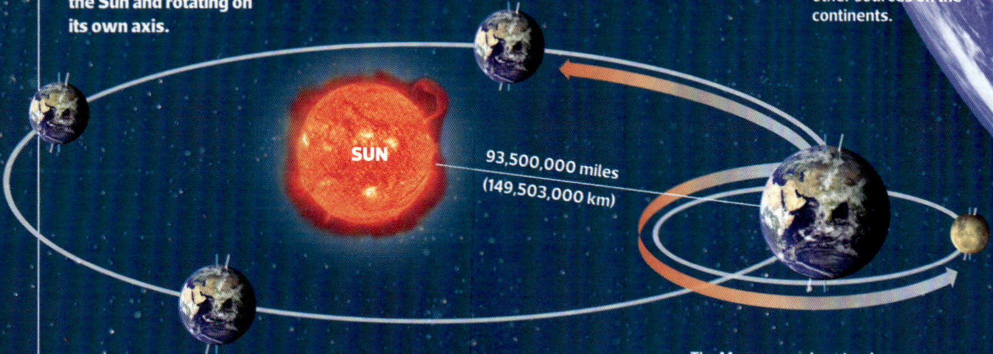

ROTATION: The Earth revolves on its axis in 23 hours and 56 minutes.

REVOLUTION: It takes the Earth 365 days, 5 hours, and 57 minutes to travel once around the Sun.

The Moon, our only natural satellite, is four times smaller than the Earth and takes 27.32 days to orbit the Earth.

23.5°

This is the inclination of the Earth's axis from the vertical. As the Earth orbits the Sun, different regions gradually receive more or less sunlight, causing the four seasons.

3. PRECIPITATION

The atmosphere loses water through condensation. Gravity causes rain, snow, and hail. Dew and frost directly alter the state of the surface they cover.

2. CONDENSATION

The Earth's winds transport moisture-laden air until weather conditions cause the water vapor to condense into clouds and eventually fall to the ground as rain or other forms of precipitation.

CHARACTERISTICS

CONVENTIONAL PLANET SYMBOL

ESSENTIAL DATA

Average distance to the Sun	93 million miles (150 million km)
Revolution around the Sun (Earth year)	365.25 days
Diameter at the equator	7,930 miles (12,756 km)
Orbiting speed	17 miles per second (27.79 km/s.)
Mass*	1
Gravity*	1
Density	3.2 ounces per cubic inch (5.52 g/cu cm)
Average temperature	59° F (15° C)

*In both cases, Earth = 1

AXIS INCLINATION

23.5°

One rotation lasts 23.56 hours.

Magnetism and Gravity

The Earth's magnetic field originates in the planet's outer core, where turbulent currents of molten iron generate both electric and magnetic fields. The orientation of the Earth's magnetism varies over time, causing the magnetic poles to fluctuate.

The Earth's core works as a magnet.

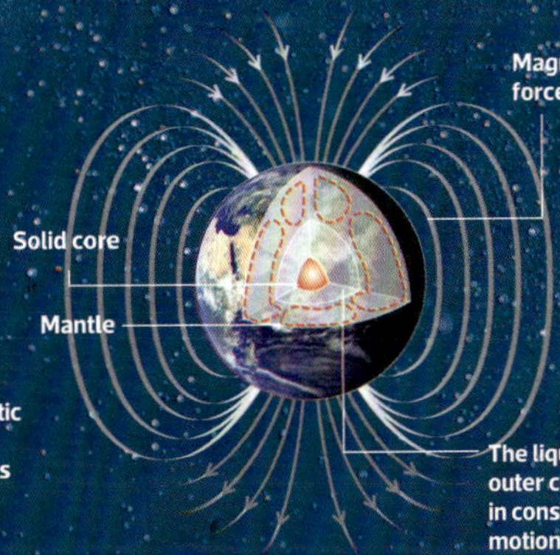

The Earth's magnetic field is created by convective currents in its outer core.

WHAT IT DOES

The magnetic field protects the Earth from the radiation of the solar wind.

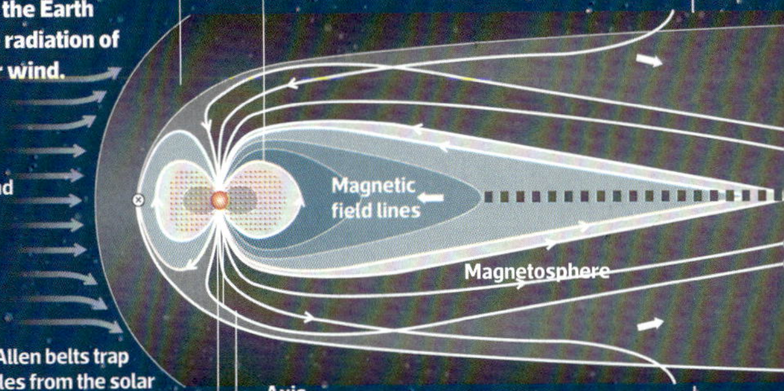

The Van Allen belts trap the particles from the solar wind, causing phenomena like the auroras.

GRAVITY AND WEIGHT

Weight is the force of the gravity that acts on a body.

24 pounds (11 kg)
ON THE MOON
The Moon has less mass than the Earth and, as a result, less gravity.

154 pounds (70 kg)
ON EARTH
The object is drawn toward the Earth's center.

390 pounds (177 kg)
ON JUPITER
Jupiter has 300 times more mass than the Earth and therefore more gravity.

Journey to the Center of the Earth

We live on the Earth, but do we know what we are standing on? The planet is made up of layers of various materials, such as solid and molten rock, which in turn are composed of such elements as iron, nickel, and silicon. Our atmosphere is the layer of gases surrounding our planet. One of these gases, oxygen, does a very special job—it permits life to exist.

Internal Structure

We live on a rocky surface similar to a shell. The rocks we live with are made mostly of oxygen and silicon, but underneath them is the mantle, made of much heavier rocks. The mantle also surrounds the inner and outer cores with a region of constantly boiling liquid metals, creating the convective currents that generate the Earth's magnetic field. The inner core, solid because of the great pressure put upon it, is the densest part of the planet.

HOW FAR HUMANS HAVE GONE

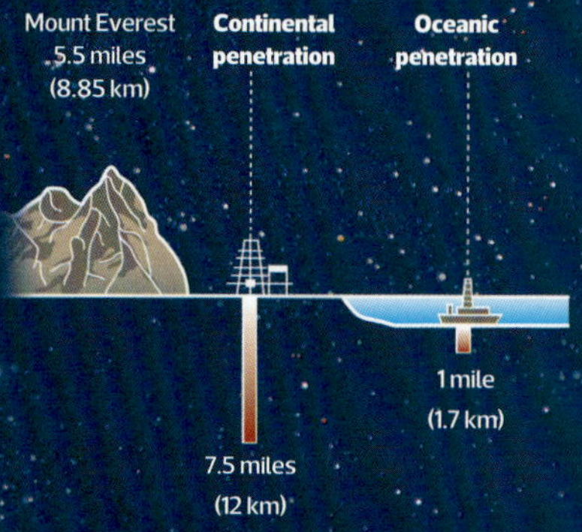

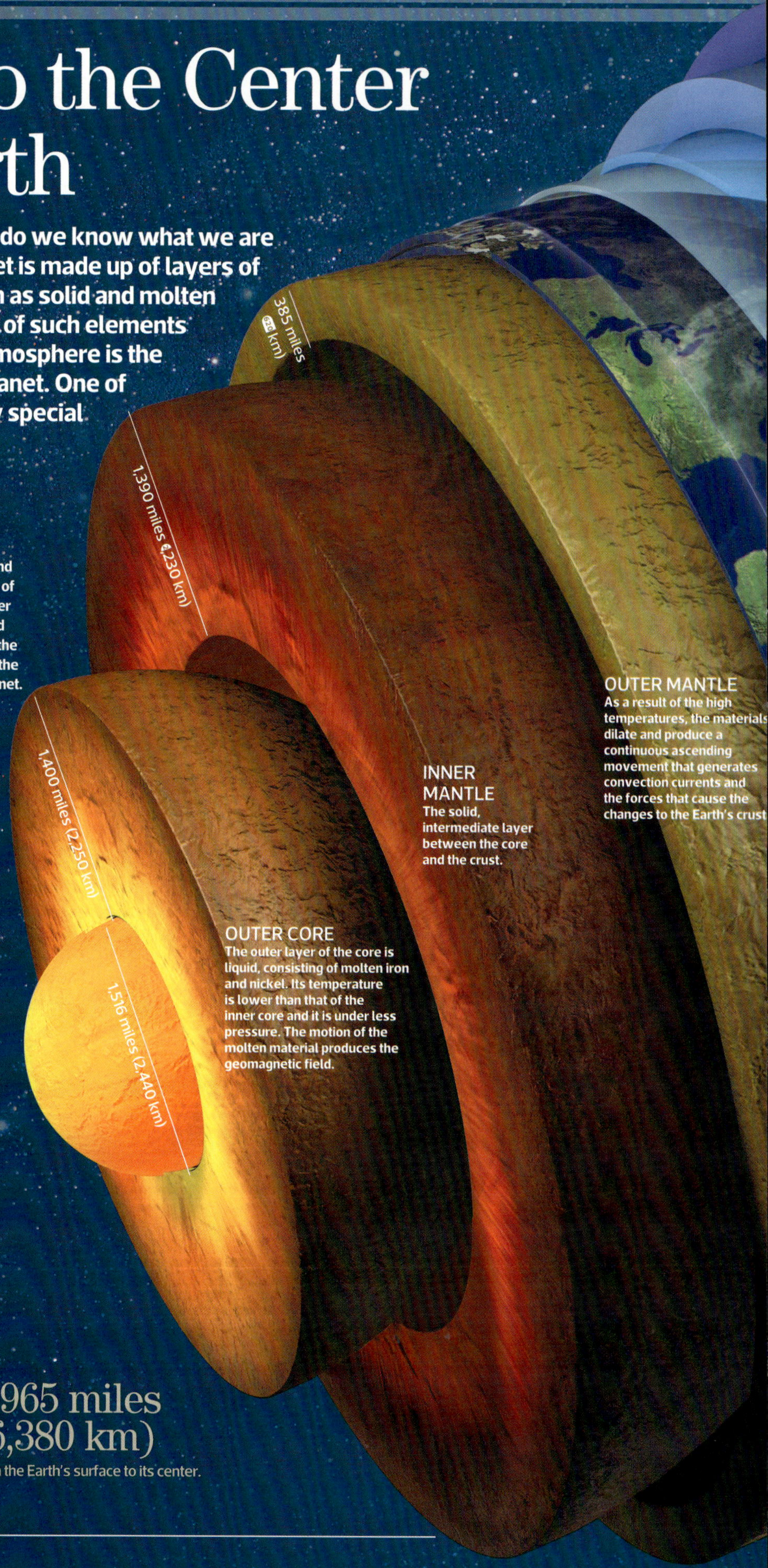

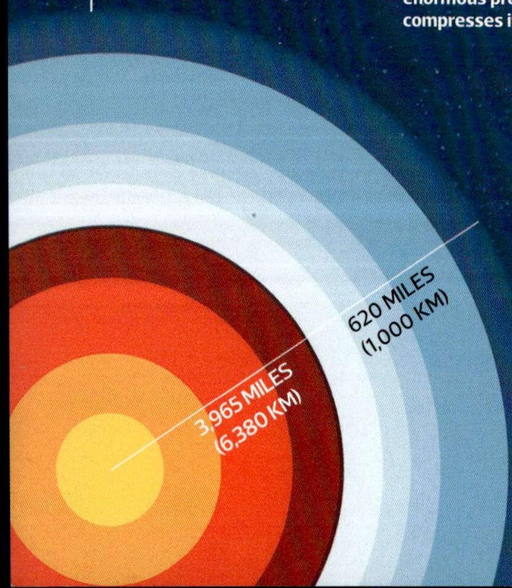

3,965 miles (6,380 km)

from the Earth's surface to its center.

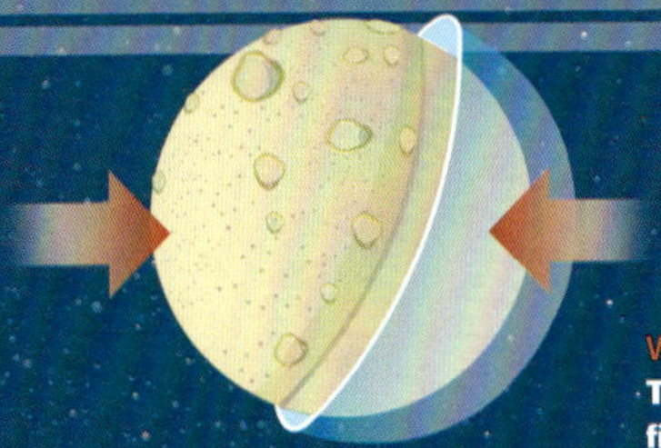

Above the Surface

The existence of life on our planet would be impossible without the atmosphere that provides the air we breathe and the water we drink; it also protects us from the Sun's harmful radiation, while simultaneously maintaining mild temperatures by retaining the Sun's warmth. The atmosphere is about 435 miles thick (700 km) but lacks defined limits.

Lithosphere and Hydrosphere

The hydrosphere, the liquid part of the Earth, includes the oceans, lakes, rivers, underground waters, snow, and ice. It almost completely covers the crust, surrounds the shores of the continents, and covers 71 percent of the Earth's surface. The lithosphere is a superficial, elastic region that is 4 to 7 miles (6 to 11 km) thick under the oceans and up to 43 miles (70 km) thick under mountain ranges.

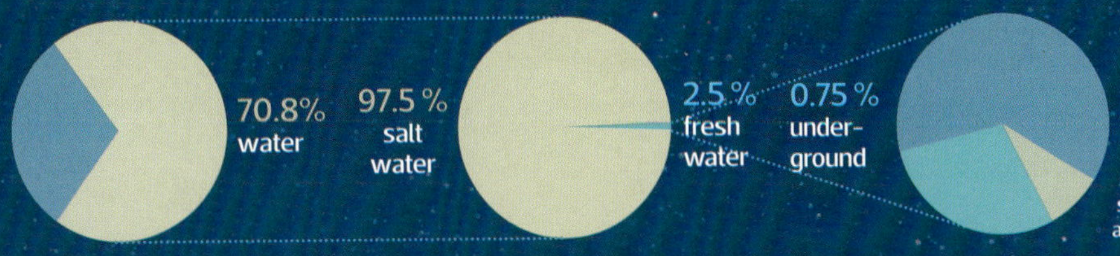

Once Upon a Time

The Earth probably formed from material in the solar nebula—the cloud of gas and dust that led to the formation of the Sun. This material gradually grew into a larger and larger body that became a red-hot ball of rock and metal. Later the rocky crust formed, its surface cooling enough to allow the continents to appear. Even later the oceans arrived, as well as the tiny organisms that released oxygen into the atmosphere. Although much of this gas was initially consumed in chemical reactions, over time, it allowed the development of multicellular organisms and an explosion of life that took place at the start of the Paleozoic Era, 542 million years ago.

Continental Drift

We live on the continents, which are part of movable plates that drift across the Earth's surface at the rate a fingernail grows. India, Africa, Australia, and Antarctica were part of the same continent 250 million years ago. When tectonic plates rub against each other, land and oceanic crust earthquakes occur. Where the plates separate, a rift forms. The mid-ocean ridges that run beneath the oceans are formed by lava that emerges from the rifts between tectonic plates. Where plates collide, a process called subduction takes place, in which the rocks of the oceanic floor are drawn under the continent and melt, reemerging in the form of volcanoes.

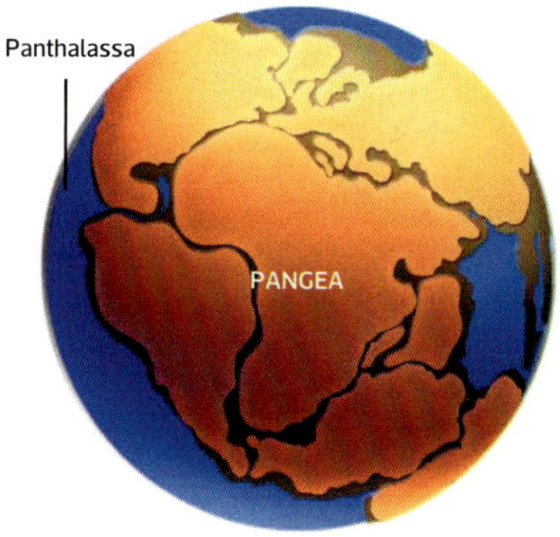

1 290 MILLION YEARS AGO
The supercontinent called Pangea formed. An immense ocean called Panthalassa surrounded it.

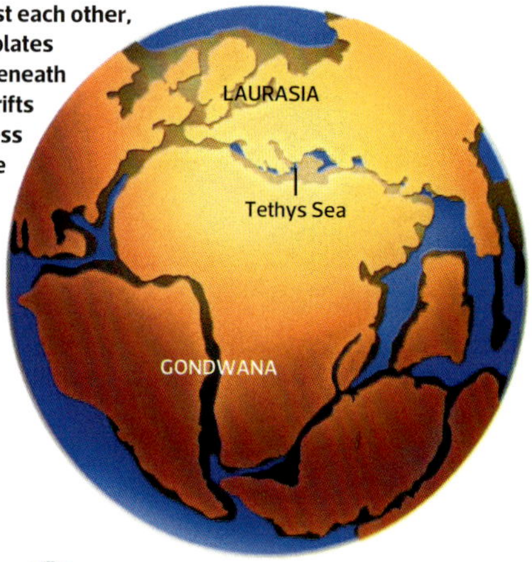

2 250 MILLION YEARS AGO
The Tethys Sea slowly split Pangea, creating two continents, known as Laurasia and Gondwana.

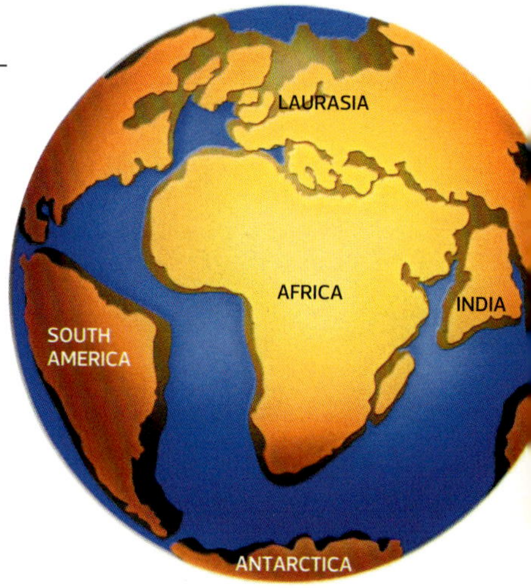

3 163 MILLION YEARS AGO
Gondwana split, forming Africa and South America as the southern Atlantic Ocean was created.

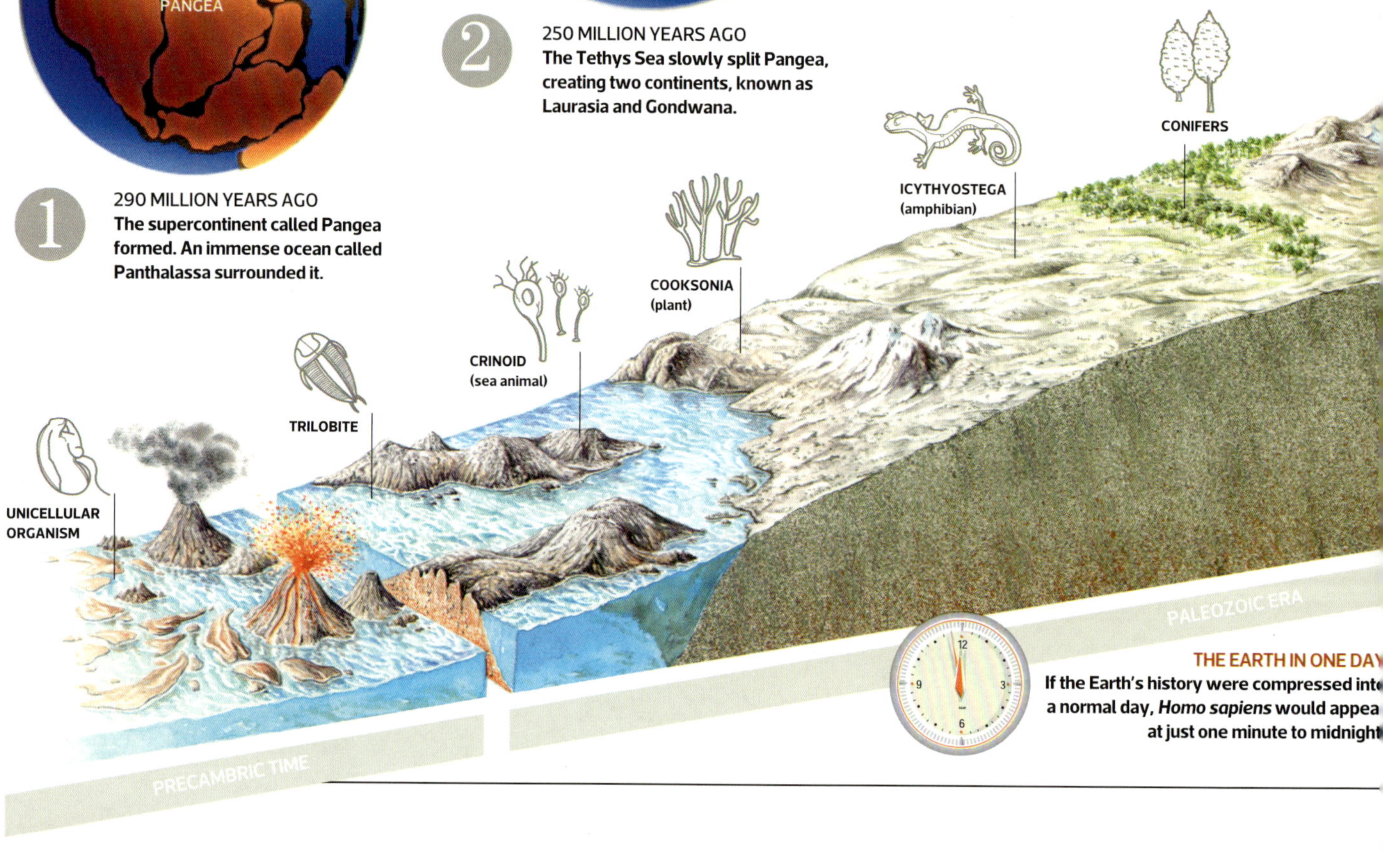

THE EARTH IN ONE DAY
If the Earth's history were compressed into a normal day, *Homo sapiens* would appear at just one minute to midnight.

rigin of the Earth

The Earth was formed 4.6 billion years ago from a cloud of dust and gas. In the beginning, it was a molten, constantly active, mass. As time passed, the rth began to cool, and the atmosphere began to clear as n fell, creating the oceans.

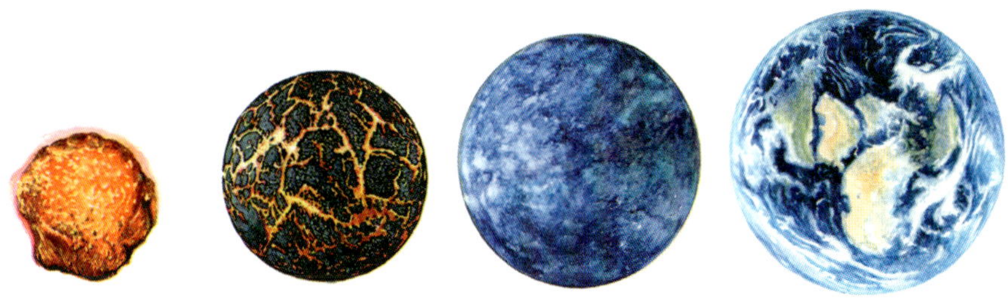

A Ball of fire The Earth was created from small particles that coalesced in the solar nebula.

B The planet cooled The atmosphere was created as the planet cooled and began to emit gases and steam.

C The crust forms Lava poured across the surface of the Earth. As it cooled, it formed the Earth's crust.

D Water appeared on the Earth 3.9 billion years ago. Water-rich Earth is the only planet in the solar system known to have life.

4 60 MILLION YEARS AGO
The northern Atlantic Ocean slowly separated, completing the formation of Europe and North Africa.

Chronology

Geology is the study of rocks in the Earth's crust. It divides the Earth's history into different eras, periods, and epochs lasting millions of years. Geology also helps us catalog the processes of evolution—changes in generations as species adapt to their environment and their competitors.

Through the study of fossils—remains of creatures buried in the Earth's various sedimentary layers and consequently at different times in the past– geology helps us trace the timeline of evolutionary history.

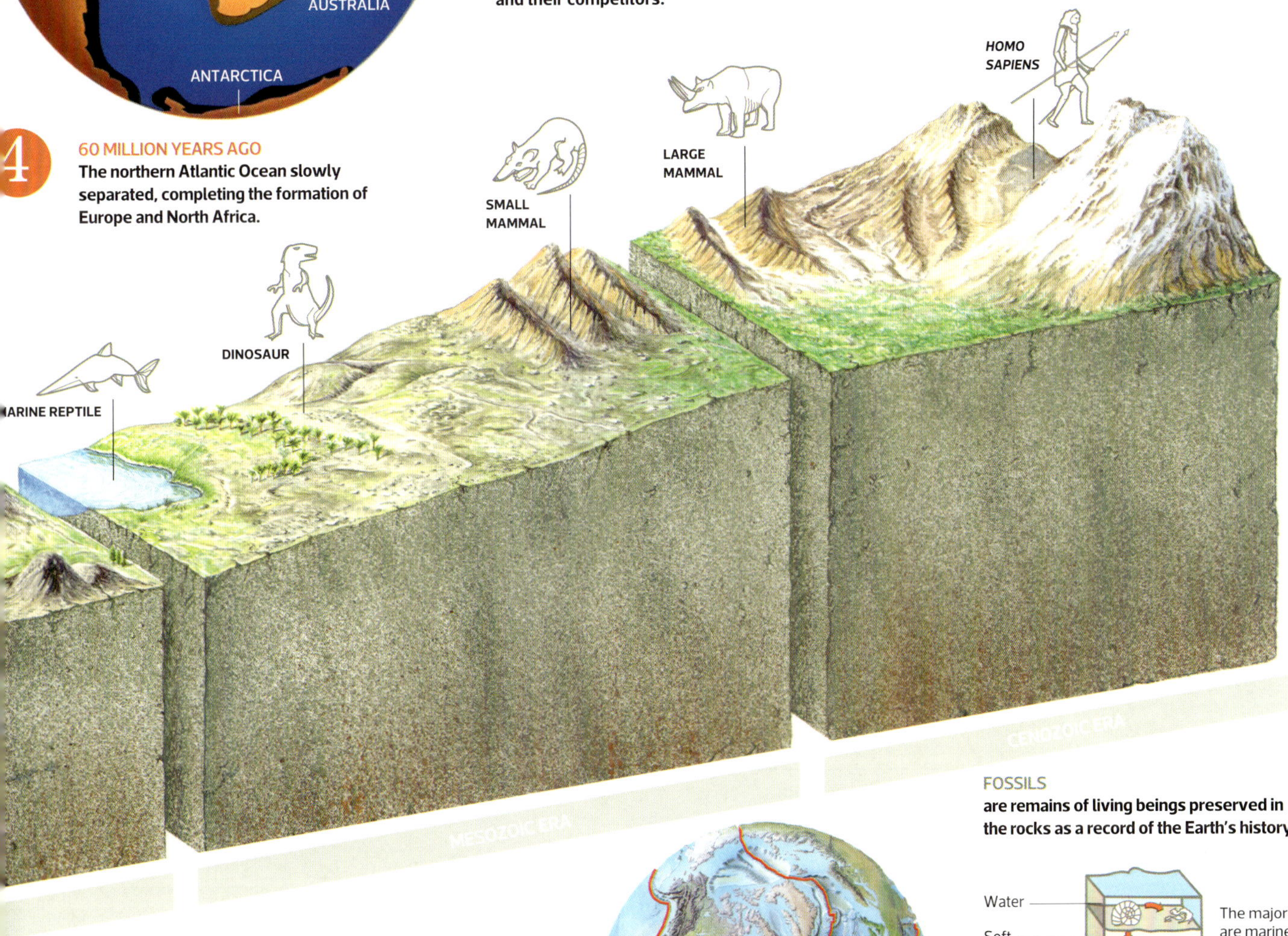

FOSSILS
are remains of living beings preserved in the rocks as a record of the Earth's history.

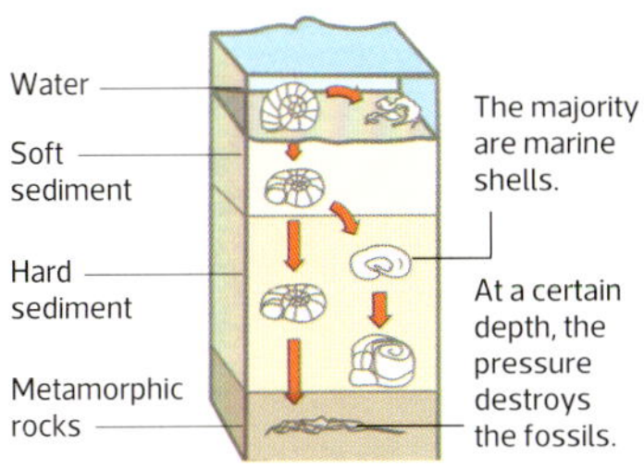

Tectonic Plates

The surface of the Earth is shaped by tectonic plates. There are eight major plates, some of which even encompass entire continents. The plates' borders are marked by ocean trenches, cliffs, chains of volcanoes, and earthquake zones.

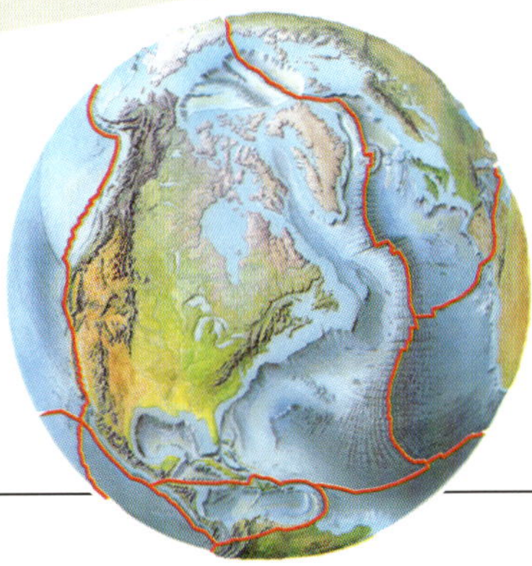

Movements and Coordinates

Yes, it moves. The Earth rotates on its axis while simultaneously orbiting the Sun. The natural phenomena of night and day, seasons, and years are caused by these movements. To track the passage of time, calendars, clocks, and time zones were invented. Time zones are divided by meridians and assigned a reference hour according to their location. When traveling east, an hour is added with each time zone. An hour is subtracted during westbound travel.

The Earth's Movements

Night and day, summer and winter, new year and old year result from the Earth's various movements during its orbit of the Sun. The most important motions are the Earth's daily rotation from west to east on its own axis and its revolution around the Sun. (The Earth follows an elliptical orbit that has the Sun at one of the foci of the ellipse, so the distance to the Sun varies slightly over the course of a year.)

ROTATION

1 DAY

The Earth revolves once on its axis in 23 hours and 56 minutes. We see this as day and night.

REVOLUTION

1 YEAR

The Earth's orbit around the Sun lasts 365 days, 5 hours, and 57 minutes.

NUTATION

18.6 YEARS

is a sort of nod made by the Earth, causing the displacement of the geographic poles by nine arc seconds.

PRECESSION

25,800 YEARS

A slow turning of the direction of the Earth's axis (similar to that of a top), caused by the Earth's nonspherical shape and the gravitational forces of the Sun and the Moon

Equinox and Solstice

Every year, around June 21, the Northern Hemisphere reaches its maximum inclination toward the Sun (a phenomenon referred to as the summer solstice in the Northern Hemisphere and the winter solstice in the Southern Hemisphere). The North Pole receives sunlight all day, while the South Pole is covered in darkness. Between one solstice and another the equinoxes appear, which is when the axis of the Earth points toward the Sun and the periods of daylight and darkness are the same all over our planet.

June 20 or 21

Summer solstice in the Northern Hemisphere and winter solstice in the Southern Hemisphere. **Solstices exist because of the tilt of the Earth's axis. The length of the day and the height of the Sun in the sky are greatest in summer and least in winter.**

March 20 or 21

Spring equinox in the Northern Hemisphere and autumn equinox in the Southern Hemisphere. **The Sun passes directly above the equator, and day and night have the same length.**

September 21 or 22

Autumn equinox in the Northern Hemisphere and spring equinox in the Southern Hemisphere. **The Sun passes directly abov the equator, and day and nigl have the same length.**

MEASUREMENT OF TIME

Months and days are charted by calendars and clocks, but the measurement of these units of time is neither a cultural nor an arbitrary construct. Instead, it is derived from the natural movements of the Earth.

PERIHELION

The point where the orbiting Ear most closely approaches the Su (91 million miles [147 million km

December 21 or 22

Winter solstice in the Northern Hemisphere and summer solstice in the Southern Hemisphere.

Solstices exist because of the tilt of the Earth's axis. The length of the day and the height of the Sun in the sky are greatest in summer and least in winter.

APHELION

The point in the Earth's orbit where it is farthest from the Sun (94 million miles [152 million km]). This occurs at the beginning of July.

Geographic Coordinates

Thanks to the grid formed by the lines of latitude and longitude, the position of any object on the Earth's surface can be easily located by using the intersection of the Earth's equator and the Greenwich meridian (longitude 0°) as a reference point. This intersection marks the midpoint between the Earth's poles.

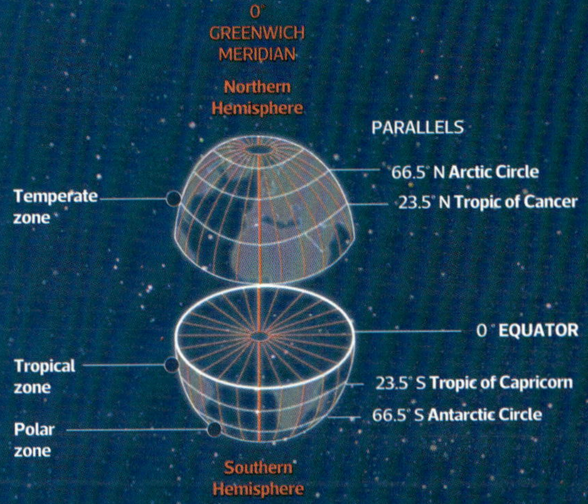

Time Zones

The Earth is divided into 24 areas, or time zones, each one of which corresponds to an hour assigned according to the Coordinated Universal Time (UTC), using the Greenwich, England, meridian as the base meridian. One hour is added when crossing the meridian in an easterly direction, and one hour is subtracted when traveling west.

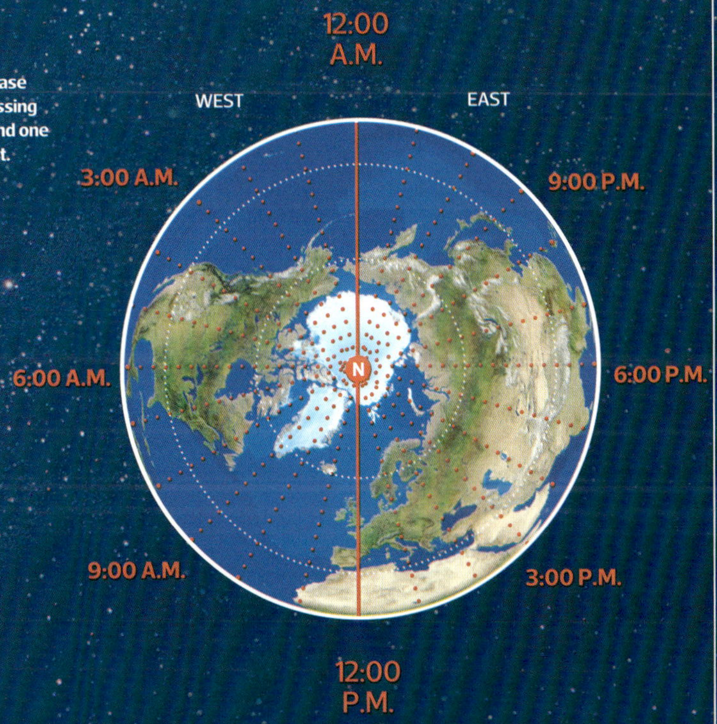

ET LAG

he human body's biological clock responds to the rhythms of light and dark based on he passage of night and day. Long air flights east or west interrupt and disorient the ody's clock, causing a disorder known as jet lag. It can cause fatigue, irritability, nausea, eadaches, and difficulty sleeping at night.

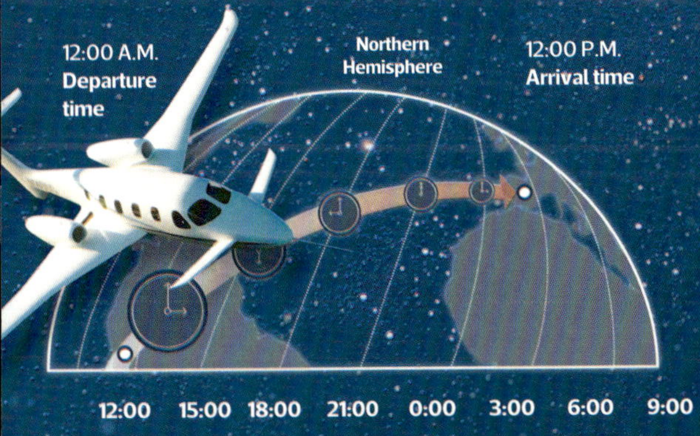

The Moon and Tides

Romance and terror, mystery and superstition—all these emotions are responses to the Moon, the Earth's one natural satellite, which always hides one of its two faces. However, whatever symbolic meanings are attributed to the Moon, its gravitational pull has a concrete effect on the Earth—it is a cause of the tides. Depending on the distance of the Moon from the Earth, the gravitational pull exerted by the Moon varies in strength and so can high tides and low tides. To reach full height, tides need large open areas of ocean. For this reason, tides in closed or small bodies of water are much lower.

ORIGIN OF THE MOON
The most widely accepted theory of the Moon's origin suggests that an object the size of Mars collided with the Earth during its formation.

THE MOON'S MOVEMENTS

As the Moon orbits the Earth, it revolves on its own axis in such a way that it always shows the Earth the same side.

LUNAR MONTH
It takes 29.53 days to complete its phases.

SIDEREAL MONTH
It takes 27.32 days to orbit the Earth.

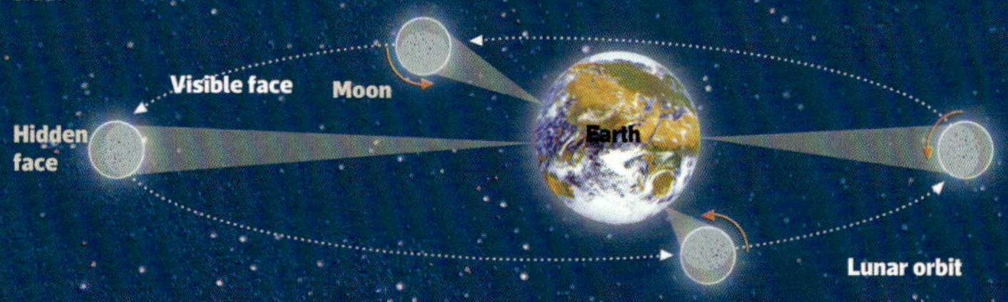

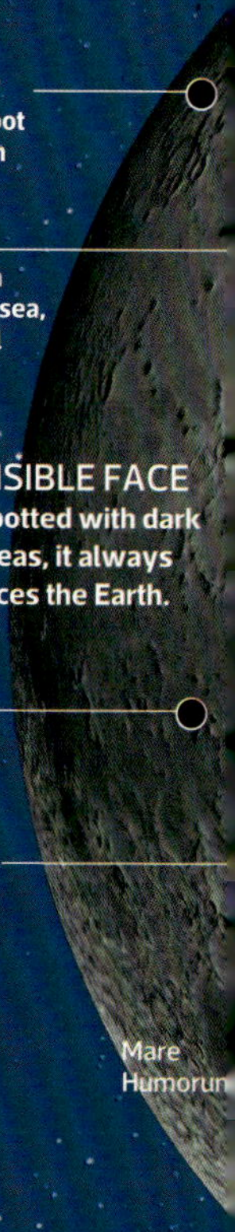

The Tides

The water on the side of the Earth closest to the Moon feels the Moon's gravitational pull most intensely, and vice versa. Two tides are formed, and they track the Moon in its orbit around the Earth. However, they precede the Moon instead of being directly in line with it.

1 NEW MOON
SPRING TIDE
When the Sun and the Moon are aligned, the highest high tides and lowest low tides are produced.

2 FIRST QUARTER
NEAP TIDE
The Moon and the Sun are at right angles to the Earth, producing the lowest high tides and the highest low tides.

3 FULL MOON
SPRING TIDE
The Sun and the Moon align once again, and the Sun augments the Moon's gravitational pull, causing a second spring tide.

4 THIRD QUARTER
NEAP TIDE
The Moon and the Sun again form a right angle, causing a second neap tide.

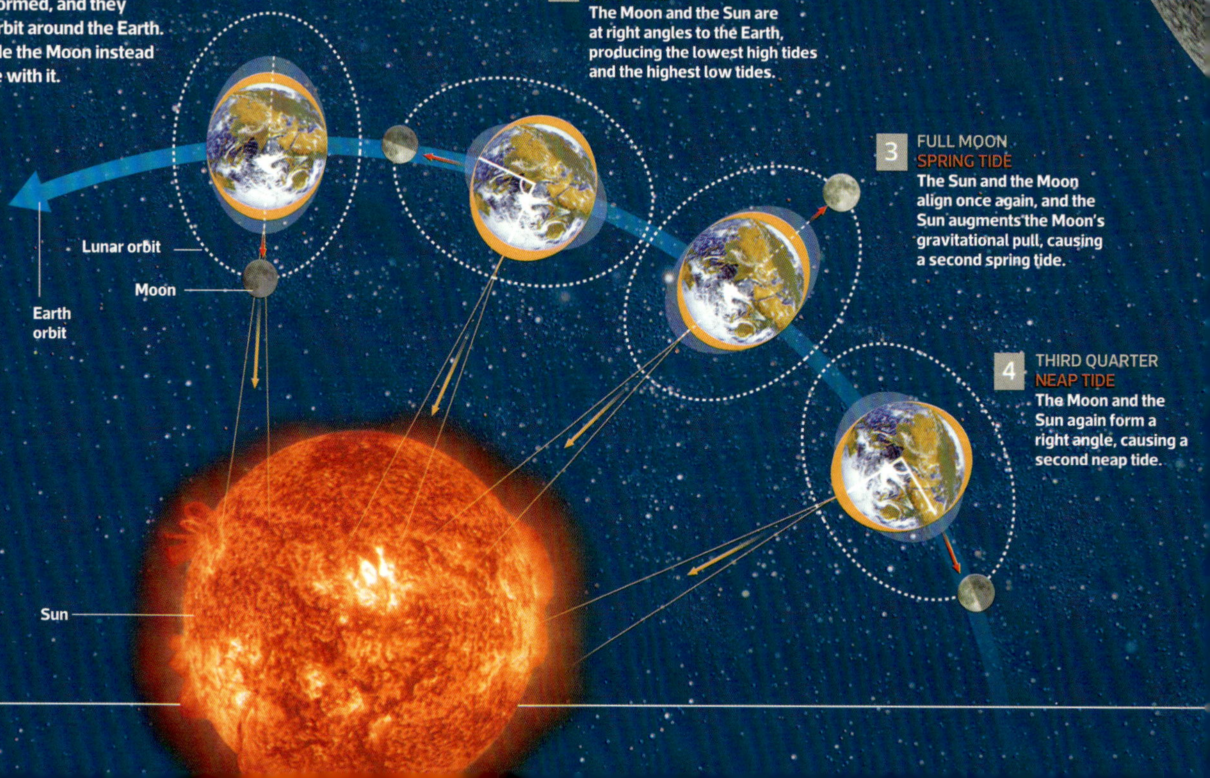

KEY
- Gravitational pull of the Moon
- Gravitational pull of the Sun
- Influence on the tide by the gravitational pull of the Moon
- Influence on the tide by the gravitational pull of the Sun

INNER STRUCTURE

Various seismic analyses of the Moon suggest that its core is solid or semisolid.

2,160 miles (3,476 km)

The diameter of the Moon is one fourth of the Earth's.

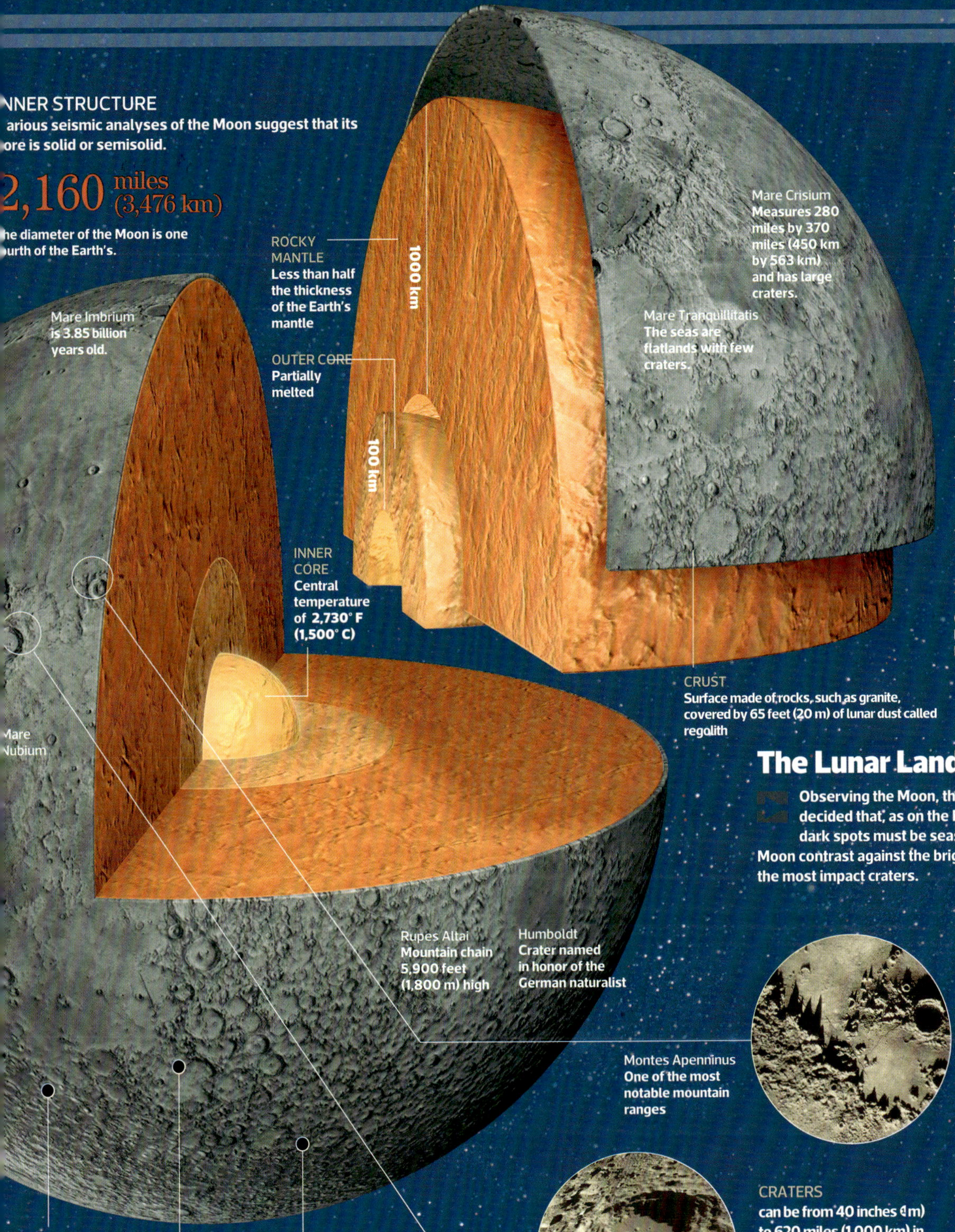

CHARACTERISTICS

CONVENTIONAL PLANET SYMBOL ☾

ESSENTIAL DATA

Average distance from the Earth	226,400 miles (364,400 km)
Revolution around the Earth	27.3 days
Diameter at the equator	2,160 miles (3,476 km)
Orbiting speed	0.6 miles per second (1.02 km/s)
Mass*	0,01
Gravity*	0,17
Density	2 ounces per cubic inch (3.34 g/cu cm)
Temperature	302° F (150° C) (day) -148° F (-100° C) (night)
Volume*	0.02

*Earth = 1

AXIS INCLINATION

5.14°

One rotation lasts 27.32 Earth days.

The Lunar Landscape

Observing the Moon, the ancient astronomers decided that, as on the Earth, its plainly visible dark spots must be seas. These dark regions of the Moon contrast against the bright ones, the highlands with the most impact craters.

MOUNTAIN RANGES
When a meteorite strikes the lunar surface, a mountain range forms from the material ejected during the cratering process.

CRATERS
can be from 40 inches (1 m) to 620 miles (1,000 km) in diameter and are formed by meteorites that strike the Moon's surface with incredible force.

SEAS
cover almost 16 percent of the Moon's surface and were formed by flowing lava. Today the Moon has no volcanic activity.

THE PHASES OF THE MOON

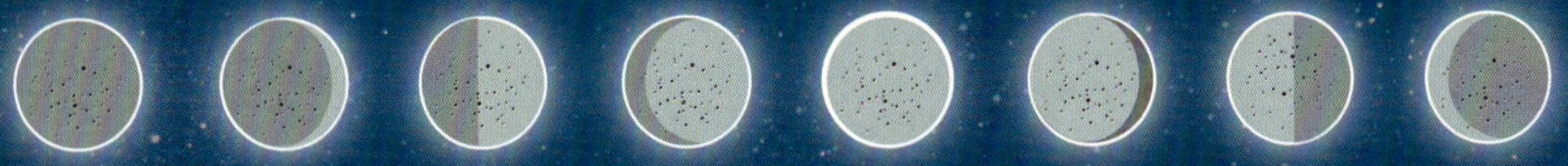

Unique

The Moon is the Earth's only natural satellite.

Eclipses

Typically four times a year, during the full or new moon, the centers of the Moon, the Sun, and the Earth become aligned, causing one of the most marvelous celestial phenomena: an eclipse. At these times, the Moon either passes in front of the Sun or passes through the Earth's shadow. The Sun—even during an eclipse—is not safe to look at directly, since it can cause irreparable damage to the eyes, such as burns on the retina. Special high-quality filters or indirect viewing by projecting the Sun's image on a sheet of paper are some of the ways in which this celestial wonder can be watched. Solar eclipses provide a good opportunity for astronomers to conduct scientific research.

TOTAL LUNA ECLIPSE, SEE FROM THE EART

The orange color comes fr sunlight that has been refract and colored by the Eart atmosphe

ANNULAR ECLI OF THE SUN, S FROM THE EA

Solar Eclipse

Solar eclipses occur when the Moon passes directly between the Sun and the Earth, casting a shadow along a path on the Earth's surface. The central cone of the shadow is called the umbra, and the area of partial shadow around it is called the penumbra. Viewers in the regions where the umbra falls on the Earth's surface see the Moon's disk completely obscure the Sun—a total solar eclipse. Those watching from the surrounding areas that are located in the penumbra see the Moon's disk cover only part of the Sun—a partial solar eclipse.

ALIGNMENT

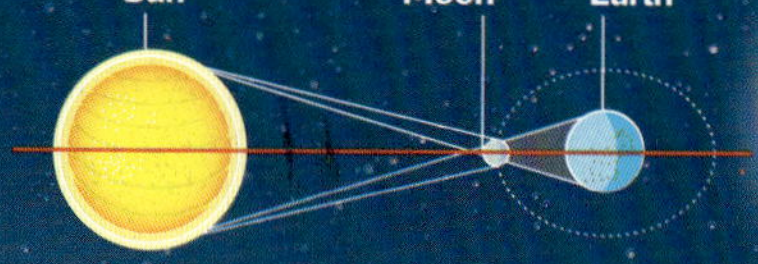

During a solar eclipse, astronomers take advantage of the blocked view of the Sun in order to use devices designed to study the Sun's atmosphere.

TYPES OF ECLIPSES

TOTAL The Moon is between the Sun and the Earth and creates a cone-shaped shadow.

ANNULAR The Sun appears larger than the Moon, and it remains visible around it.

PARTIAL The Moon does not cover the Su completely, so t Sun appears as a crescent.

SUN'S APPARENT SIZE
400 times larger than the Moon

DISTANCE FROM THE S THE EARTH
400 times great the distance Earth to the

unar Eclipse

When the Earth passes directly between the full Moon and the Sun, a lunar eclipse (which could be total, partial, or penumbral) curs. Without the Earth's atmosphere, during each nar eclipse, the Moon would become completely visible (something that never happens). The ally eclipsed Moon's characteristic reddish lor is caused by light refracted by the Earth's mosphere. During a partial eclipse, on the other nd, part of the Moon falls in the shadow cone, hile the rest is in the penumbra, the outermost, lest part. It is not dangerous to look at a lunar lipse directly.

ALIGNMENT

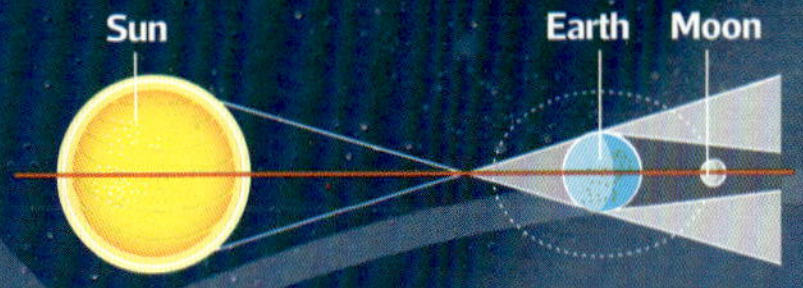

During an eclipse, the Moon is not completely black but appears reddish.

TYPES OF ECLIPSES

TOTAL
The Moon is completely in the shadow cone.

PARTIAL
The Moon is only partially inside the shadow cone.

PENUMBRAL
The Moon is in the penumbral cone.

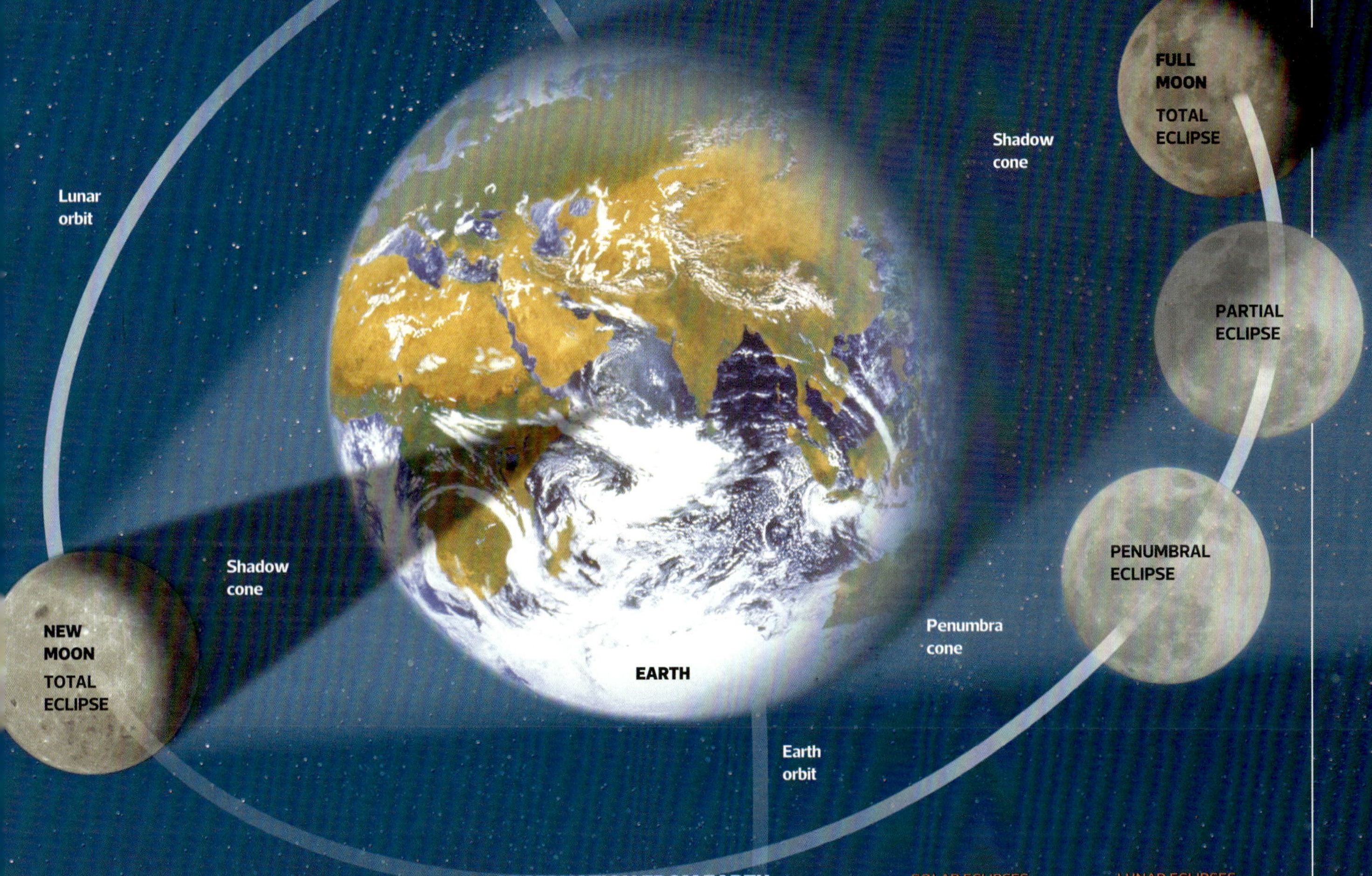

HE ECLIPSE CYCLE

lipses repeat every 223 lunations—18 years and 11 days. ese are called Saros periods.

CLIPSES IN A YEAR

7	4
nimum Maximum	Average

ECLIPSES IN A SAROS

41	29	70
of the Sun	of the Moon	Total

OBSERVATION FROM EARTH

A black, polymer filter, with an optical density of 5.0, produces a clear orange image of the Sun.

Prevents retinal burns

SOLAR ECLIPSES are different for each local observer.

MAXIMUM DURATION
8 minutes

LUNAR ECLIPSES are the same for all observers.

MAXIMUM DURATION
100 minutes

CLIPSES IN 2006 AND BEYOND

THE ...N (Sun)

3/29	Total
9/22	Total
3/19	Partial
9/11	Partial
2/07	Total
1/26	Total
7/22	Total
1/15	Total
7/11	Total
1/4	Partial
11/25	Partial
5/20	Annular
11/13	Annular
5/10	Annular
11/3	Hybrid
4/29	Annular
10/23	Partial
3/20	Total
9/13	Partial

2006 2007 2008 2009 2010 2011 2012 2013 2014 2015 2016

THE ...OON (Moon)

3/14	Partial
9/07	Partial
3/03	Total
8/28	Total
2/21	Total
8/16	Partial
2/9	Partial
7/7	Partial
6/26	Partial
12/21	Total
6/15	Total
12/10	Total
6/4	Partial
12/28	Partial
4/25	Partial
10/18	Partial
4/15	Total
10/08	Total
4/4	Total
9/28	Total

Observing the Universe

Astronomy was born out of humankind's need to measure time and seasons, marking the best times to plant. In ancient times, the study of the stars was mixed with superstition and ritual. The megalithic monument Stonehenge, found in southern England, is an example of this. Today, thanks to advances in new technologies, such as the giant telescopes

ONEHENGE
cated in Wiltshire (England), it was built in several ases over some 600 years—between 2200 and 00 BCE. The placement of most of its large stones s a relationship to the Moon and the Sun.

nstalled in various locations around he planet, we have discovered many new things about the universe. The VLT Very Large Telescope), astronomy's new monster telescope located in Chile, is part of an attempt to find planets beyond the solar system, because many astronomers suspect that life is not exclusive to the Earth. ●

Astronomical Theories

For a long time, it was believed that the Earth was stationary. The Sun, the Moon, and the planets were thought to orbit it. To study the sky and calculate its movements, people began to build instruments, such as the astrolabe, armillary sphere, and telescope. The telescope revolutionized the conception of the universe. Instead of the Earth being at the center of the universe, it was suggested that the Earth and other planets travel around the Sun. The Roman Catholic Church opposed the idea and, for a time, persecuted dissident astronomers and banned their theories.

Geocentric Model

Before telescopes, binoculars, and modern observatories existed, little was known about the Earth. Many believed that the Earth was fixed and that the Sun, the Moon, and the five known planets orbited it in circles. This geocentric model was promoted by the Egyptian astronomer Claudius Ptolemy, who in the 2nd century CE compiled the astronomical ideas of the ancient Greek astronomers (in particular, those of Aristotle, who had proposed the Earth as the center of the universe, with the celestial objects revolving around it). Although other ancient astronomers, such as Aristarchus of Samus, proposed that the Earth was round and rotated around the Sun, Aristotle's ideas were accepted as true for 16 centuries, and at times Aristotle's ideas were defended and preserved by the Roman Catholic Church.

MEASUREMENTS

Noticing that the Sun, the Moon, and the stars moved in cycles, ancient civilizations found they could use the sky as both a clock and a calendar. However, ancient astronomers had difficulties performing the complex calculations needed to predict the positions of stars accurately enough to create a truly precise calendar. A useful tool developed to perform this task was the astrolabe. Its engraved plates reproduce the celestial sphere in two dimensions, allowing the elevations of the celestial bodies to be measured.

TIME This astrolabe was used by ancient Persians. To them, astronomy functioned as a kind of agricultural calendar.

COSMIC CHARACTERS

2nd Century
Claudius Ptolemy
100–170

Resurrected and compiled the works of great Greek astronomers into two books. His postulates held undisputed authority for centuries.

16th Century
Nicolaus Copernicus
1473–1543

In his *De revolutionibus orbium coelestium*, the Polish astronomer postulated that the Sun—not the Earth—was the center of the universe. This concept is the foundation of our own astronomy.

17th Century
Johannes Kepler
1571–1630

The German astronomer, believ in Copernicus's heliocentric mo formulated three famous laws of planetary movement, which encouraged Galileo to publis his research.

Heliocentric Model

In 1543, a few months before his death, Nicolaus Copernicus published the book *De revolutionibus orbium coelestium*, inaugurating what is now known as the Copernican Revolution. The Polish astronomer developed the heliocentric theory (from *helios*, the Greek word for "the Sun"), which contradicted the geocentric theory. Copernicus's new postulate inverted the traditional relationship of the Sun and the Earth, identifying the Sun as the center of the universe and the Earth as one of many solar satellites. Copernicus argued that spheres moved in endless, circular orbits. Since the universe and all the celestial bodies were thought to be spherical, he argued that their movements must also be circular and uniform (the Ptolemaic system considered the planets' circuits to be irregular). Copernicus reasoned that, since the movements of the planets appeared to be irregular, the Earth must not be the center of the universe. These discoveries were contrary to the views promulgated by the Roman Catholic Church. In fact, both Roman Catholics and Protestants suppressed any writings advocating these beliefs. When Galileo Galilei was brought to trial by the Roman Catholic Church for advocating the Copernican theory, he was forced to renounce his views.

GALILEO'S TELESCOPE

The telescope is thought to have been invented in 1609 by the Dutch optician Hans Lippershey but had no real scientific application until Galileo Galilei improved and adapted it to observe celestial bodies. Galileo's first telescope, made of a leather tube covered by a lens at each end (one lens convex and the other concave), magnified objects up to 30 times. Using the telescope, Galileo discovered that the Sun's surface had imperfections (sunspots), that the Moon had mountains and craters, and that there were four moons, or satellites, that traveled around Jupiter.

THE TRAVELERS

After many years and great advancements in technology, scientists decided that space observation conducted only from the Earth's surface was insufficient. In 1959, the first space probe was launched, an automatic vehicle that flew to the Moon and photographed its hidden face. The space probes Voyager 1 and 2 explored the planets Jupiter, Saturn, Uranus, and Neptune, a milestone in space exploration. The probes continue to explore the frontier of the solar system. Both carry with them golden discs, named Sounds of Earth, containing sounds and images portraying the diversity of life on Earth.

7th Century

alileo Galilei
54-1642

ilt the first telescope, a mitive device with which he covered sunspots, four of iter's moons, the phases Venus, and craters on Moon's surface.

17th Century

Isaac Newton
1642-1727

He built upon the ideas of Galileo and developed the theory of universal gravitation, asserting that the movements of the Earth and the celestial bodies are governed by the same natural laws.

20th Century

Edwin Hubble
1889-1953

In 1929, he began to investigate the expansion of the galaxies, allowing scientists to obtain an idea of the true scale of the universe as well as refine the big bang theory.

Sprinkled with Stars

Constellations are groups of stars thought to represent different animals, mythological characters, and other figures. Constellations were invented by ancient civilizations to serve as reference points in the Earth's sky. There are 88 of these collections of stars. Although each star in a constellation appears related to the others, it is actually very far from them. Not all the constellations are visible at the same time from any one place on the Earth.

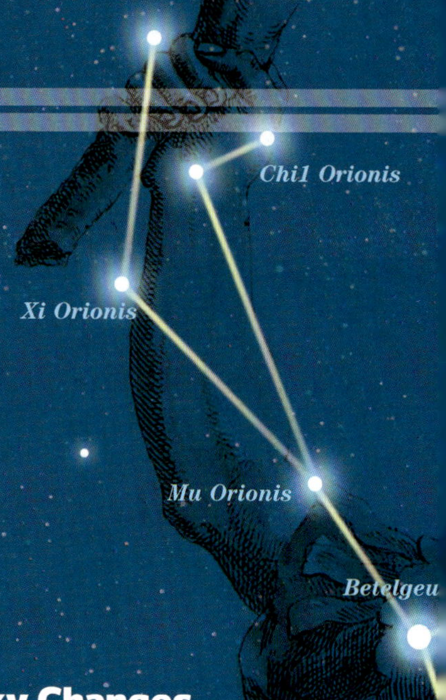

ORIGIN

The history of western culture's constellations begins with the first astronomical observations made by ancient Mesopotamian peoples. Because we inherited the constellations from Greco-Roman culture, most of the constellations are named after figures in classical mythology. All of the earliest constellations were named by the 16th century. Constellations discovered more recently bear names drawn from science or technology or from exotic fauna discovered in various places across the globe.

88

constellations

The Sky Changes

The Earth takes one year to orbit the Sun. As the planet advances in its orbit, the nighttime sky changes, allowing different parts of it to be seen. This is why some constellations can only be seen during certain seasons of the year. In addition, different constellations can be seen from different latitudes. Only near the equator is it possible to see all 88 constellations.

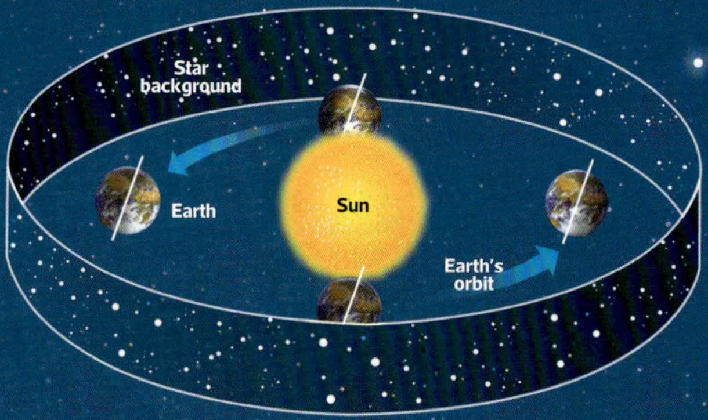

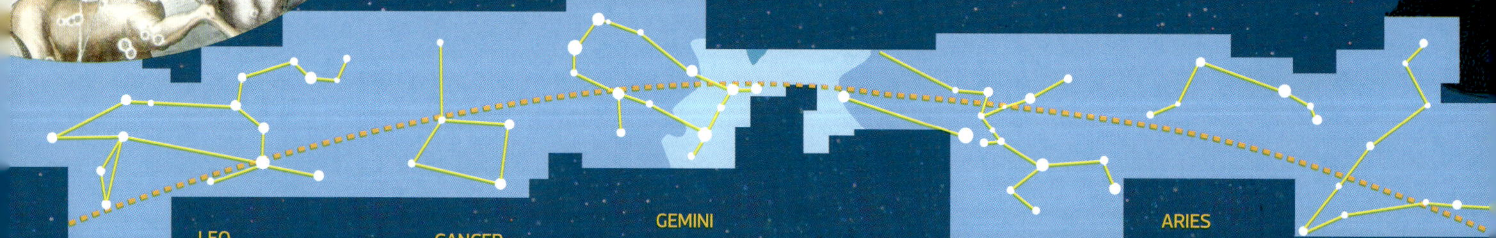

LEO

The brightest stars are those of the head and back. Regulus is prominent.

CANCER

is the least notable of the zodiac's constellations.

GEMINI

The stars Castor and Pollux form the head of the twins.

TAURUS

is visible even without binoculars. The brightest star, Aldebaran, is red.

ARIES

has only one very bright star, Hamal, the Arabic word for "sheep."

PISCES

Not a very noteworthy constellation, it has no very bright stars.

The Constellations of the Zodiac

The 13 constellations located within the elliptical plane—through which the Sun passes as seen from Earth—are called the constellations of the zodiac. Twelve of these constellations have long formed the foundation of astrology, but Ophiuchus, the 13th, is ignored by astrologers as a new addition.

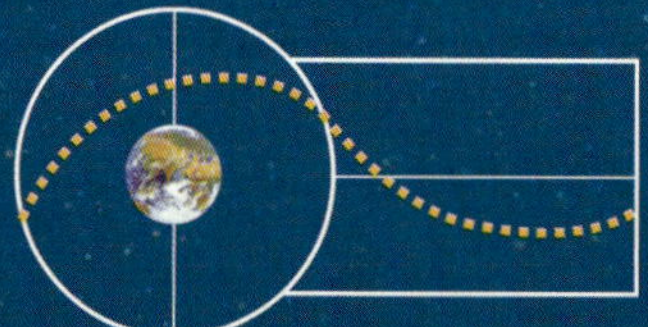

OBSERVING THE CONSTELLATIONS

Observers in both hemispheres can see the constellations of the zodiac. In the Northern Hemisphere, the southern constellations, such as Scorpius, are difficult to see, and in the Southern Hemisphere, northern constellations, such as Gemini, are difficult to study.

Mythological Characters

Since ancient times, animal figures have been seen represented in the sky by groups of stars. The constellation of Taurus takes its name from its resemblance to a bull. Orion, Cassiopeia, Andromeda, and Perseus were named after characters of Greek tragedies.

Different Cultures

In antiquity, each culture recognized certain constellations that other civilizations did not. The Chinese see smaller, more detailed patterns in the stars, allowing for more precise positional information. Various cultures also tend to use varied names for the same constellation. Scorpius is recognized by the people of Mesopotamia, Greece, Rome, Mesoamerica, and Oceania—under different names.

SCORPIUS
In Greco-Roman mythology, Orion and Scorpius are closely linked. Orion is the giant, handsome, seductive hunter.

URSA MAJOR
The bear represented by this constellation is unusual because of its long tail. The constellations' shapes rarely agree perfectly with their namesakes.

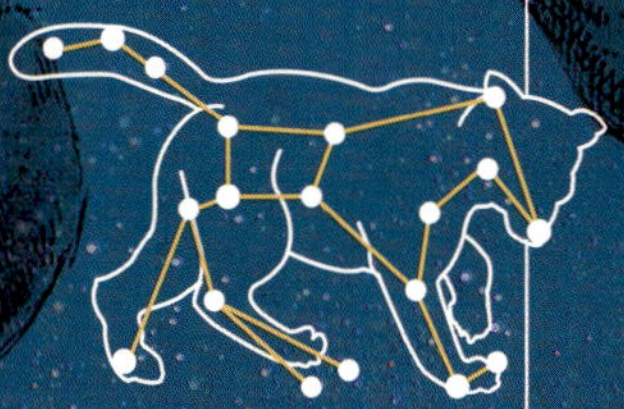

THE CENTAUR
is a creature from Greek mythology, half man and half horse. The centaur accompanied Orion during his quest to recover his sight.

13

OPHIUCHUS
Although it is the 13th constellation of the zodiac, Ophiuchus is not a part of the zodiac. When astrology began 3,000 years ago, the constellation was far from the zodiac.

Babylon

The Babylonians conceived of the zodiac 2,000 years ago as a way of measuring time, using it as a symbolic calendar.

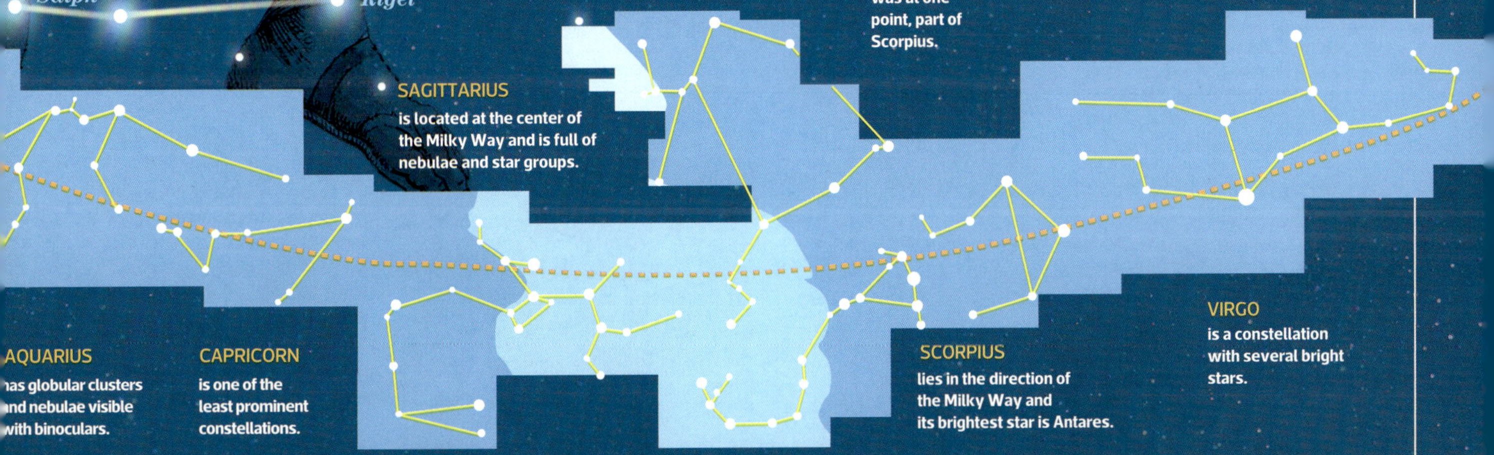

Celestial Cartography

As on the Earth, so in heaven. Just as terrestrial maps help us find locations on the surface of the planet, star charts use a similar coordinate system to indicate various celestial bodies and locations. Planispheres, or star wheels, are based on the idea of a celestial sphere (an imaginary globe on which the stars appear to lie and that surrounds the planet). Two common types are polar and bimonthly star maps.

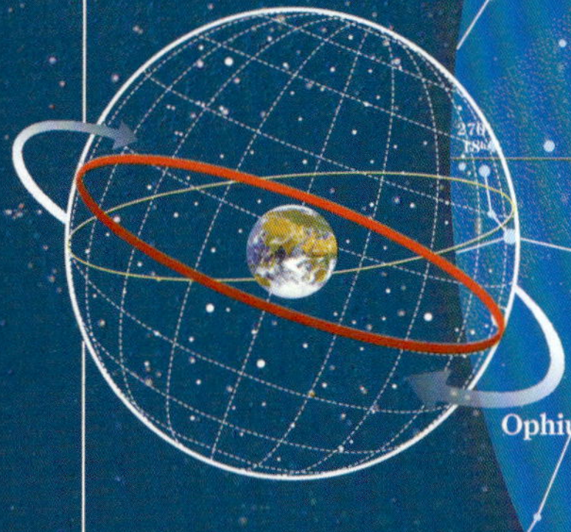

THE CELESTIAL SPHERE

The celestial sphere is imagined to extend around the Earth and forms the basis for modern star cartography. The sphere is divided into a network of lines and coordinates corresponding to those used on the Earth, allowing an observer to locate constellations on the sphere. The celestial equator is a projection of the Earth's equator, the north and south celestial poles align with the axis of the Earth, and the elliptic coincides with the path along which the Sun appears to move.

Measuring Distances

Once a star or constellation has been located in the sky, hands and arms can serve as simple measuring tools. A single extended finger, shown in the first illustration, can form a one-degree angle from the observer's line of sight and is useful for measuring short distances between stars. The closed palm of the hand forms a 10° angle, and the open hand measures 20°.

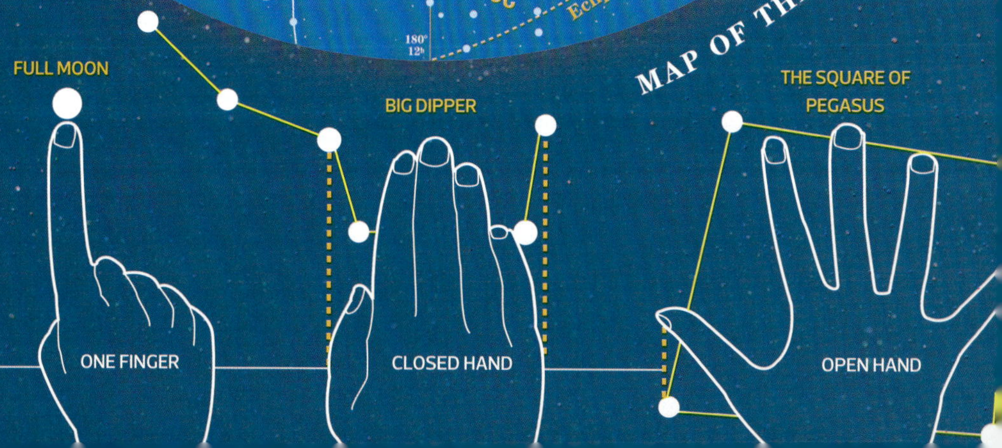

OW TO READ A MAP OF THE SKY

stronomers divide the celestial sphere into sections, llowing them to study the sky in detailed, systematic ays. These maps can show a particular region bserved from a certain place at a certain time, or hey can merely concentrate on a specific location. o specify the position of a point on the surface of e Earth, the geographic coordinates called latitude nd longitude are used. With the celestial sphere, eclination and right ascension are used instead. bservers located at the equator see the celestial quator pass directly over their heads.

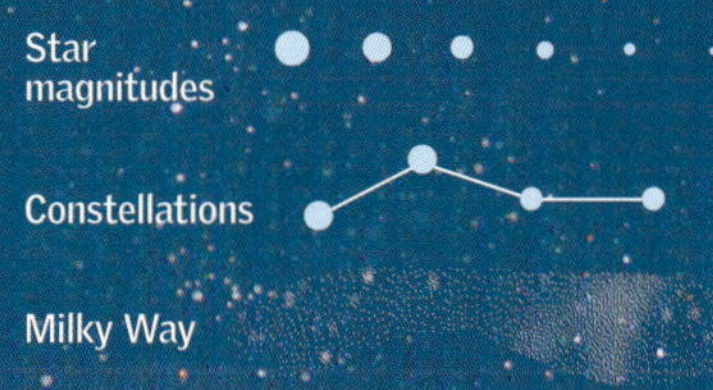

F THE STELLAR SOUTH POLE

Stellar Movements

The visible regions of the celestial sphere and the ways in which stars move through the sky depend upon the observer's latitude. As an observer moves north or south, the visible portion of the celestial sphere will change. The elevation of the north or south celestial pole above the horizon determines the apparent motion of the stars in the sky.

AT THE POLES
At the North Pole, the stars appear to rotate around the observer's head. The effect is the same at the South Pole but in the opposite direction.

IN MIDDLE LATITUDES
some stars can be seen all year long, but others are only visible during certain months.

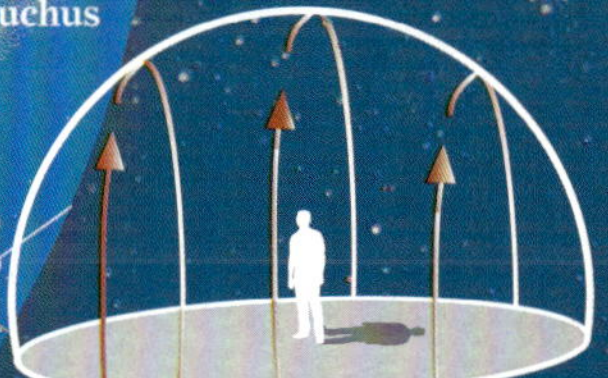

AT THE EQUATOR
stars can be seen throughout the year, rising in the east and setting in the west.

ifferent Types of Charts

Throughout the year, different constellations are visible because the Earth moves along its orbit. As the Earth's place in its orbit changes, the night side of the planet ces different regions of space. To compensate for this shifting erspective, there are various kinds of planispheres: north and uth polar maps and bimonthly equatorial maps.

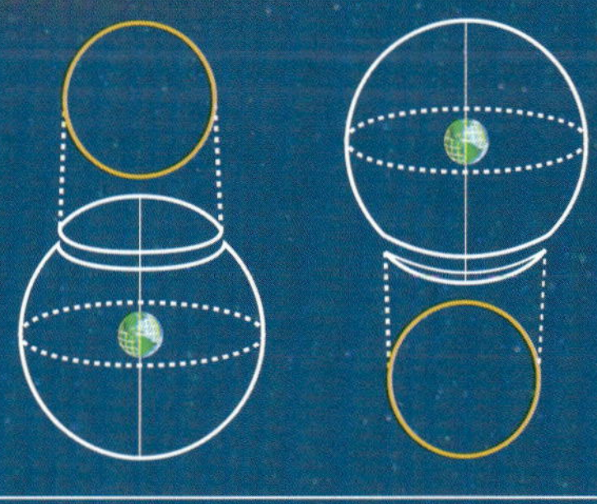

POLAR
The celestial sphere is generally divided into two polar maps: north and south.

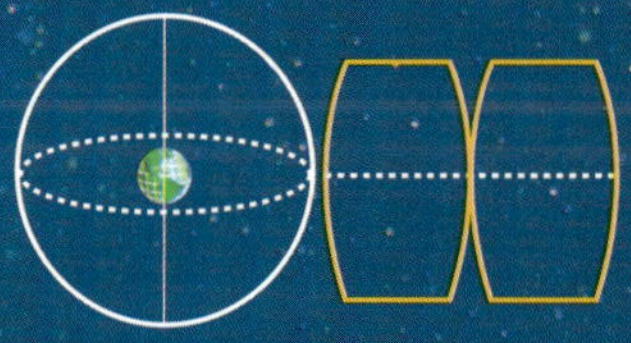

EQUATORIAL
Six bimonthly maps depict all 88 constellations, which can be seen over the course of the year.

From the Home Garden

Stargazing is not difficult. After learning to locate celestial objects, many people find the hobby very gratifying. With the aid of a star map, you can recognize galaxies, nebulae, star clusters, planets, and other objects. Some of these treasures of the universe are visible with the unaided eye, but others require binoculars or even more sophisticated telescopes. Familiarity with the night sky is useful in many ways.

Basics

Before stepping out to observe the night sky, make sure you have everything you need. If you collect all your supplies beforehand, you will avoid having to expose your eyes to bright light once they have adjusted to darkness. In addition to binoculars, star maps, and a notebook, you should bring warm clothes, a comfortable seat, and something to drink.

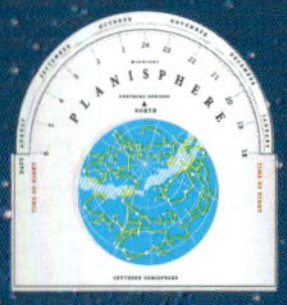

Planisphere

Compass

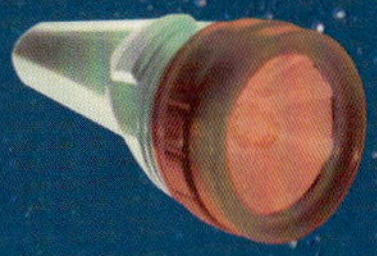

Flashlight with red cellophane

How to Look at the Moon

Under various degrees of magnification, the Moon and stars take on different appearances. In some cases, you can make observations of the Moon with the unaided eye as well as with binoculars or a telescope.

Normal view

View with binoculars

View with telescope

THE MOTION OF CONSTELLATIONS

The Earth's rotation makes the planets and stars appear to move through the nighttime sky in a general east-to-west direction. When the southern constellation Orion, visible from November through March, is viewed from the Northern Hemisphere, it appears to move from left to right.

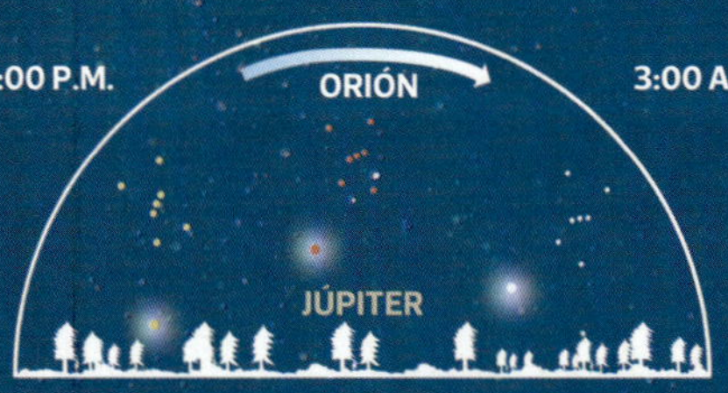

Observable Objects

The sky is a very busy place. Not only are there stars and planets, but there are also satellites, airplanes, comets, and meteorites. Fortunately, all become recognizable by their appearance as well as their movement.

SHOOTING STARS
Very short flashes of light lasting only a fraction of a second

MOON
The illuminated face of the Moon can always be seen at some time during the night, at least partially, except around the new moon.

VENUS
can generally be seen above the horizon at dusk or dawn.

SATELLITES
The bigger ones are brighter than some stars. Some take a while to cross the sky.

COMETS
visible to the naked eye appear every one to two years and are visible for weeks or even months.

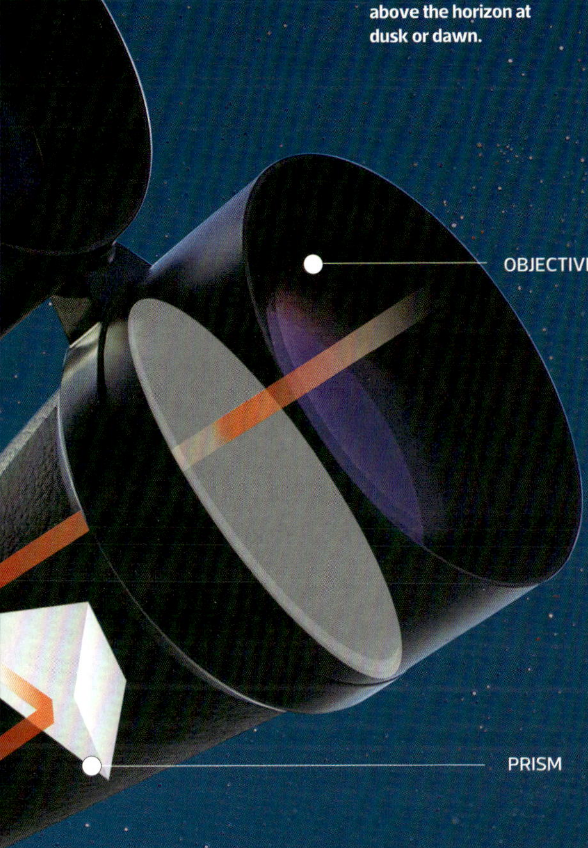

Flat Perspective

A constellation is a group of stars that, when viewed from a certain angle, seem to assume a specific shape. However, these stars that seem closely joined together are, in fact, separated by great distances.

Measurement methods

A planisphere is a circular star chart that is used to locate celestial bodies in the celestial sphere. To identify a particular object, your own arms and body can be used to measure its direction and altitude in relation to the horizon.

MEASUREMENT OF ELEVATION

MEASURING DIRECTION

Starting at the horizon, extend one of your arms until it is perpendicular to the other.

To measure a 45° angle, move your arm halfway up from the horizon.

The planisphere indicates the principal direction of a star. Place the arms at 90°, using north or south as the base.

A star to the southwest could be located with your arms at 45°. Combine the directional angles with your hand measurements for elevation.

A Four-Eyed Giant

The Paranal Observatory, one of the most advanced in the world, is located in the region of Antofagasta, Chile. It uses four identical telescopes to obtain enough light-gathering power that it could see the flame of a candle on the surface of the Moon. This sophisticated collection of digital cameras, reflecting mirrors, and other instruments is mounted in the interior of four metallic structures weighing hundreds of tons. The Very Large Telescope (VLT) is operated by a scientific consortium drawn from fourteen European countries. One of their stated objectives is to discover new worlds orbiting other stars.

CLIMATIC CONDITIONS

Cerro Paranal is located in the driest part of the Atacama desert, where the conditions for astronomical observation are extraordinarily favorable. It is an 8,645-foot- (2,635-m-) tall mountain that has about 350 cloudless nights a year.

10.9 (750)
LB PER SQ IN (MBAR)
Air pressure

0.06 (0.96)
LB PER CU FT (KG/M3)
Air density

18–77° (-8–25°)
FAHRENHEIT (CELSIUS)
Average temperature

5 to 20
PERCENT
Humidity

ARMILLARY SPHERE
Invented by Eratosthenes in the year 225 BCE, it was used as a teaching aid and became especially popular in the Middle Ages thanks to Danish astronomer Tycho Brahe.

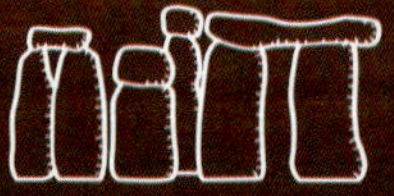

2500–2000 BCE
STONEHENGE
Located in Wiltshire, England, it is an observatory temple dating from the Neolithic Period.

1000 CE
CARACOL
It is located in the ruins of the Mayan city of Chichén Itzá. The structure was used for venerating the Sun, the Moon, and Venus.

Cerro Paranal Observatory

The ESO's Very Large Telescope is located to the north of the Atacama desert, on Cerro Paranal. Completed in 2006, it has four 26.9-foot- (8.2-m-) wide reflector telescopes capable of observing objects four billion times fainter than those visible to the unaided eye. It also has four 5.9-foot- (1.8-m-) wide movable auxiliary telescopes that are used in conjunction with the larger ones to simulate the light-gathering power of a 52-foot- (16-m-) wide mirror (with the resolution of a 656-foot- [200-m-] long telescope). This is enough to see an astronaut on the Moon. The above technique is called interferometry.

215,000 SQ FT
(20,000 SQ M) TOTAL SURFACE

7,759 FEET
(2,365 M) ABOVE SEA LEVEL

Telescope units

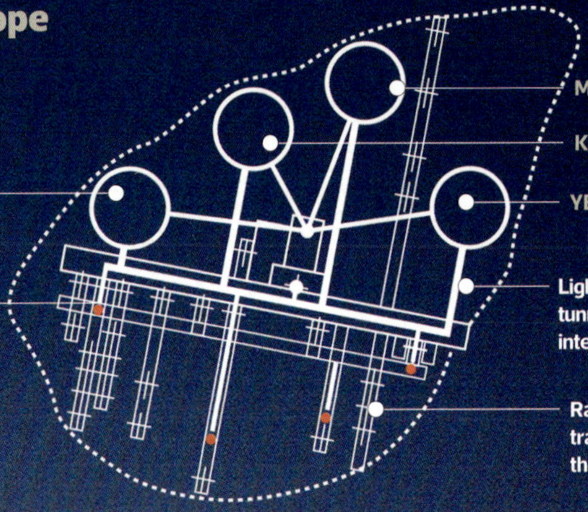

The Telescope

The main feature of the VLT is its revolutionary optical design. By using adaptive and active optics, it achieves resolution similar to that possible from space.

ACTIVE OPTICS

ACTIVE OPTICS

To prevent the primary mirror from deforming because of gravitational effects, the VLT has an active optics system that maintains the mirror in optimal shape, with 150 supporting pistons that continually adjust the shape of the mirror.

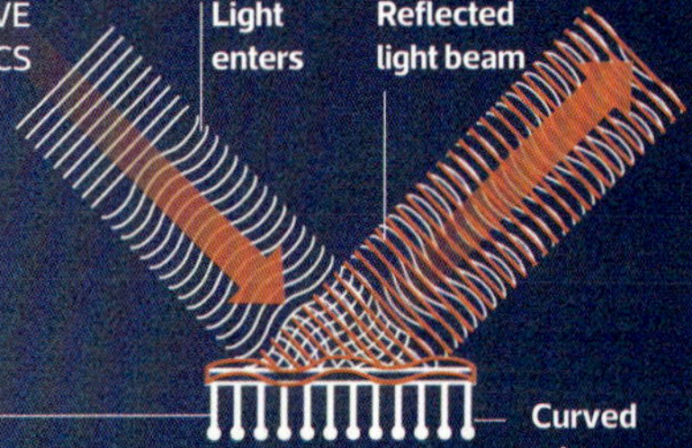

VLT
ACRONYM FOR
Very Large
Telescope

726
AIPUR
ocated in India, it was built by he maharajah Sawai Jai Singh nd has a large sextant and a eridional chamber.

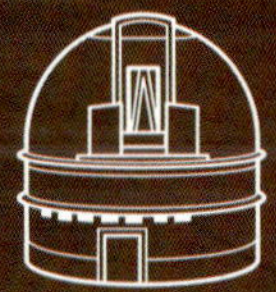

1888
LICK
Located on 4,265-foot- (1,300-m-) high Mount Hamilton. It was the first observatory to be located on a mountain.

1897
YERKES
Located in Wisconsin, it contains the largest refracting telescope in the world.

1979
MAUNA KEA
An international complex located in Hawaii, with large British, French-American, and American observatories

Glossary

Annihilation

Total destruction of matter in a burst of energy, as when it encounters antimatter.

Antigravity

Hypothesized force, equal to gravity and diametrically opposed to it.

Antimatter

Matter formed from subatomic particles with shared properties. Its electrical charge is opposite that of normal matter.

Aperture

Diameter of the main mirror of a telescope or eyepiece. The larger the aperture, the more light the device receives.

Aphelion

The point in a celestial body's orbit farthest from the Sun. The Earth reaches aphelion on or about July 4, when it is 95,000,000 miles (152, 600,000 km) from the Sun.

Apogee

The farthest position from the Earth reached by the Moon or any of the artificial satellites that orbit the planet.

Asteroids

Minor bodies of the solar system, formed by rock, metal, or a mixture of both. Most asteroids orbit the Sun between the orbits of Mars and Jupiter. Their size ranges from dozens of feet to hundreds of miles.

Astrolabe

Ancient astronomical instrument for measuring both the positions and the movements of celestial objects.

Astronomy

Science that studies the universe. It is concerned with the physical characteristics, movements, distances, formation, and interactions of galaxies, stars, planets, moons, comets, asteroids, and other celestial bodies.

Atmosphere

Layer of gas retained around a planet by its gravity. It is also the outer layer of matter in a star, where the energy produced in the star's interior is emitted in the form of radiation.

Atom

The smallest part of an element that partakes of all the element's properties. It is generally composed of three subatomic particles: the neutron, the proton, and the electron.

Aurora

Luminous phenomenon, with red and green layers, visible in the skies of the polar regions. The auroras are caused by the collision of solar particles with the Earth's atmosphere.

Austral

Related to the Southern Hemisphere.

Big Bang

Cosmological theory asserting that the universe began to exist as a result of a great explosion that occurred some 14 billion years ago.

Big Crunch

Cosmological theory asserting that the universe would undergo a final, complete collapse if it were to begin to contract.

Black Hole

Celestial body so dense that not even light can escape its gravity.

Black Hole, Stellar-Mass

Black hole produced by the explosion of a massive star as a supernova. Its mass is typically about 10 times that of the Sun.

Black Hole, Supermassive

Black hole located at the center of a galax and formed by material that falls into the central region of the galaxy. Its mass can b a billion times that of the Sun.

Carbon

One of the most common elements in the universe, produced by stars. All known life carbon-based.

Chromosphere

The lowest layer of the Sun's atmosphere. It emits a pinkish-red light that can be see only when the brighter photosphere is obscured during a total eclipse.

Circumpolar Star

Any star always visible to an observer on t Earth as it rotates about the celestial pole.

Comet

Object made of ice and rock dust. When a comet approaches the Sun, the growing heat causes the ice to evaporate, forming a gaseous head and a tail of dust and gas pointing away from the Sun.

Constellation

Group of stars in the sky. Constellations tend to bear the names of mythological characters or creatures. To astronomers, th constellations demarcate regions of the sk

Core

In a planet, a solid, high-pressure central mass; in a star, the central region undergoi nuclear fusion; in a galaxy, the innermost light-years.

Corona

Upper atmosphere of the Sun. It is visible a a pearly halo during a total solar eclipse.

osmos

nother name for the universe.

rater

rcular depression formed by the impact of meteorite on the surface of a natural satellite a planet.

rust

ocky layer of the surface of a planet or natural atellite.

urvature of Light

istortion of light rays when passing through egions with strong gravitation.

ecay

ocess by which radioactive elements and nstable particles become stable substances. lso the way in which black holes eventually sappear.

ensity

egree of solidity of a body (its mass divided by s volume).

clipse

sual concealment of one celestial body by nother. A lunar eclipse occurs when the Moon asses into the Earth's shadow, and a solar clipse takes place when the Earth passes into ne Moon's shadow.

cliptic

naginary line around the sky along which the un moves during the year. The orbits of the arth and the other planets generally lie along ne ecliptic.

lectrical Charge

roperty of particles causing them to either ttract or repel each other because of electrical orces. Electrical charges are either positive or egative.

Electromagnetic Radiation

Radiation composed of magnetic and electric fields moving at the speed of light. It encompasses radio waves (long wavelengths), visible light, and gamma rays (very short wavelengths).

Element

A basic substance of nature that cannot be diminished without losing its chemical properties. Each element (such as hydrogen, helium, carbon, oxygen) has its own characteristics.

Elliptical Orbit

Orbit shaped like a flattened circle. All orbits are elliptical. A circle is a special form of an ellipse.

Energy

The capacity to do work.

Event Horizon

The edge of a black hole.

Extraterrestrial

Foreign to the Earth.

Force

Something that changes the motion or shape of a body.

Galactic Filament

Structure formed by superclusters of galaxies stretching out through great portions of space. Filaments are the largest structures in the universe and are separated by great voids.

Galaxy

Collection of billions of stars, nebulae, dust, and interstellar gas held together by gravity.

Galaxy Cluster

Group of galaxies linked together by gravity.

Gamma Rays

Form of electromagnetic radiation with greatest energy and shortest wavelength. It is generated by only the most powerful phenomena in the universe, such as supernovae or the fusion of neutron stars.

General Relativity

Theory formulated by Albert Einstein in 1915. In part, it holds that gravity is a natural consequence of the curvature of space-time caused by the presence of a massive body. In general relativity, the phenomena of classical mechanics (such as the orbit of a planet or the fall of an object) are caused by gravity and are represented as inertial movements within space-time.

Gravitational Wave

Waves in space that travel at the speed of light and are produced by the movements of very massive bodies.

Gravity

Attractive force between bodies, such as between the Earth and the Moon.

Greenhouse Effect

Temperature increase caused by gases (such as carbon dioxide and methane) that prevent the surface heat of a planet from escaping into space.

Heliosphere

The region of space around the Sun in which its effects are evident. It extends some 100 astronomical units around the Sun.

Helium

The second most common and second lightest element in the universe. It is a product of the big bang and of nuclear fusion of stars.

Hubble Constant

Number that measures the rate of expansion of the universe. It is expressed in kilometers per second per millions of parsecs. It is currently estimated at 70 km/s/Mpc.

Hydrogen

The most common and lightest element in the universe; the main component of stars and galaxies.

Hypernova

Destruction of a massive star, which emits a wave of gamma rays extending great distances across the universe.

Implosion

Collapse of a body upon itself in response to great external pressure.

Infrared Radiation

Heat radiation, with a wavelength between visible light and radio waves.

Intergalactic Space

Space between galaxies.

Interstellar Space

Space between the stars.

Ionosphere

Region of the Earth's atmosphere that is electrically charged and is located between 30 and 370 miles (50 and 600 km) from the Earth's surface.

Kuiper Belt

Region of the solar system that is home to millions of frozen objects, such as comets. It stretches from the orbit of Neptune to the inner limit of the Oort cloud.

Light

Electromagnetic radiation with a wavelength visible to the human eye.

Light Pollution

Brightness of the sky originating in street illumination and other artificial lighting, which impedes the observation of dim celestial objects.

Light-Year

Standard astronomical measurement unit equivalent to the distance traveled by light, or any form of electromagnetic radiation, in one year. Equivalent to 6,000,000,000,000 miles (10,000,000,000,000 km).

Lunar Mare

The large, dark regions of the surface of the Moon. They were originally thought to be seas, but they are actually great depressions covered by lava.

Magnetic Field

The area near a magnetic body, electric current, or changing electric field. Planets, stars, and galaxies have magnetic fields that extend into space.

Magnetosphere

Sphere that surrounds a planet with a magnetic field strong enough to protect the planet from the solar wind.

Mantle

Layer that lies between the crust and the core of a planet.

Mass

Measure of the amount of matter in an object.

Matter

The substance of a physical object, it occupies a portion of space.

Meteorite

Rocky or metallic object that strikes the surface of a planet or satellite, where it can form a crater.

Milky Way

The galaxy to which the Sun and the solar system belong. It is visible as a pale band of light that crosses our night sky.

Molecule

Smallest unit of a pure substance that has the composition and chemical properties of the substance. It is formed by one or more atoms.

Moon

The Earth's natural satellite is called the Moon The natural satellites of other planets are commonly known as moons and have their own proper names.

Nebulae

Clouds of gas and dust in space. Nebulae can be seen when they reflect starlight or when they obstruct light from sources behind them.

Neutron

Electrically neutral subatomic particle. It makes up part of an atom's nucleus (with the exceptio of ordinary hydrogen).

Neutron Star

Collapsed star consisting mostly of neutrons.

Nova

Star that increases greatly in brightness for several days or weeks and then slowly fades. Most novae probably occur in binary-star systems in which a white dwarf draws in matte from its companion star.

Nuclear Fusion

Nuclear reaction in which relatively light elements (such as hydrogen) form heavier elements (such as helium). Nuclear fusion is th source of energy that makes stars shine.

Oxygen

Chemical element vital to life and to the expansion of the universe. Oxygen makes up 2 percent of the Earth's atmosphere.

Particle

In particle physics, a tiny, individual component of matter with characteristic mass, electrical charge, and other properties.

ʼerihelion

he point in a celestial body's orbit closest to ne Sun. The Earth reaches perihelion on or bout January 4, when it is 92,000,000 miles 47,500,000 km) from the Sun.

ʼhoton

lemental particle responsible for lectromagnetic radiation. Photons are the nost common particles in the universe.

ʼlanet

toughly spherical object made of rocks or gas rbiting a star. A planet cannot generate its own ght but reflects the light of its parent star.

ʼolestar

ʼolaris, a star that lies near the celestial north ole. Polaris is commonly called the North Star.)ver thousands of years, other stars will ecome the polestar.

ʼroton

ubatomic particle with positive electrical harge. It forms part of the nucleus of an atom.

ładio Galaxy

ctive galaxy emitting energy as both radio vaves and light. Most of the radio emission riginates at the core of the galaxy.

olar Flare

nmense explosion produced on the surface of the Sun by the collision of two loops of the olar magnetic field.

olar Mass

tandard unit of mass against which other bjects in the universe can be compared. he Sun has 333,000 times as much mass as he Earth.

Space

The medium through which all celestial bodies move.

Space-Time

Four-dimensional conception of the universe in which length, width, and height constitute three dimensions and time acts as the fourth.

Spectral Analysis

Study of spectral lines that provide information about the composition of stars or galaxies and their redshifts.

Spectrum

The result of dispersing the electromagnetic radiation of an object so that the wavelengths of which it is composed can be seen.
Dark lines that originate from elements that are present and punctuate the spectrum at specific wavelengths reveal the composition of the object.

Speed of Light

The distance traveled by light in a vacuum in one second (approximately 186,000 miles, or 300,000 km). No object can move faster than the speed of light.

Star

Enormous sphere of gas (generally hydrogen) that radiates light and heat. The Sun is a star.

Star Cluster

Group of stars linked together by gravity. Open clusters are scattered groups of several hundred stars. Globular clusters are dense spheres of several million old stars.

Sunspots

Dark, relatively cool spots on the surface of the Sun. They tend to be located on either side of the solar equator and are created by the solar magnetic field.

Supernova

Explosion of a massive star at the end of its life.

Tide

The effect of the gravitational pull of one astronomical object upon the surface of another. Ocean tides on Earth are an example.

Unstable

Tendency to change from one state into another less energetic one. Radioactive elements decay into more stable elements.

Vacuum

Space occupied by little or no matter.

Van Allen Belt

Radiation zone surrounding the Earth, where the Earth's magnetic field traps solar particles.

Wavelength

Distance between the peaks of any wave of electromagnetic radiation. Radiation with a short wavelength (such as X-rays) has more energy than radiation with a longer wavelength (such as radio waves).

Zenith

Point in the sky 90° above the horizon (that is, immediately above an observer).

Zodiac

Twelve constellations through which the Sun, the Moon, and the planets appear to move.

For More Information

Association of Science – Technology Centers

818 Connecticut Avenue, NW

7th Floor

Washington, DC 20006-2734

(202) 783-7200

Website: www.astc.org

Through strategic alliances and global partnerships, the Association of Science-Technology Centers (ASTC) strives to increase awareness of the valuable contributions its members make to their communities and the field of informal STEM learning.

Canada Science and Technology Museum

PO Box 9724, Station T

Ottawa, Ontario K1G 5A3

Canada

(866) 442-4416

Website: cstmuseum.techno-science.ca

The Canada Science and Technology Museum is the largest of its kind in Canada and fulfills its mission through its collection, its permanent, temporary, and traveling exhibitions, as well as special events, school programs, and workshops.

H. R. MacMillan Space Centre

1100 Chestnut Street (Vanier Park)

Vancouver, British Columbia V6J 3J9

Canada

(604) 738-7827

Website: www.spacecentre.ca

The H. R. MacMillan Space Centre is a nonprofit community resource. Through innovative programming, exhibits, and activities, the centre's goal is to educate, inspire, and evoke a sense of wonder about the Universe, our planet, and space exploration.

Kennedy Space Center

Kennedy Space Center Visitor Complex

R 405

:usville, FL 32899

77) 404-3769

ebsite: www.kennedyspacecenter.com

ennedy Space Center Visitor Complex is organized into Mission Zones, where attractions and tours are grouped by chronological era. From e dawn of space exploration to current and ongoing missions, you can get an up-close, hands-on feel for the story of humans in space.

iberty Science Center

berty State Park 222

rsey City Boulevard

rsey City, NJ 07305

01) 200-1000

ebsite: www.lsc.org

berty Science Center is a 300,000-square-foot (28,000-square-meter) learning center dedicated to bringing the excitement of science to eople of all ages.

ose Center for Earth and Space – American Museum of Natural History

5-208 79th Street at Central Park West

ew York, NY 10024

12) 769-15100

ebsite: www.amnh.org/exhibitions/permanent-exhibitions/rose-center-for-earth-and-space

ne Rose Center for Earth and Space encompasses the spectacular Hayden Sphere and exhibitions that explore the vast range of sizes in the osmos, the 13-billion-year history of the universe, the nature of galaxies, stars, and planets, and the dynamic features of planet Earth.

ebsites

ecause of the changing nature of internet links, Rosen Publishing has developed an online list of websites related to the subject of this book. This site is odated regularly. Please use this link to access the list:

tp://www.rosenlinks.com/VES/universe

For Further Reading

Dickinson, Terence. *Hubble's Universe: Greatest Discoveries and Latest Images.* Ontario, Canada: Firefly Books, 2014.

DK Publishing. *Space!* New York, NY: DK Publishing, 2015.

DK Publishing. *Space Exploration.* New York, NY: DK Publishing, 2014.

Gilliland, Ben. *How to Build a Universe: From the Big Bang to the End of the Universe.* New York, NY: Sterling, 2015.

Miller, Ron. *Spaceships: An Illustrated History of the Real and the Imagined.* Washington, DC: Smithsonian Books, 2016.

Sagan, Carl. *Cosmos.* New York, NY: Ballantine Books, 2013.

Schilling, Govert. *Deep Space: Beyond the Solar System to the End of the Universe and the Beginning of Time.* New York, NY: Black Do and Leventhal Publishers, 2014.

Shetterly, Margot Lee. *Hidden Figures: The American Dream and the Untold Story of the Black Women Mathematicians Who Helped W the Space Race.* New York, NY: HarperCollins Publishers, 2016.

Smith, Robert W., and David H. Devorkin. *The Hubble Cosmos: 25 Years of New Vistas in Space.* Washington, DC: National Geographic, 2015.

Snedden, Robert. *A Brief Illustrated History of Space Exploration.* North Mankato, MN: Capstone Press, 2017.

Index

A

B

C

H

I

J

K

L

M

N

O

P

Q

R